IMAGES
of America

Quabbin Valley
Life As It Was

On the Cover: The Quabbin Valley was heavily forested with oak, maple, hemlock, pine, and ash trees. Clearing the land for agriculture required extensive logging, which provided year-round employment. These loggers may have stopped for their noon meal, which would have been brought to them by the wives and might include beef or venison stew, baked beans, thick chowder, homemade bread or biscuits, cake, pies, and plenty of hot coffee. The workday usually lasted from dawn to dark. The location of this mill is unknown. (Courtesy of Swift River Valley Historical Society.)

IMAGES
of America

QUABBIN VALLEY
LIFE AS IT WAS

Elizabeth Peirce

ARCADIA
PUBLISHING

ISBN 978-1-4671-2281-8

Published by Arcadia Publishing
Charleston, South Carolina

Printed in the United States of America

Library of Congress Control Number: 2014944277

For all general information, please contact Arcadia Publishing:
Telephone 843-853-2070
Fax 843-853-0044
E-mail sales@arcadiapublishing.com
For customer service and orders:
Toll-Free 1-888-313-2665

Visit us on the Internet at www.arcadiapublishing.com

This book is dedicated in memory of the Quabbin Valley and the people who lived there from the 1700s to 1938.

Contents

ACKNOWLEDGMENTS

Many individuals have worked to keep the memories of the Quabbin Valley and its people alive by telling and retelling the story. For all the encouragement I received, my thanks. A special thank-you goes to Betty-Sue Pratt for her patience and computer skill. Without her help, this, the third book of Quabbin history (the others are *The Lost Towns of the Quabbin Valley* and *Quabbin Valley: People and Places*), would never have been accomplished. Unless otherwise noted, all pictures appear courtesy of Swift River Valley Historical Society.

INTRODUCTION

For many generations, the Nipmuc Indian tribe occupied the area known today as the Quabbin Valley. They called it "Quaben," meaning, "many waters." They were nomadic and only remained in the valley as long as the hunting and fishing was good. Then the canoe would be submerged to preserve and hide it, with the Nipmucs retrieving it the next spring, upon their return from winter quarters. One of the oldest artifacts at the Swift River Valley Historical Society in North New Salem is a dugout canoe found when the excavation was being done on Morton Pond in Enfield in the 1930s.

The Quabbin Reservoir located in central Massachusetts was built in the late 1800s to fulfill a need for clean, pure water for the growing population of Boston. The idea was brilliant, the construction, spectacular, and the cost of the project, remarkable. It came about, however, at a high cost in human suffering for the 2,500 inhabitants living in the towns of Dana, Enfield, Greenwich, and Prescott, who were forced to give up all they had worked for in a place they had thought would be their home forever. The rumors of impending evacuation had circulated for several years, but the final blow came in April 1938, when the dreaded eviction notices arrived by registered mail. No provision was made to help them relocate or find employment. That is how it was.

The Swift River Valley Historical Society in North New Salem became the repository for artifacts and remnants. It is here that the docents and staff tell and retell the stories of life in the towns of Dana, Enfield, Greenwich, and Prescott. Visitors hear about what people did for a living. They see the dishes used by the Dana Grange. They see the furniture used, the books and games in the schoolroom, the lunch pails, and even the leather punishment strap. They see the teacher's bell that was rung to signal the end of recess. In the Carriage Shed, the visitor sees farm tools and the Dana fire truck. The society's mission is to keep the memories alive by telling it as it was.

Among the many artifacts are photo albums, which became popular after the Brownie camera became affordable. People started taking pictures of everyday events—the children at play, the men at work, the pet dog and cat, the garden, the flowers. They took pictures at family reunions, Old Home Day, picnics, parades and birthday parties, and at the many camps and cottages where the good times provided good photo opportunities. These albums could be shared and enjoyed over and over. Many have come to the museum, and it is from these that images have been heavily drawn for this book.

Through the years, the Quabbin Valley has suffered many natural disasters. The terrifying tornado of 1894 caused much damage and left many scars. The hurricane that hit New England in 1938 caused massive destruction within the watershed. Fires and lightning strikes also took their toll.

The Blizzard of 1888 was one of the most talked-about events in New England history. Only word pictures exist, written by those who endured it. A blizzard is defined as a severe and prolonged storm accompanied by high winds and near-zero temperatures. In 1888, there was no way of predicting such a storm, and no way to warn people. Electricity was limited, and there were no plows or powerful trucks; no snow blowers, radios, or television; and no telephones or cell phones. On the late spring morning of March 11, 1888, it "looked like it might snow." By the end of the day, 30 to 40 inches had fallen, and high winds had caused enormous drifts. Everything came to a dead stop, including the Rabbit Train carrying 151 passengers returning home. People everywhere were forced to stay where they were. Many did not reach home for several days, and some who decided to try walking never did. Neighbors waded through drifts with food for those stranded. The sick and the elderly were a particular concern. A lot was learned about preparedness. Disasters continue worldwide, but the Blizzard of 1888 will be long remembered, and the story often retold.

Many of the people who settled in the valley came from England as early as the 1700s. They came seeking religious freedom and a place where they could bring up their children as they believed was right. These pioneers were strong in their convictions, brave, inventive, creative, and above all, optimistic. They were true Yankees—shrewd and clever. The valley was a wilderness to be conquered. Today, it is once again a wilderness, but this time, it is man-made. It covers 81,000 acres, and the Quabbin Reservoir is 13 miles long, 2.5 miles wide, and has an average depth of 45 feet. The deepest point of 141 feet is over Greenwich.

There were 7,500 gravesites removed, with most being reinterred in the beautiful Quabbin Park Cemetery in Ware. Gone are the sawmills, gristmills, cloth mills, and small factories where boxes, brooms, bricks, buttons, nails, pails, carriage wheels, palm leaf hats, and piano legs were made. Roads that once led to busy communities and businesses now end abruptly at the water's edge.

Leaving their footprints in the sands of time were the doctors, dentists, artists, poet, writes, musicians, sculptors, inventors, educators, photographers, and patriots. It is important to remember how the people of the valley enjoyed life—how they worked and played and socialized. Town meetings, neighborhood clubs, Grange meetings, 4-H Clubs, debating societies, and gold medal contests were important events in valley life. There were husking bees, taffy pulls, quilting parties, oyster and game suppers, plays, sliding and skating parties, as well as the never-to-be-forgotten dances at the Prescott Grange Hall, which lasted until the wee hours.

All is gone but not forgotten. The greatest gift of all is the gift of memory.

One

WORKING

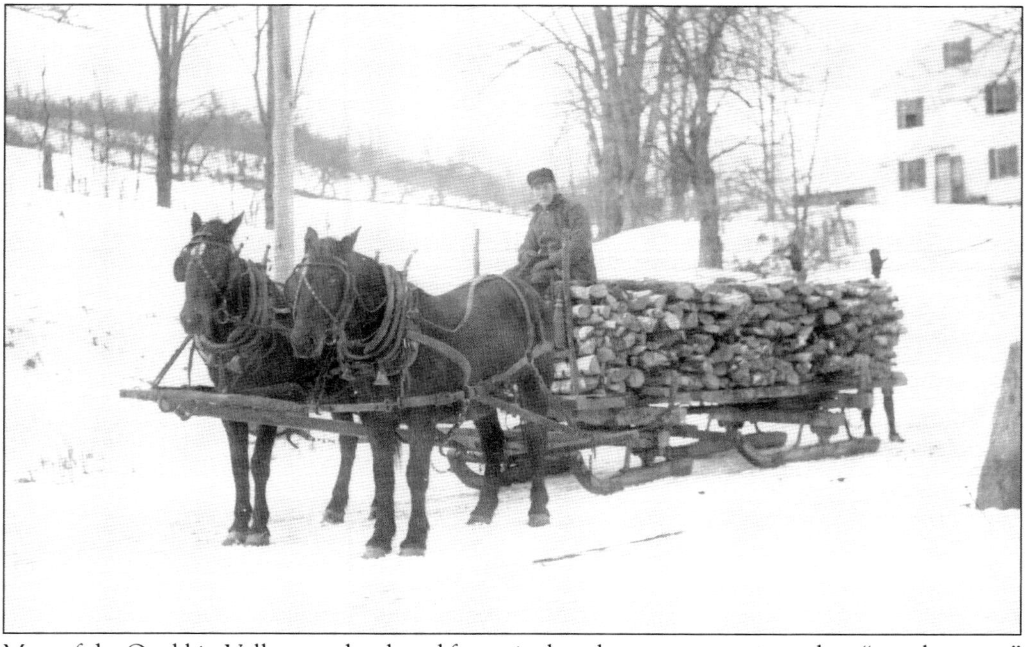

Most of the Quabbin Valley was developed for agricultural purposes at a time when "people power," oxen, and horses were the only tools available. With the help of gasoline engines, waterpower, and (much later) electricity, life became easier. Industries such as box shops, hat shops, cloth mills, sawmills, and grain mills were among the many that flourished.

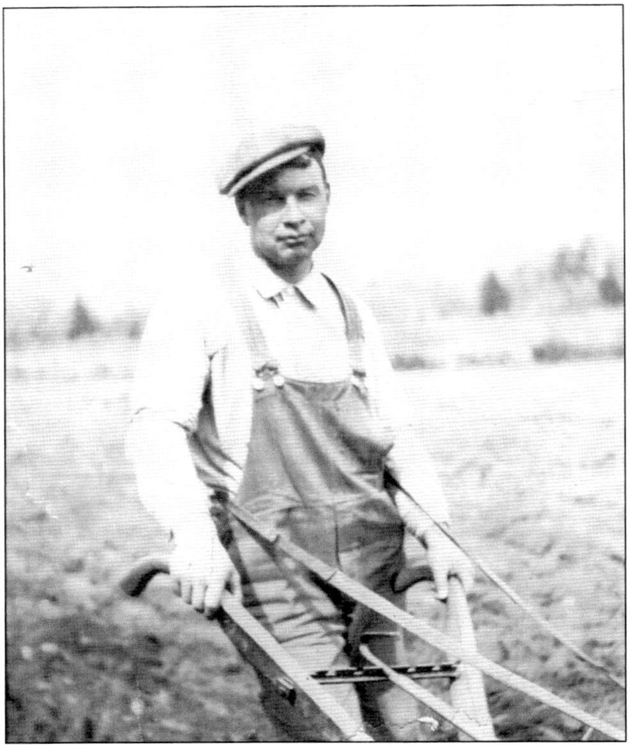

Harry Sawtell of New Salem served for many years as assessor and selectman. He was also a farmer. Here he is cultivating his garden. The reins around his waist are attached to his horse, not visible in the picture. His horse knows the routine well and is careful not to step on the plants. The date is 1916.

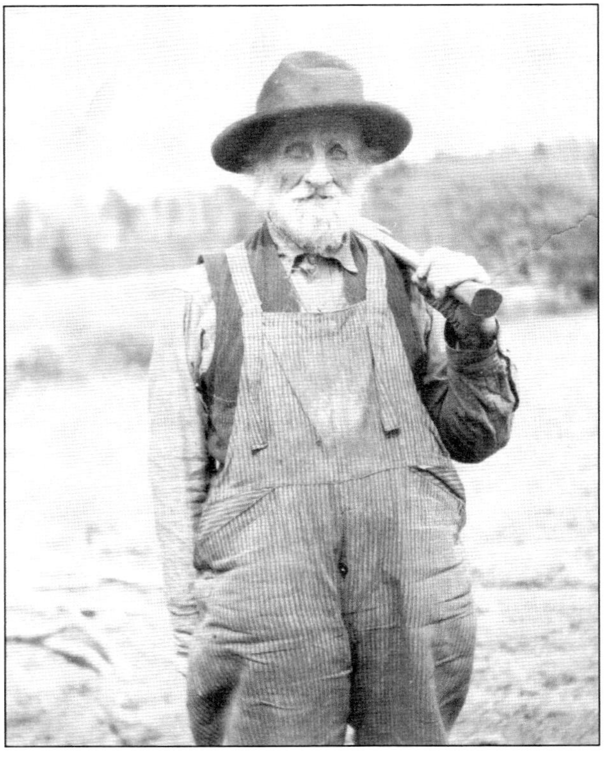

Marshall Fisher is off to chop some wood. His railroad-stripe overalls will protect his clothing, and his hat will shade his eyes. Fisher was active in town politics in New Salem for many years.

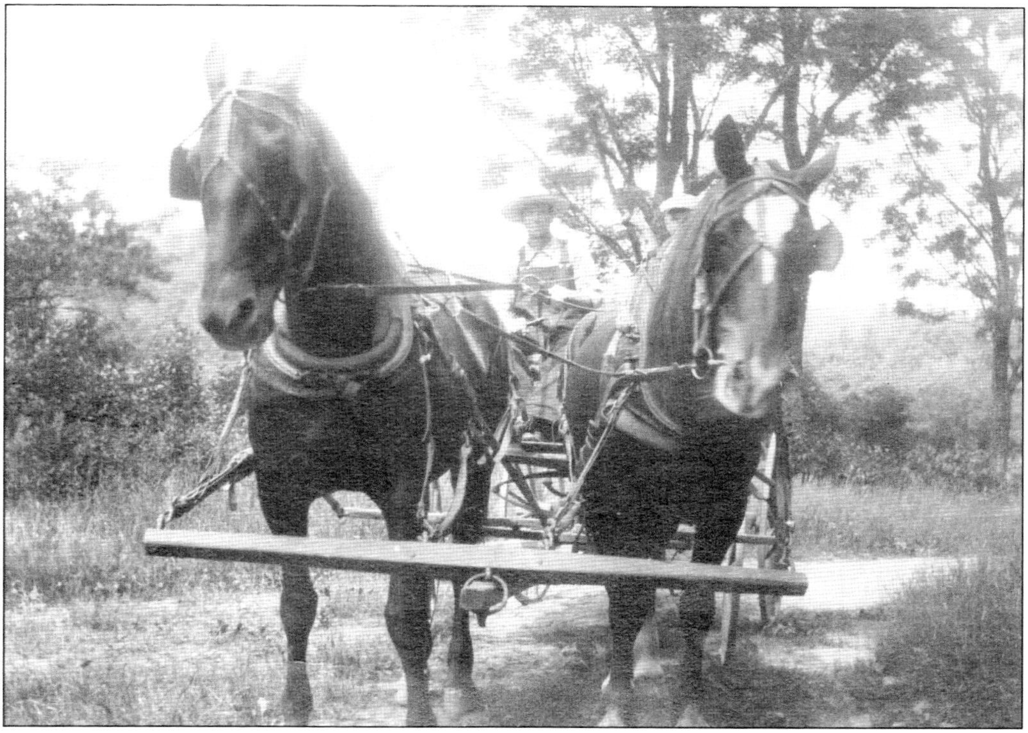

Dressed in his overalls to protect his clothing and a straw hat to protect his eyes from the hot sun, Ellis Pierce is off to rake some hay. The seat of the hay rake is very high to enable the teamster to see over the horses. On the back of the picture is written "Ellis and friends."

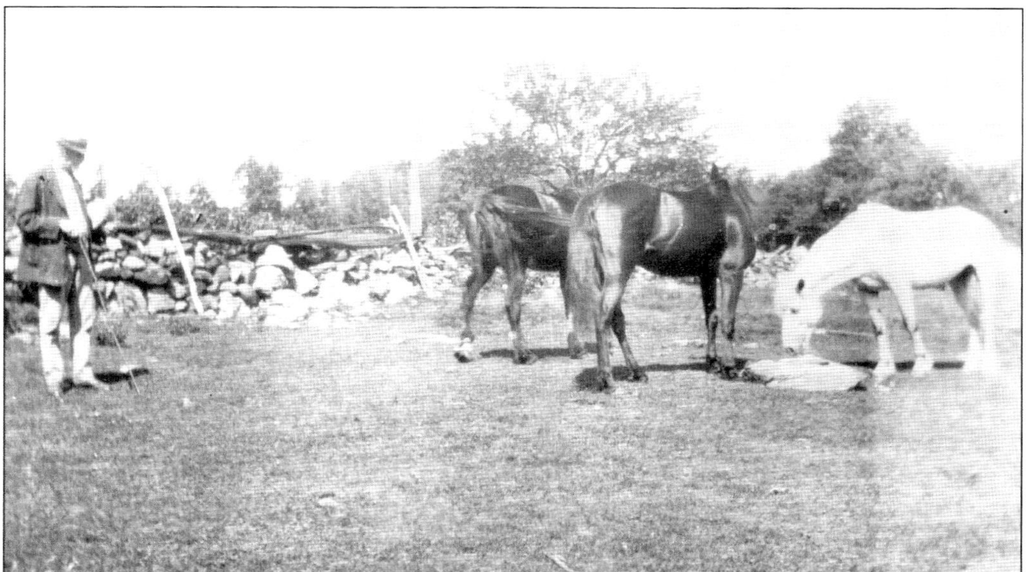

Lester Ballard visits with his horses Dexter, Dot, and Dolly on a spring morning.

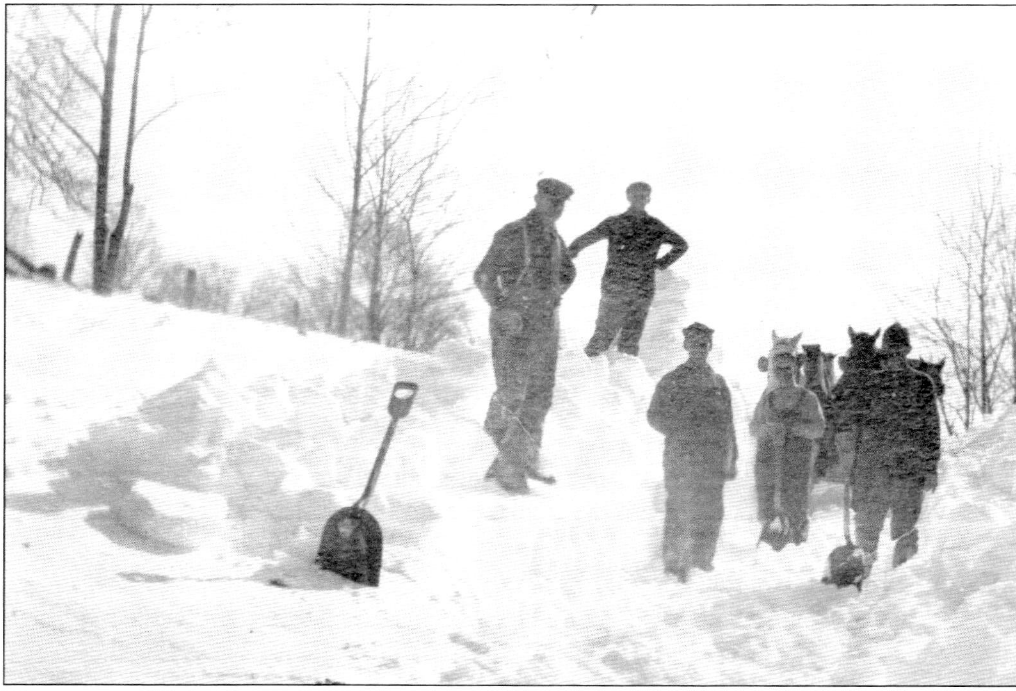

This picture shows the road to Millington in the winter of 1919–1920. Keeping roads passable was time-consuming, hard work. There were no snowplows or snowblowers.

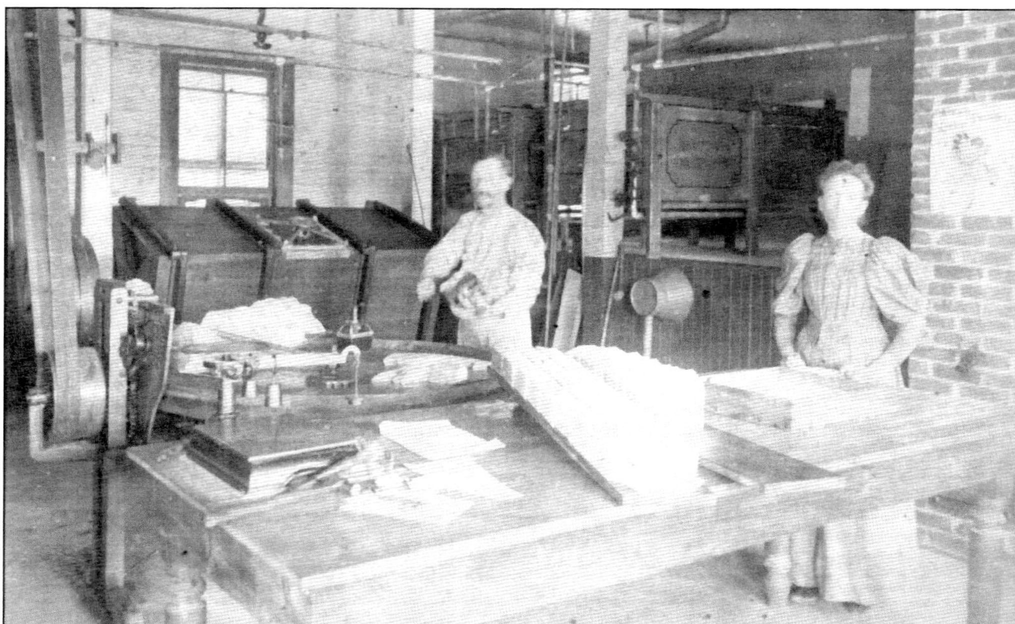

This picture shows the interior of the Creamery in Millington. Farmers who had extra milk sold it to the Creamery, where it was then separated, with the cream being churned into butter to be peddled throughout the neighboring villages. The lady at right is packaging it. Scales ensured accuracy.

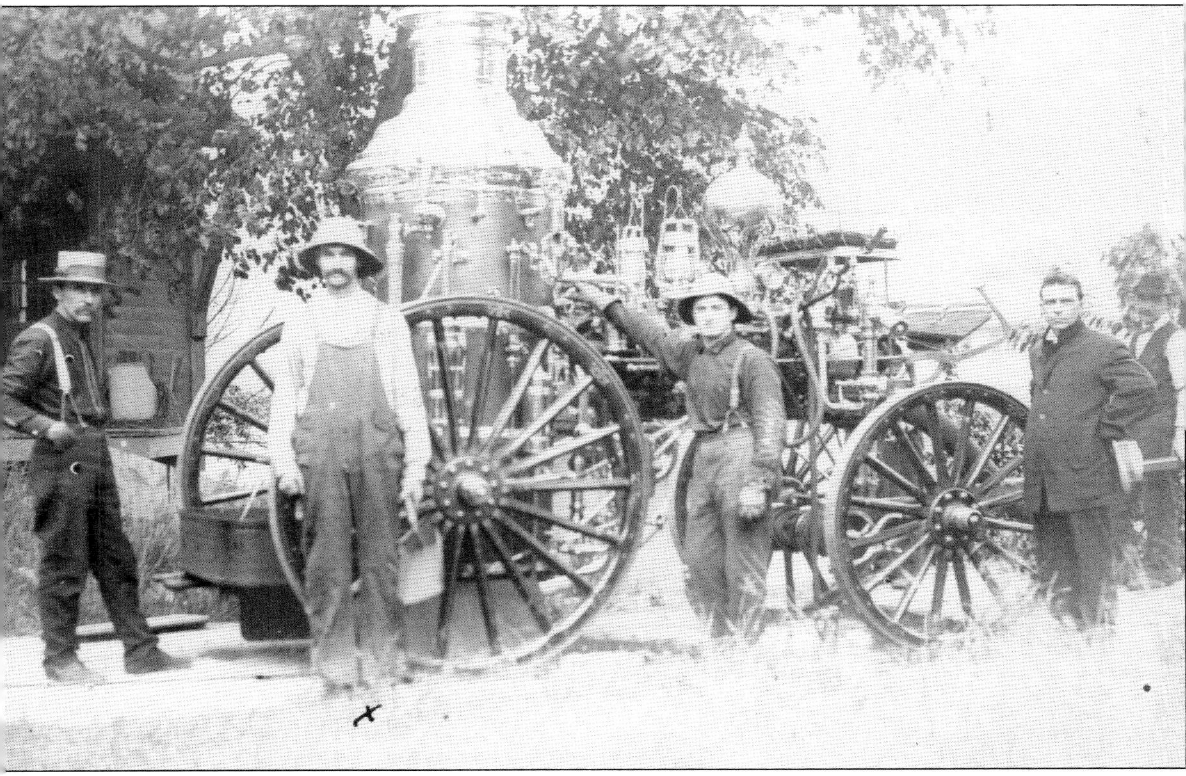

This undated picture shows the Enfield Volunteer Fire Department with its equipment. The tall can holds water. Enfield, the largest of the four towns flooded, was the scene of several devastating fires. Dana was the only town to have a motorized fire truck, a 1929 Ford. It is on display at the Swift River Valley Historical Society in North New Salem.

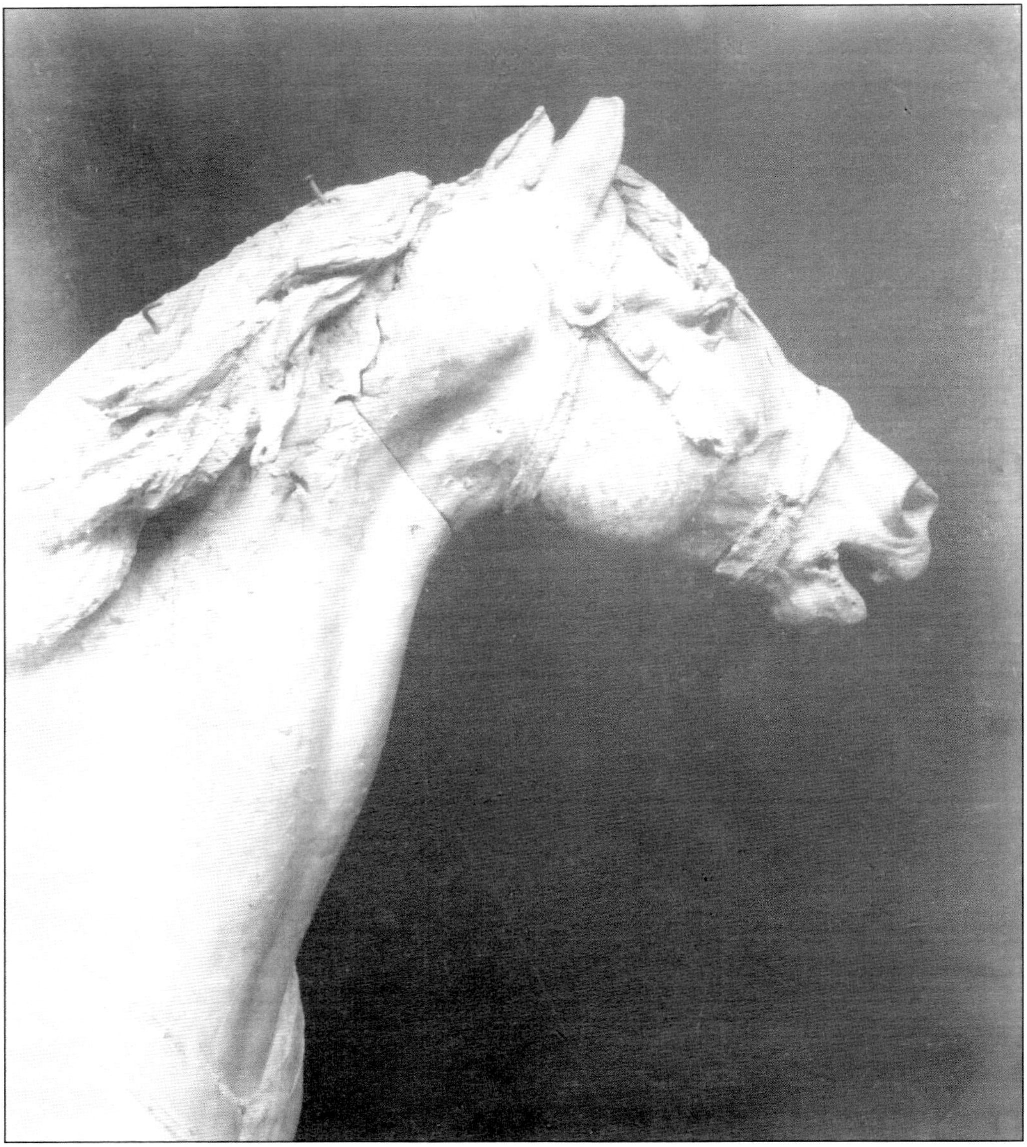

This unfinished sculpture of a horse head is by Edward C. Potter of Enfield. In collaboration with Daniel French, Potter made horses for four notable equestrian statues—one of General Grant in Philadelphia, one of General Washington in Paris, one of General Hooker in Boston, and one of General Devens in Worcester.

These pictures were taken inside the studio of Edward C. Potter, sculptor of renown. He did many other famous sculptures, including the two lions outside the entrance to the New York Public Library at Fifth Avenue and Forty-second Street.

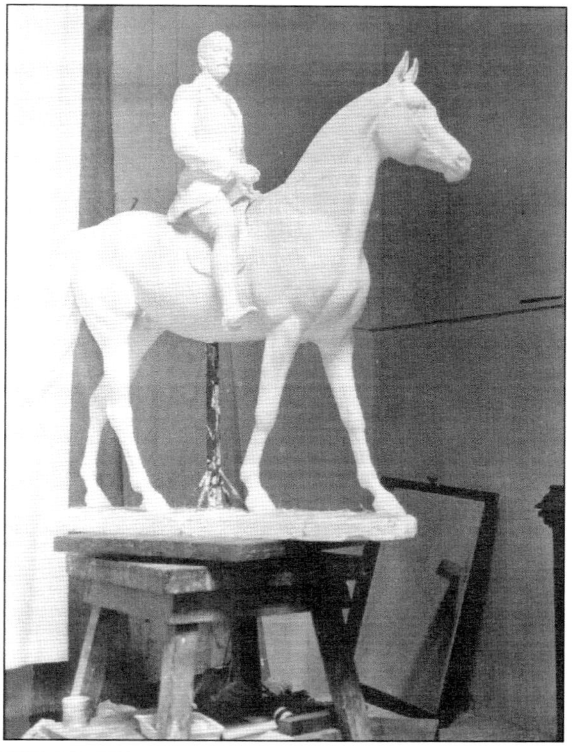

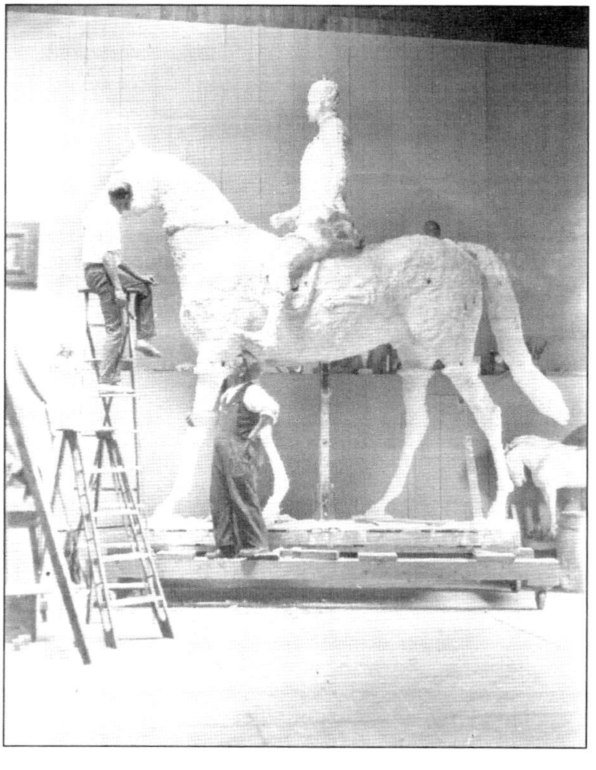

Note the size of the sculpture as measured by the two workmen.

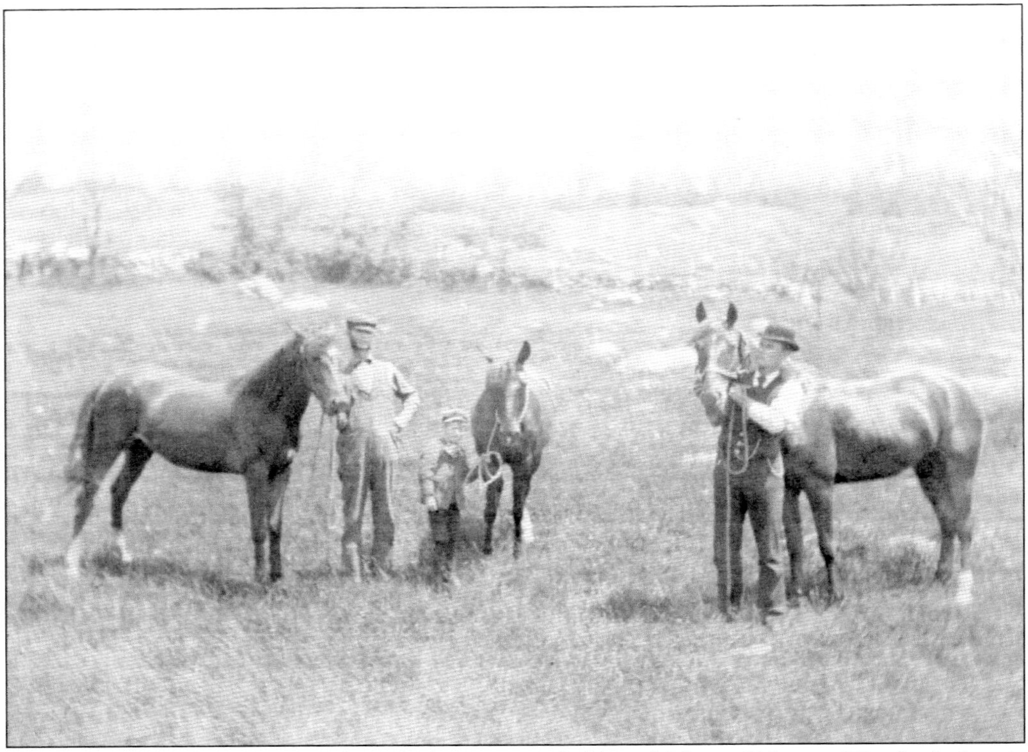

The men in this picture are identified as Henry (left) and Harry Tolman. The little boy is Louie Tolman.

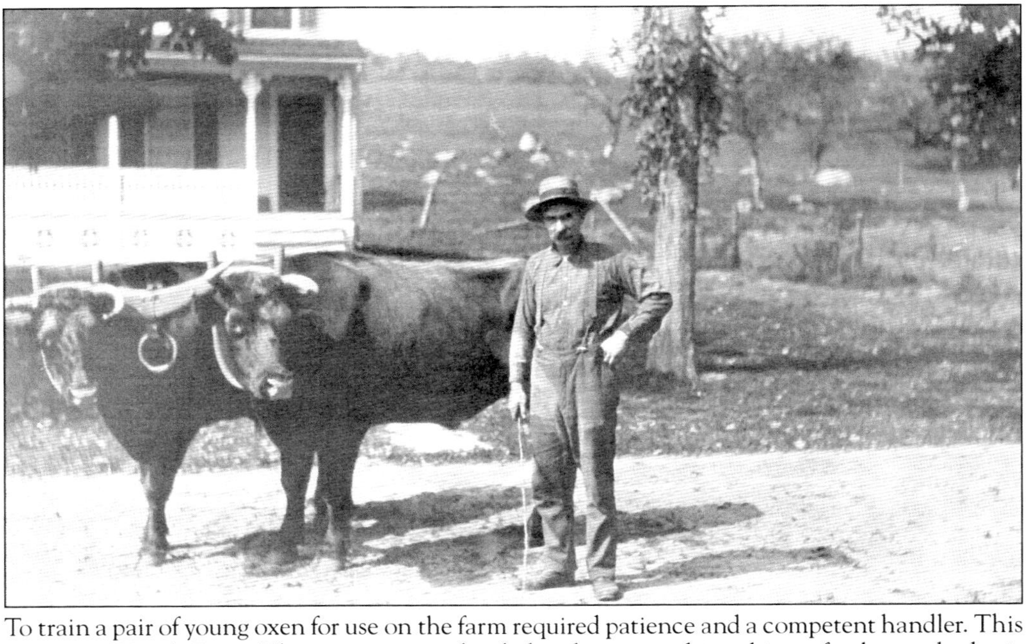

To train a pair of young oxen for use on the farm required patience and a competent handler. This scene is in North Dana. The man, using only a light whip, is teaching this perfectly matched pair of oxen to walk along under his direction.

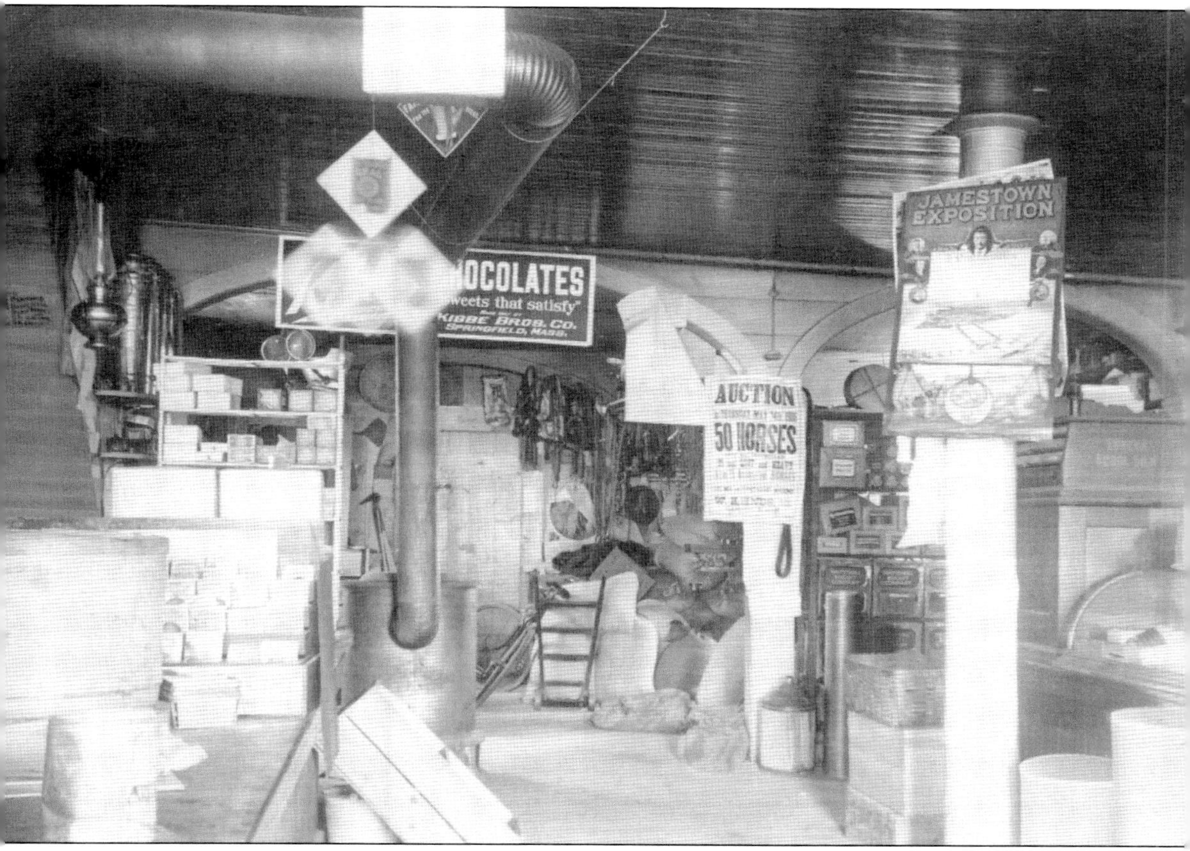

A trip to this general store in Dana was an exciting adventure, for it was the place that sold everything the shopper could want. Looking carefully, one can see a bag of grain, a kerosene lamp, a large wheel of cheese, and a glass case with pastries. Advertising posters for candy, auctions, and coming events are hung wherever handy. Note also the stove and stovepipe.

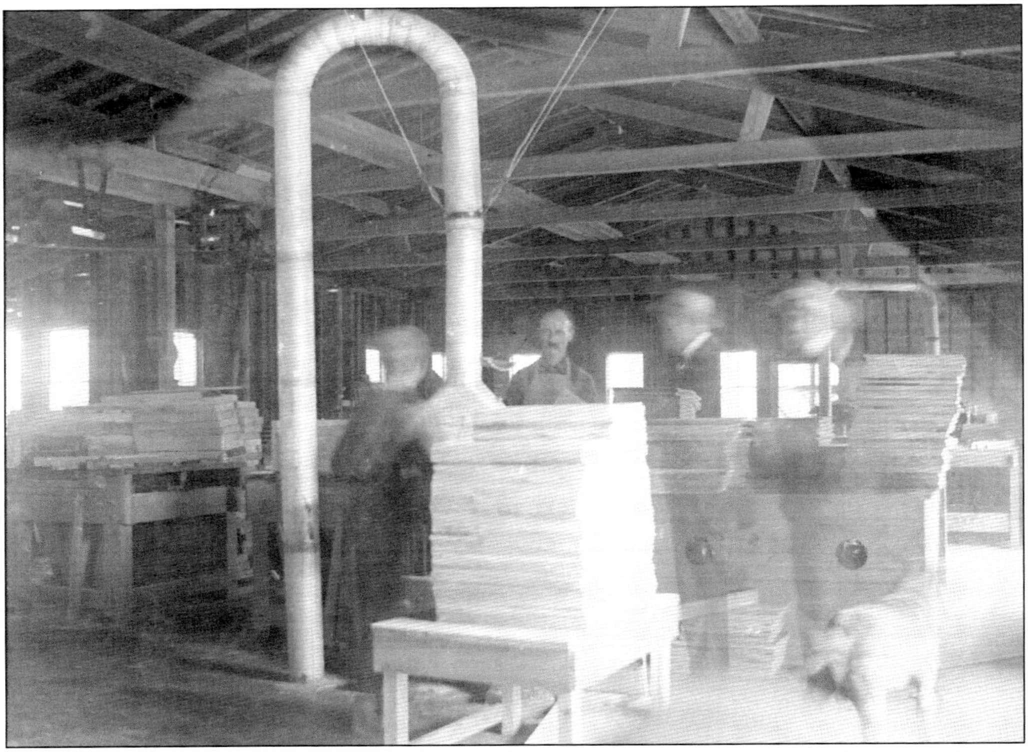

Wood was abundant and was used in many ways. This picture shows the interior of the Cyrus Forbes Box Factory in Enfield. Cyrus, second from the left, is showing the operation to some visitors.

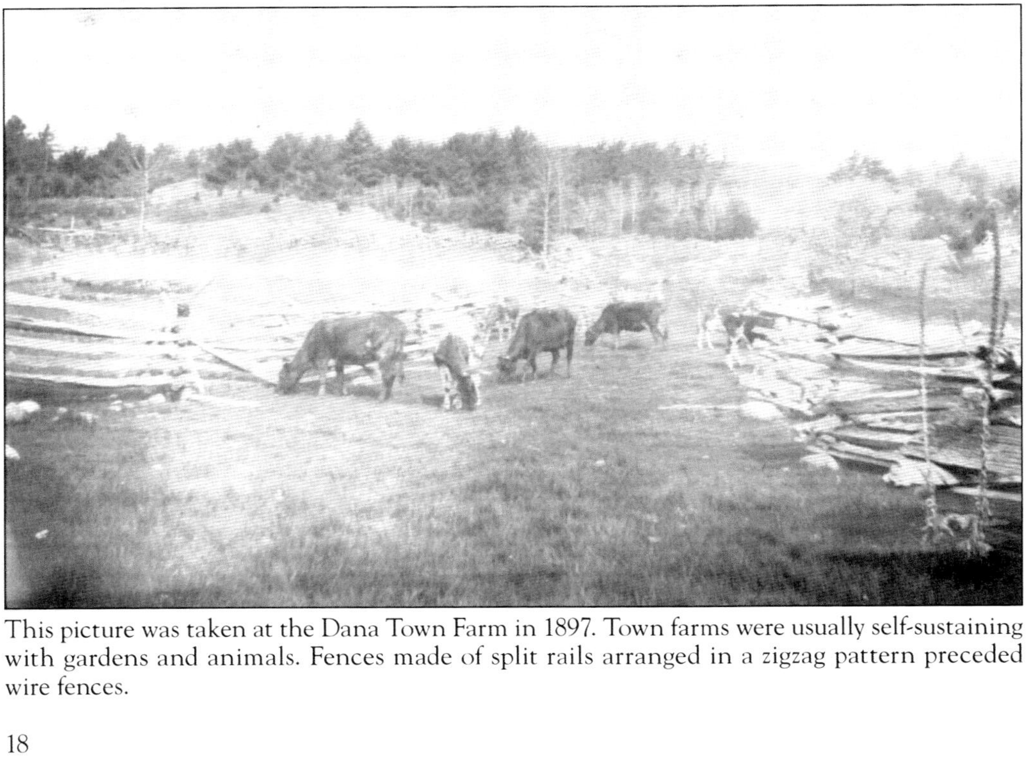

This picture was taken at the Dana Town Farm in 1897. Town farms were usually self-sustaining with gardens and animals. Fences made of split rails arranged in a zigzag pattern preceded wire fences.

This picture is labeled, "Dad, 1926 Dana, Mass." Beneath is written, "Ernest Carrington." Perhaps someone who reads this book can verify it. It looks like this man is off to rake some hay on a sunny morning.

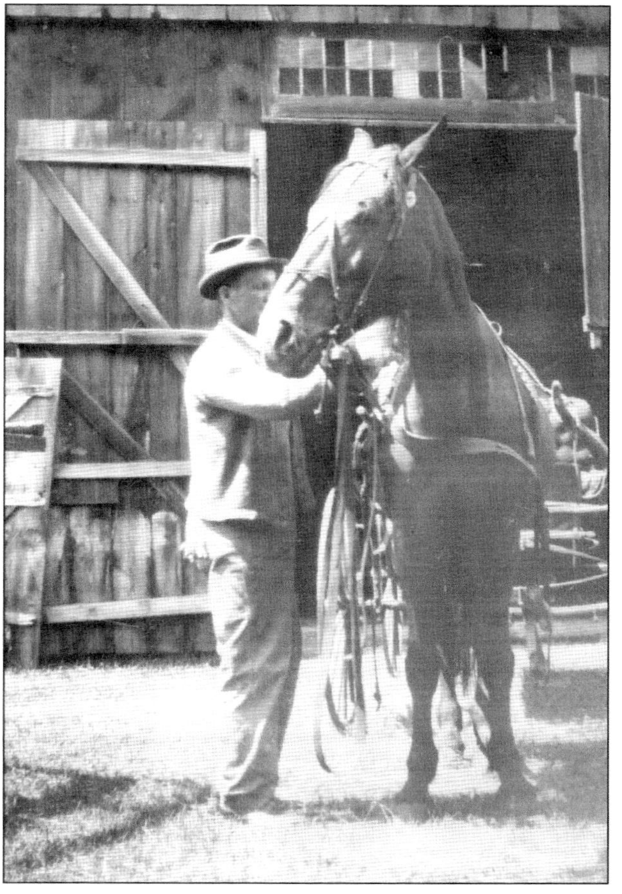

This is the Goodnow home in Millington. The 60-foot windmill drew water for household use and to water animals. There were no artesian wells. Most people had dug wells walled up with stones, and the water was drawn up with a pail. The windmill was reerected in Orange, Massachusetts, where it was used to pump water for a chicken farm. It is still stands today, but its work is done.

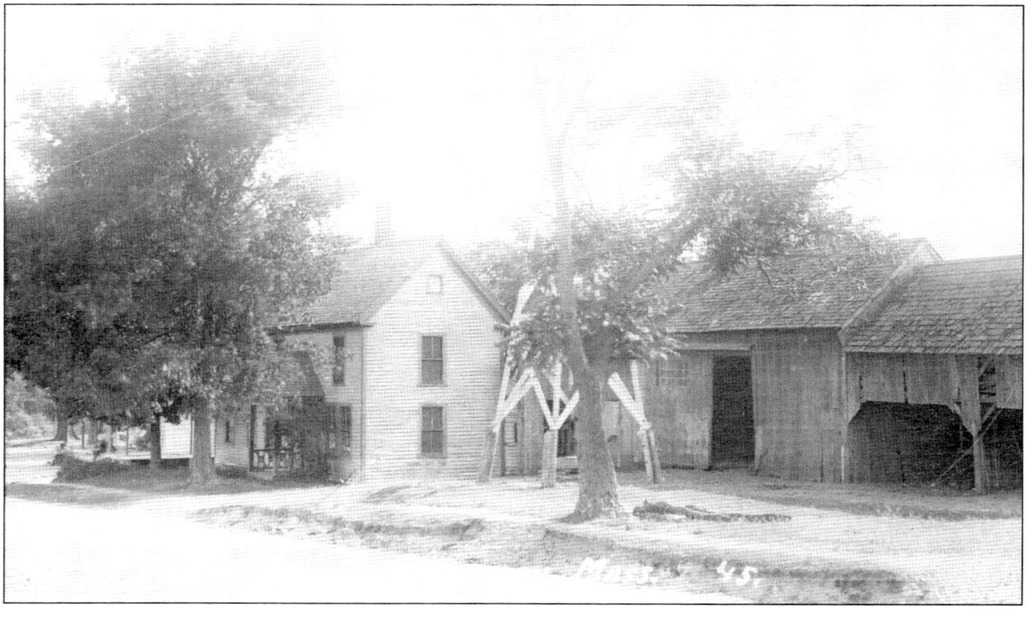

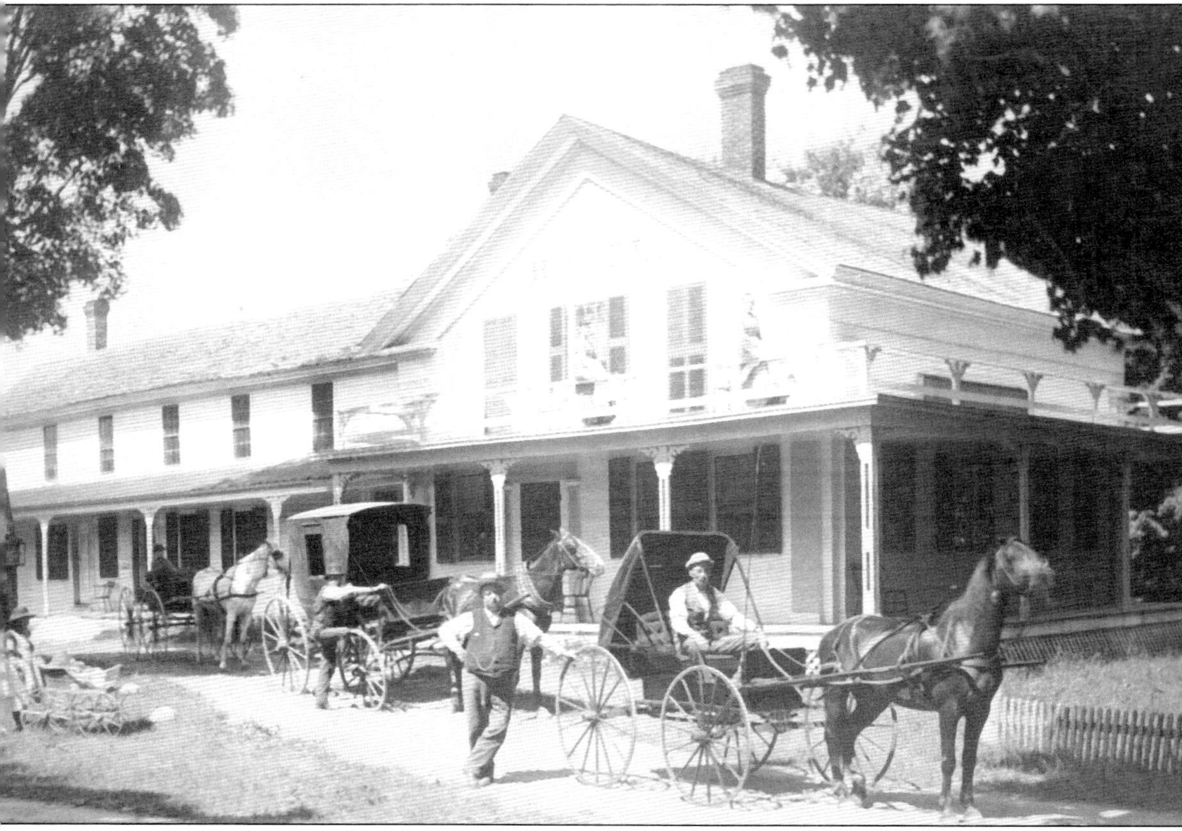

This is the Riverside Hotel in Greenwich. It burned in 1910. The guests were transferred in elegant horse-drawn carriages.

Jesse Haskins was a soldier in World War I. Prescott sent 13 men into the "war to end all wars." They were Frank A. Bowen, John W. Currier, John R. Fisher, Milfred A. Grout, Jessie L. Haskins, F. Conrad Lincoln, Robert A. Newberry, Harold F. Peirce, Harrison D. Peirce, Willis F. Shaw, Harry A. Upton, Joseph Venette, and Albert Wendemuth. Lincoln, Shaw, and Harold Peirce died as a result.

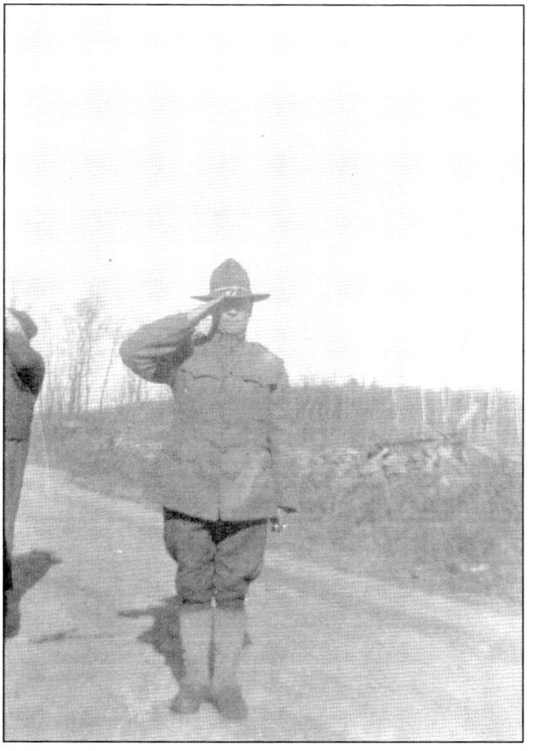

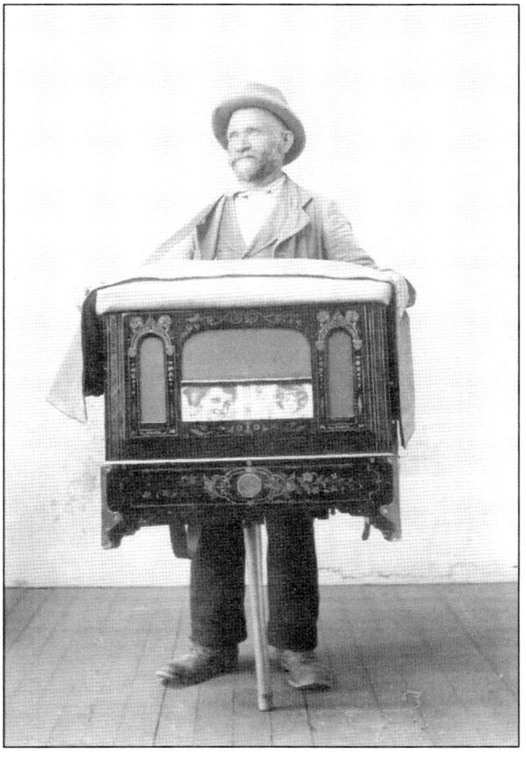

The organ grinder was a popular street entertainer in the mid-1800s. There is no identification except that this gentleman appeared often in Enfield.

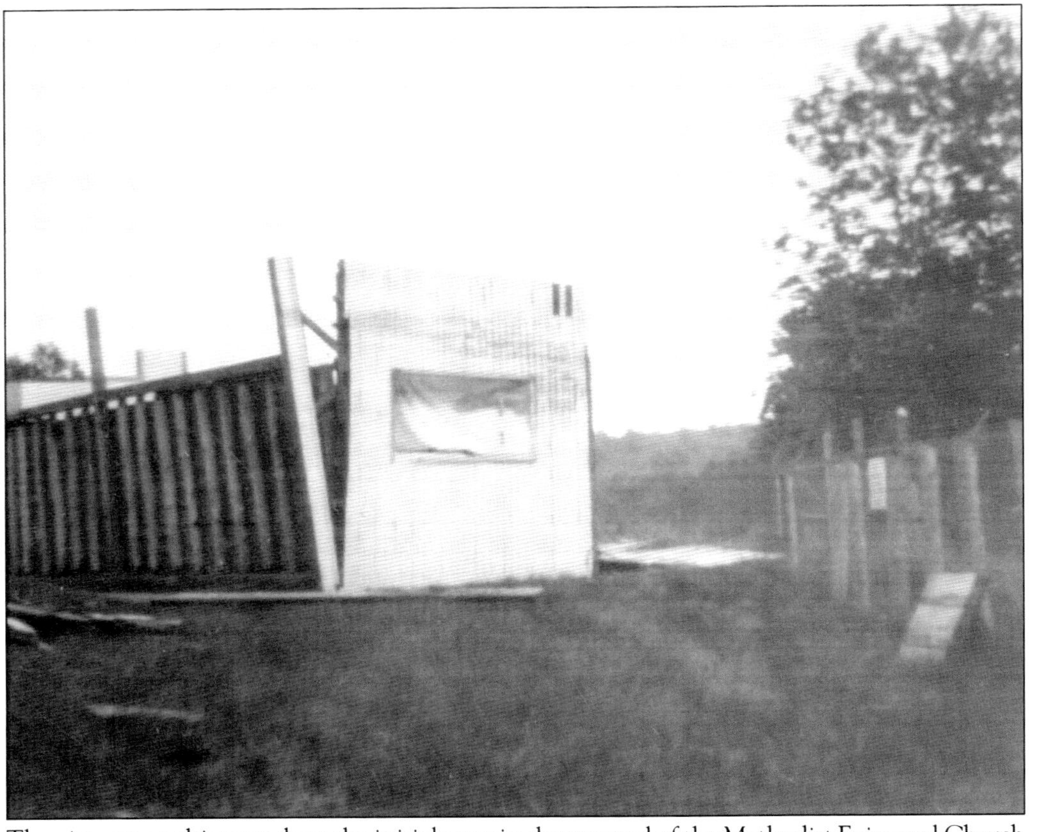

The pictures on this page show the initial steps in the removal of the Methodist Episcopal Church of Prescott from its home in Prescott to a new home in Orange. Built in 1837, it was scheduled for demolition in 1938 because it was inside the boundary line of the Quabbin watershed. The Prescott Historical Society was able to purchase the church for its museum. It was cut in thirds, moved to Orange on a flatbed trailer, and reerected.

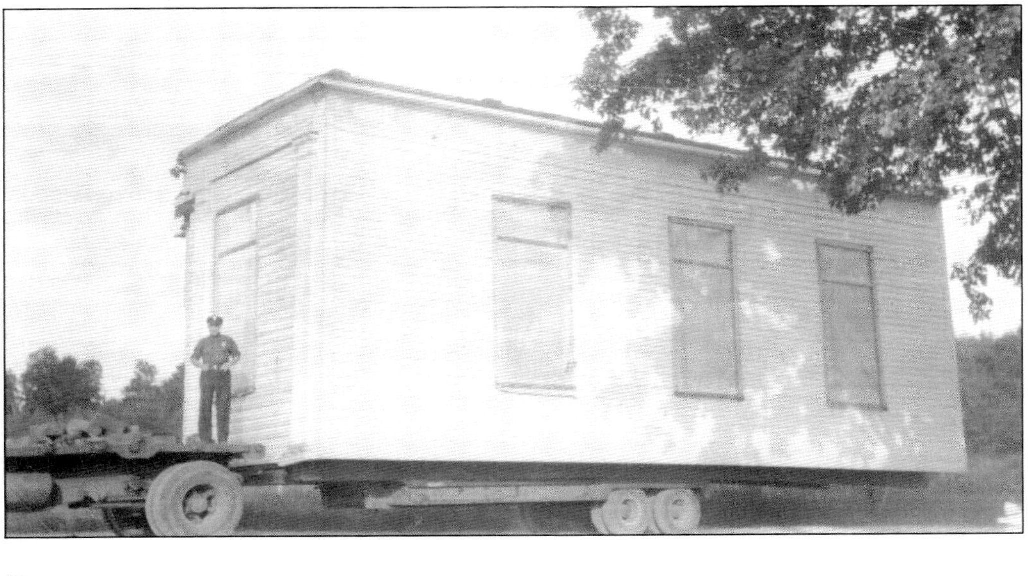

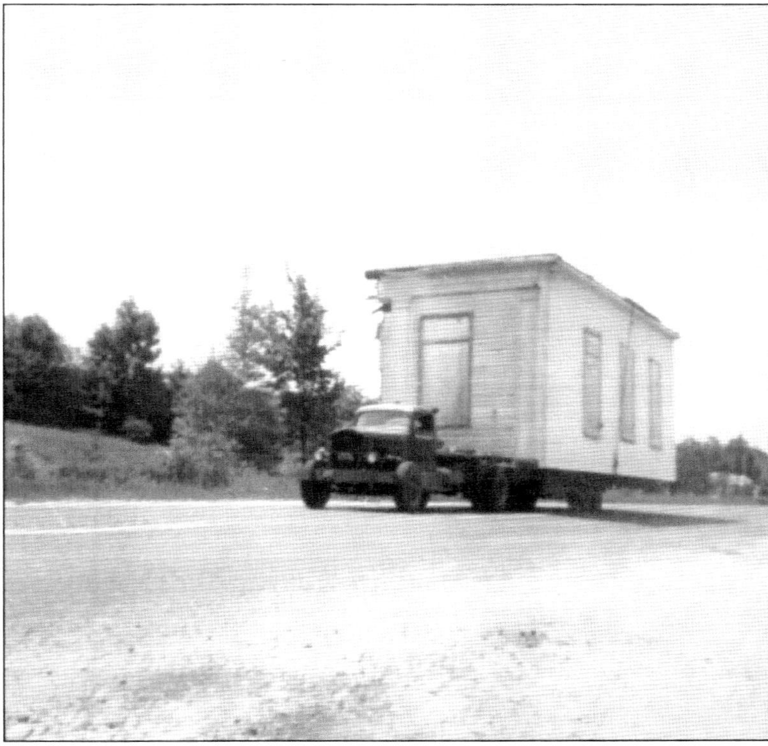

Seen here is the Methodist Episcopal church on the flatbed heading toward Orange. It was again moved in 1985, this time relocated intact to its permanent home on the grounds of the Swift River Valley Historical Society, Inc., in North New Salem.

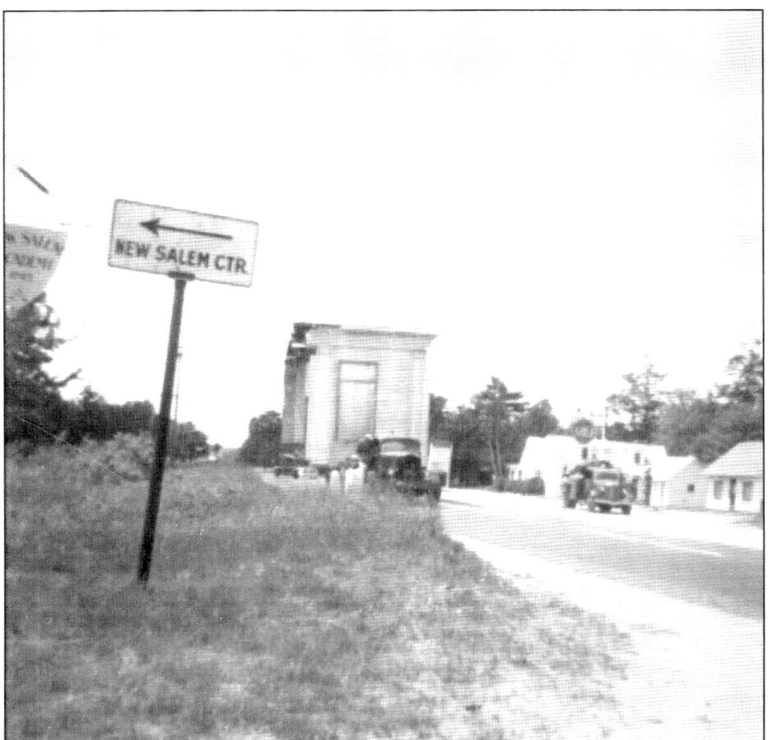

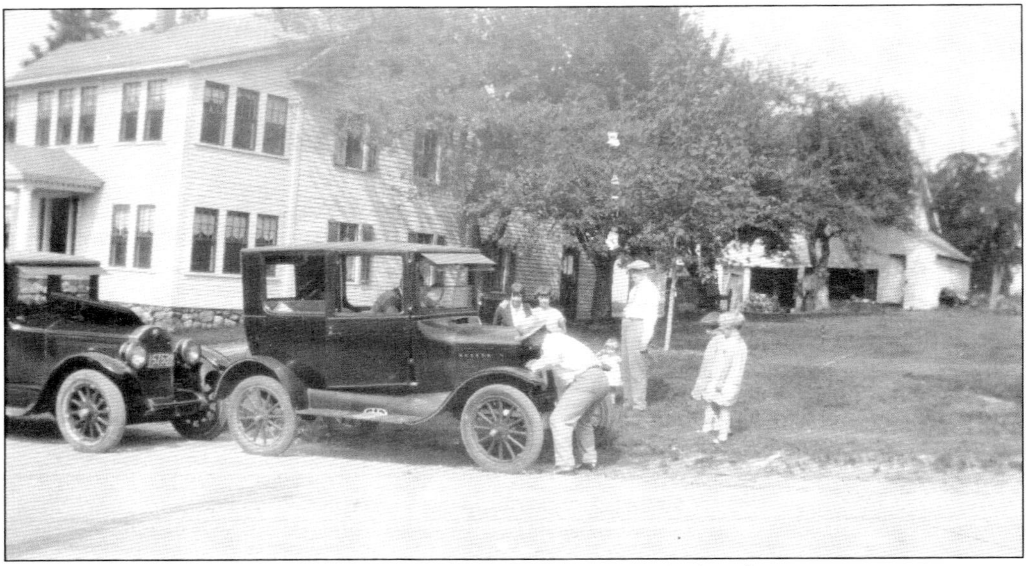

In 1923, the only way to start a Ford Model T was to crank it by hand. It was easy once one got the hang of it.

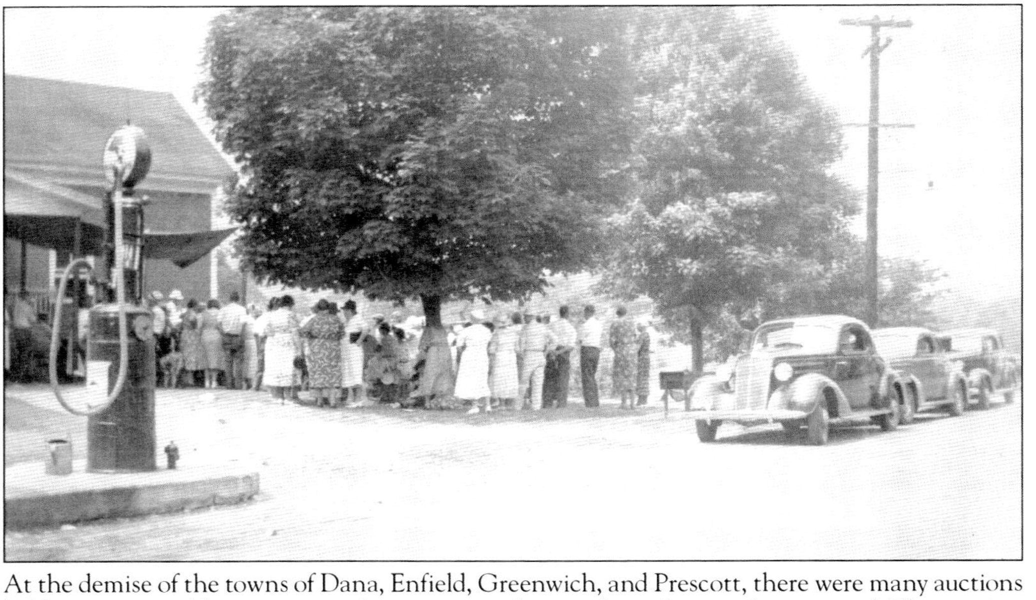

At the demise of the towns of Dana, Enfield, Greenwich, and Prescott, there were many auctions held as a way to add some income from items not being taken when residents moved. This auction is at North Dana in 1938.

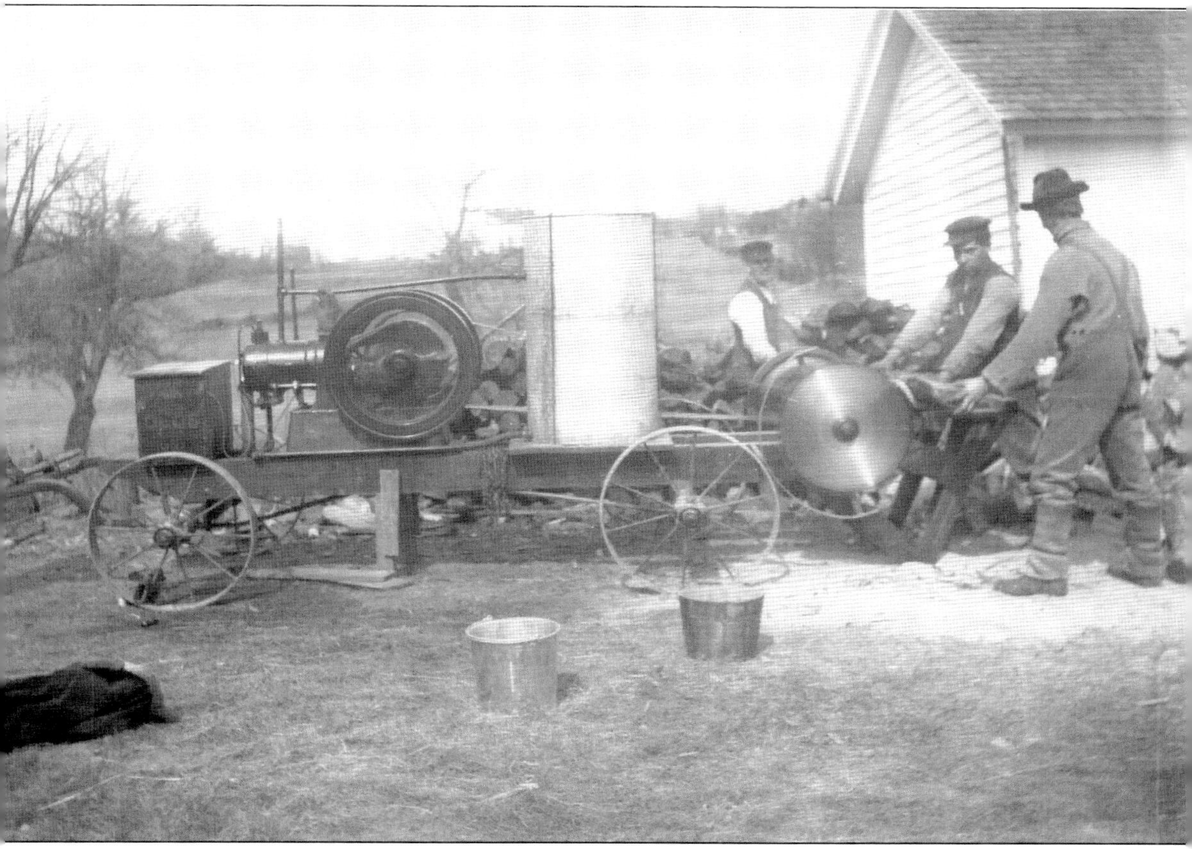

Charles Smith, at the far right of the picture, is the inventor of this portable gasoline-powered sawmill. It could easily be moved from one woodpile to another, making the work much faster, though probably as dangerous as doing it with an axe. Prescott Hill is visible in the background.

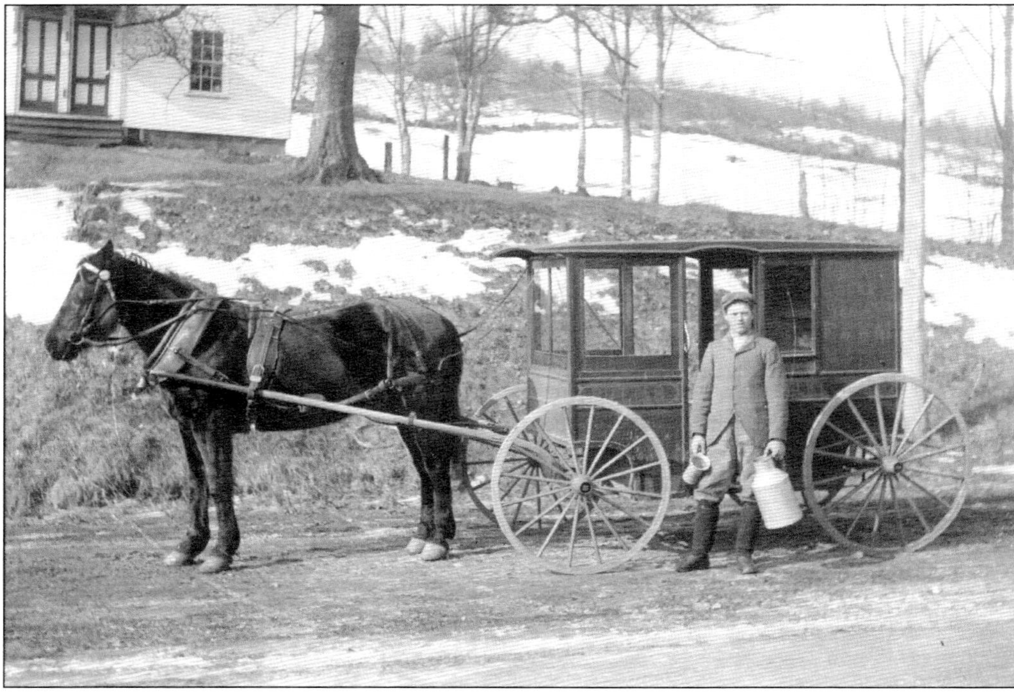

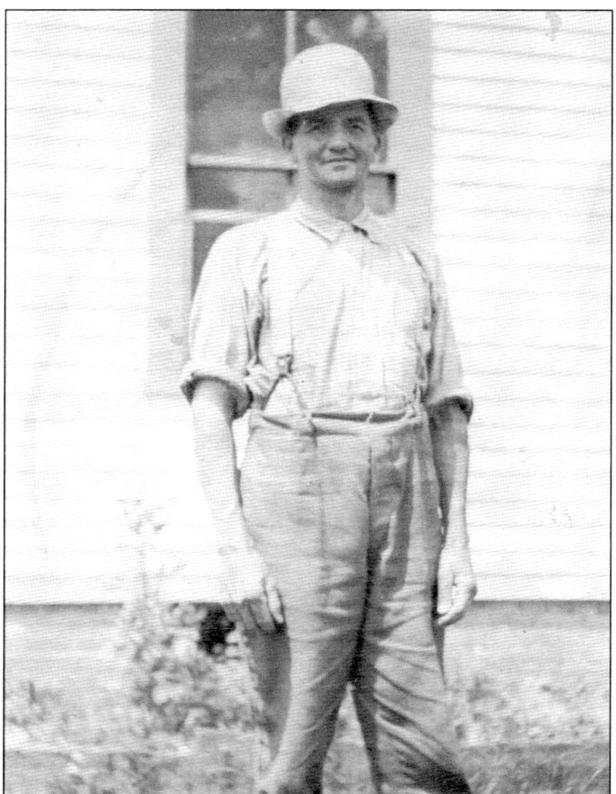

This unidentified milkman holds a one-quart measure in his right hand and a ten-quart pail of milk in his left. The horse waits patiently as they make their early-morning rounds. The customers provided their own receptacles for the amount of milk desired.

This gentleman is James Bowyer, who lived at the town farm in New Salem for several years. He and his wife took care of the needy at the farm. This picture was taken in 1916.

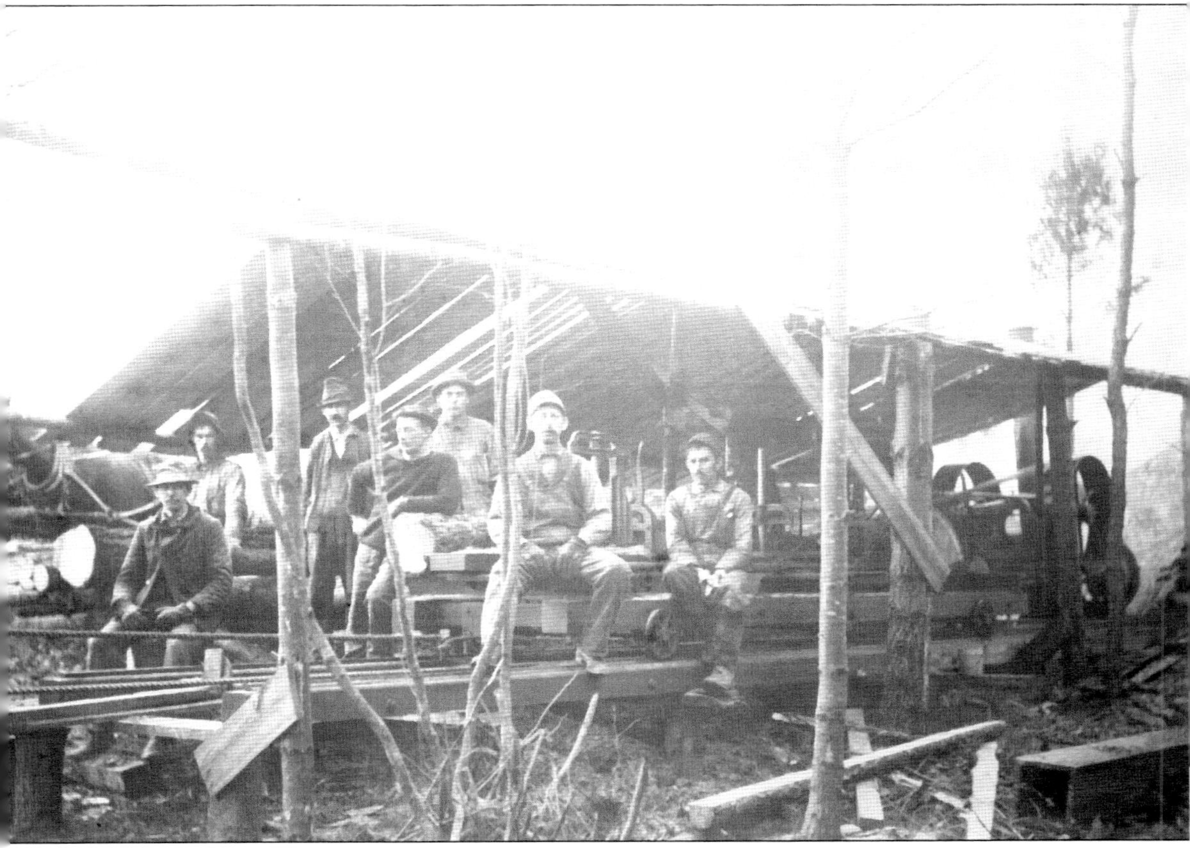

Logging provided employment for many men. Mills were moved from place to place, and makeshift shelters were constructed to house equipment. Horses or oxen were used to haul logs to the mill, where the wood was sawed into board for building projects. Pictured, from left to right, are Ed Mitchell, Everett Laplante, Harry Abbott, Miner Vaughn, Fred Moore, Linus Pierce, and Frank Jones.

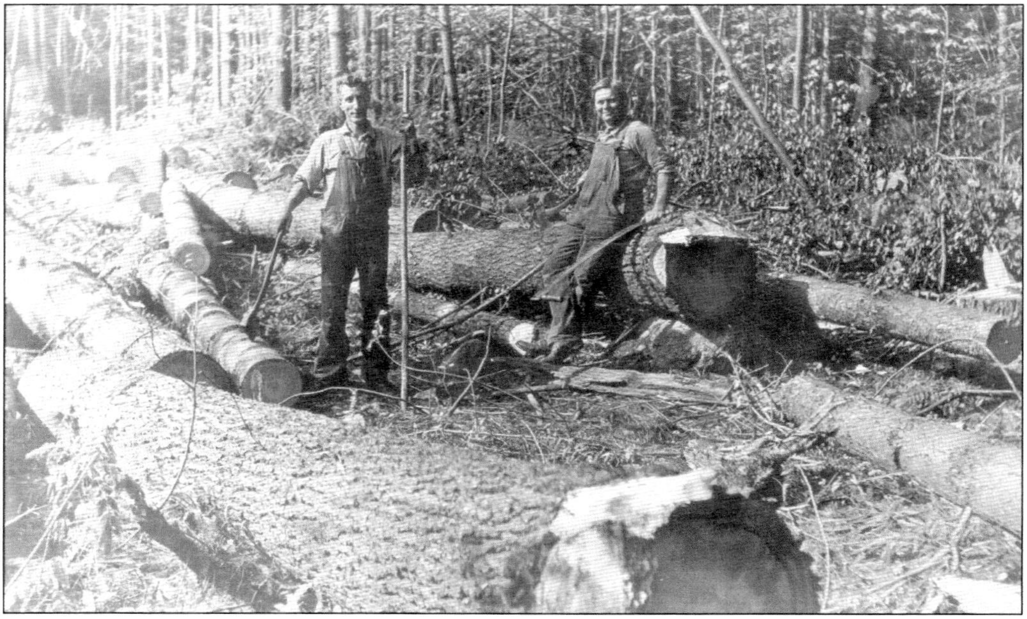

Leon Stone (left) and Jesse Haskins take a break from their logging operation. No heavy equipment was available, and the work was slow and exhausting.

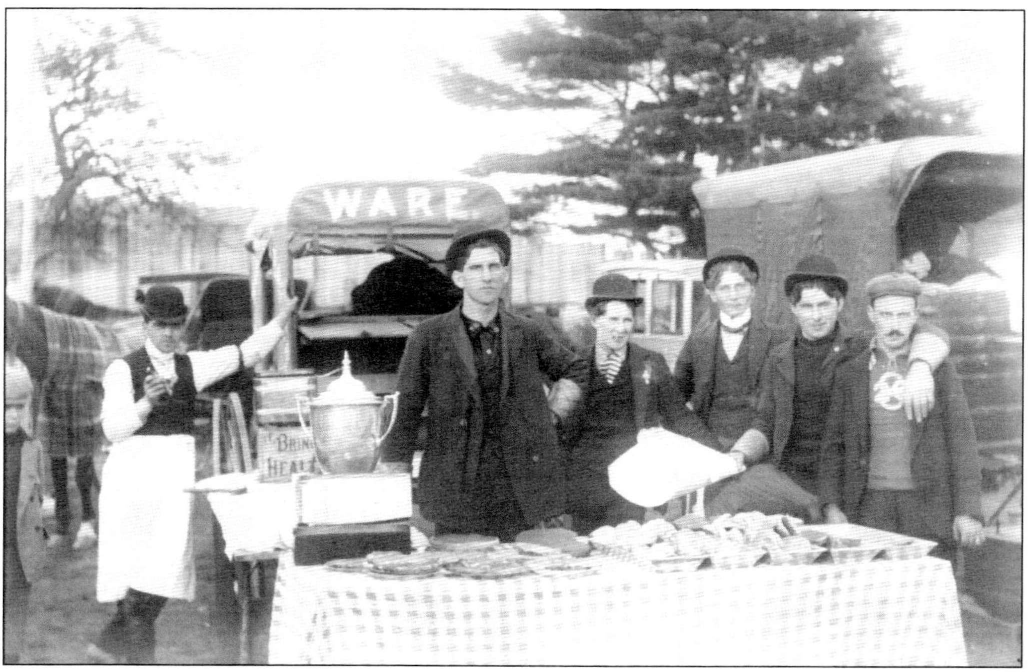

This picture shows the food concession at Tony Mason's trotting park in Enfield. As their sign says, they have come from Ware loaded down with sandwiches, cookies, and pies. Horse racing was a popular event at the park, and the crowds were large and always hungry.

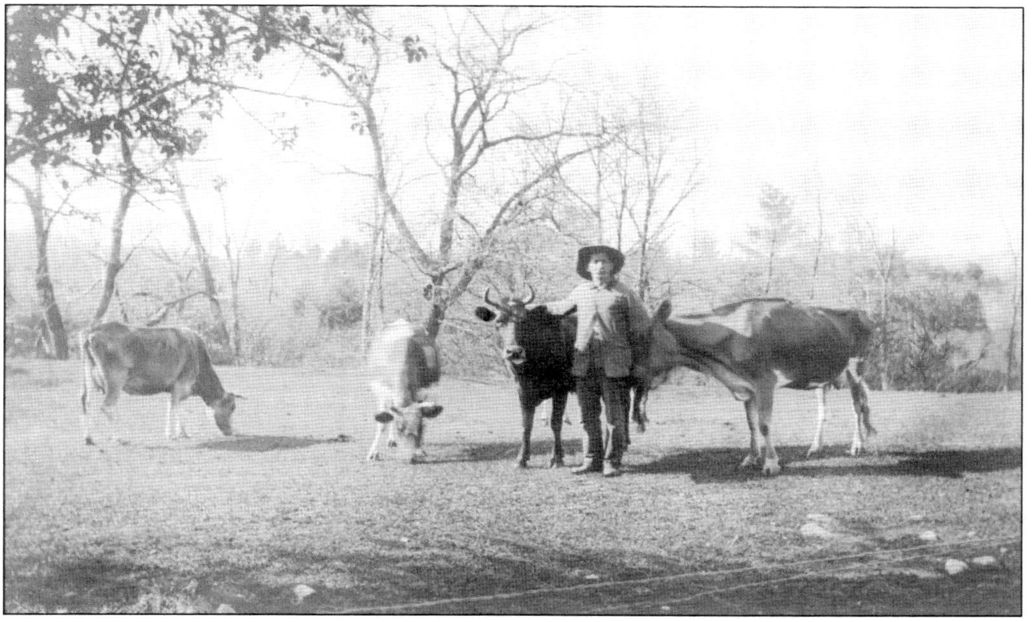

George Southworth enjoys a sunny day with his cows as they browse for a blade of green grass.

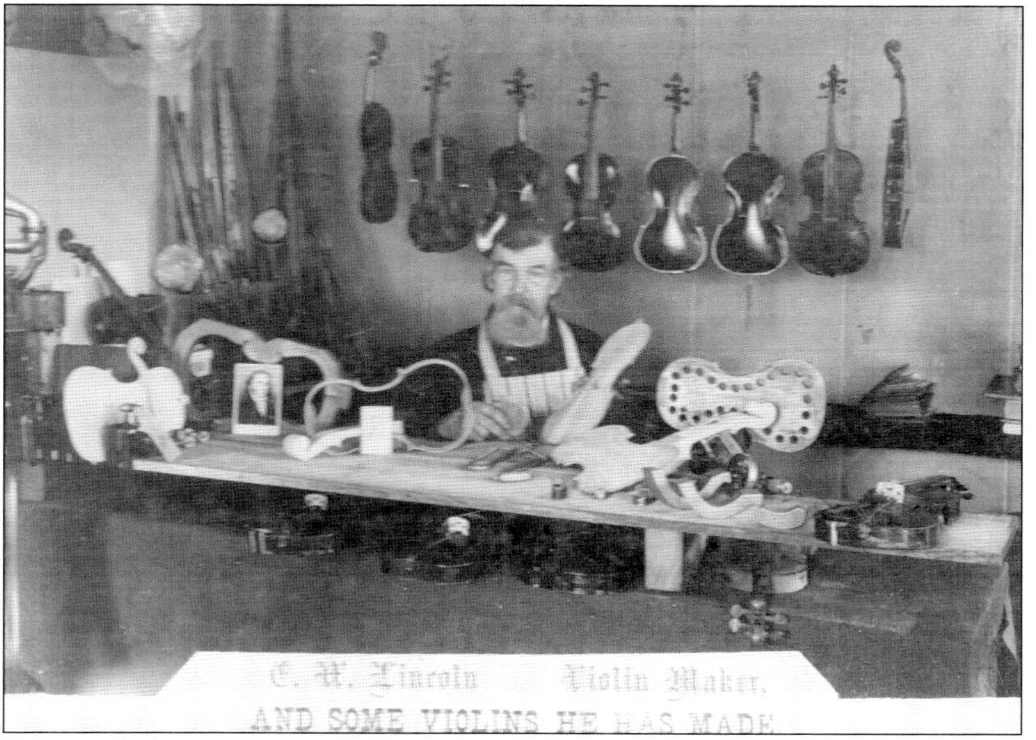

E.W. Lincoln, born in Greenwich in 1855, is pictured here in his workshop. From an early age, he was a very talented musician, playing for many occasions in many places. A machinist by trade, he had the misfortune of losing the use of his left hand and could no longer play. He turned his love of the violin into a hobby of making the instrument. His success led to a beautiful collection.

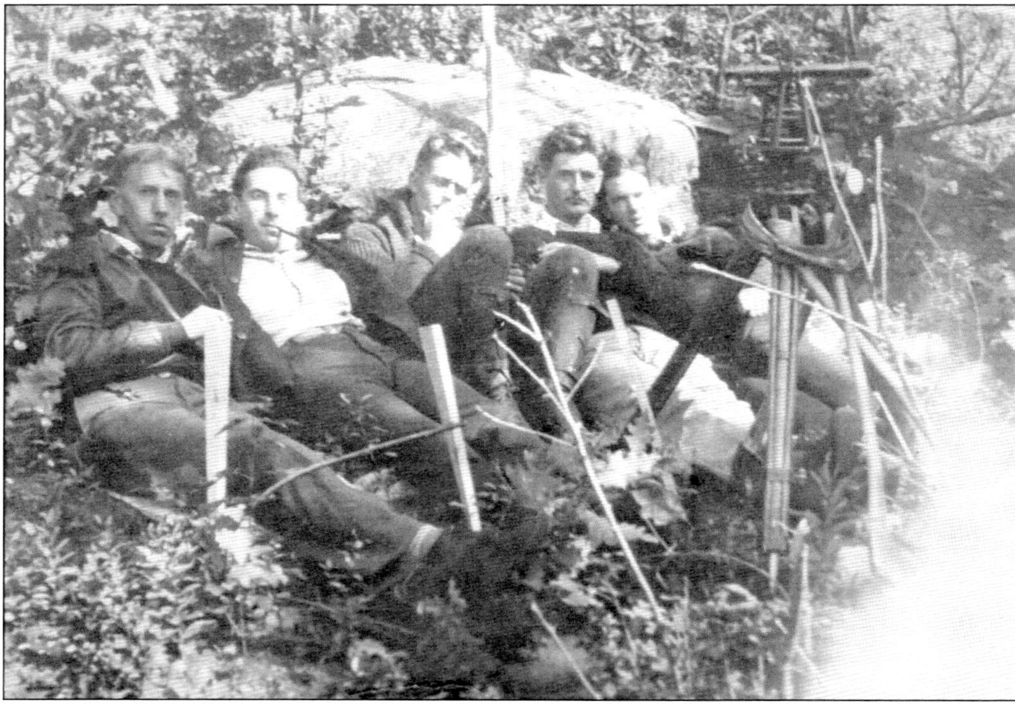

These unidentified men appear to be just too tired to work any more. The equipment shown would indicate they might be surveyors.

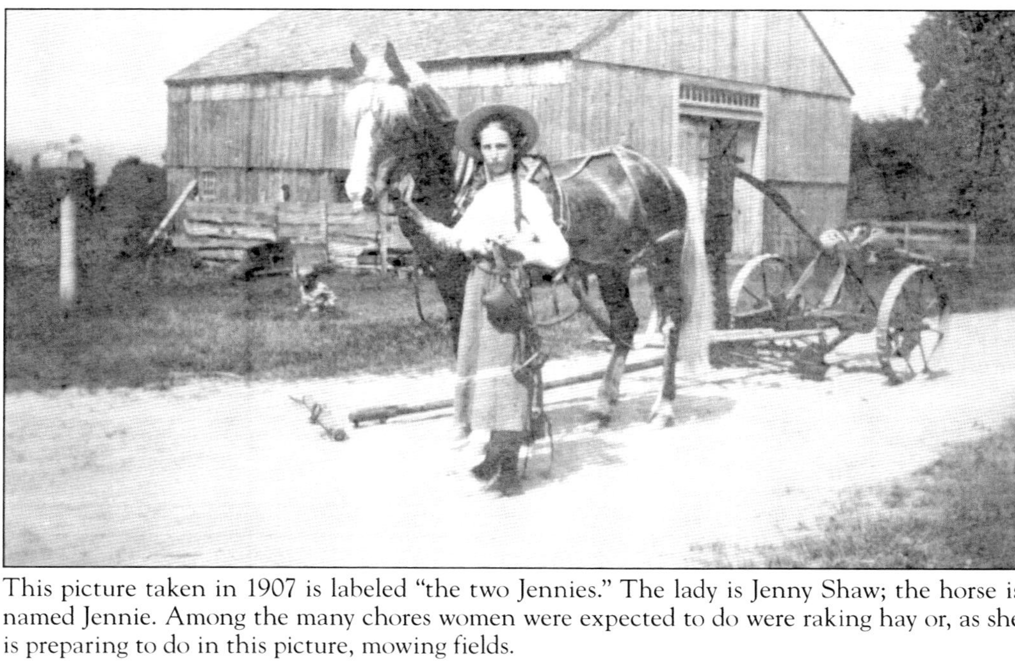

This picture taken in 1907 is labeled "the two Jennies." The lady is Jenny Shaw; the horse is named Jennie. Among the many chores women were expected to do were raking hay or, as she is preparing to do in this picture, mowing fields.

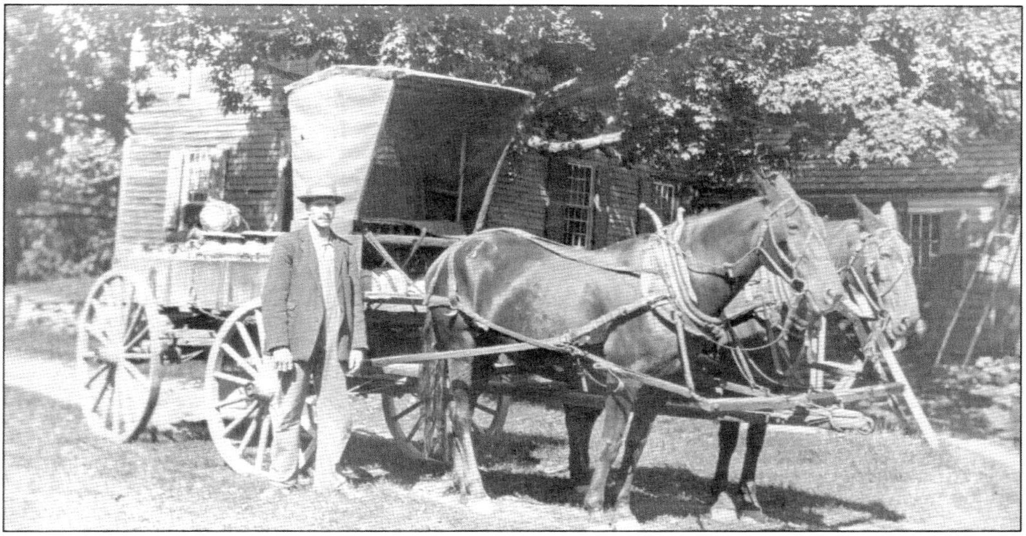

Levi Newton was the first cream gatherer in Prescott. This is Ellis Pierce, who followed him. Ellis began this job in 1907 and continued for four years.

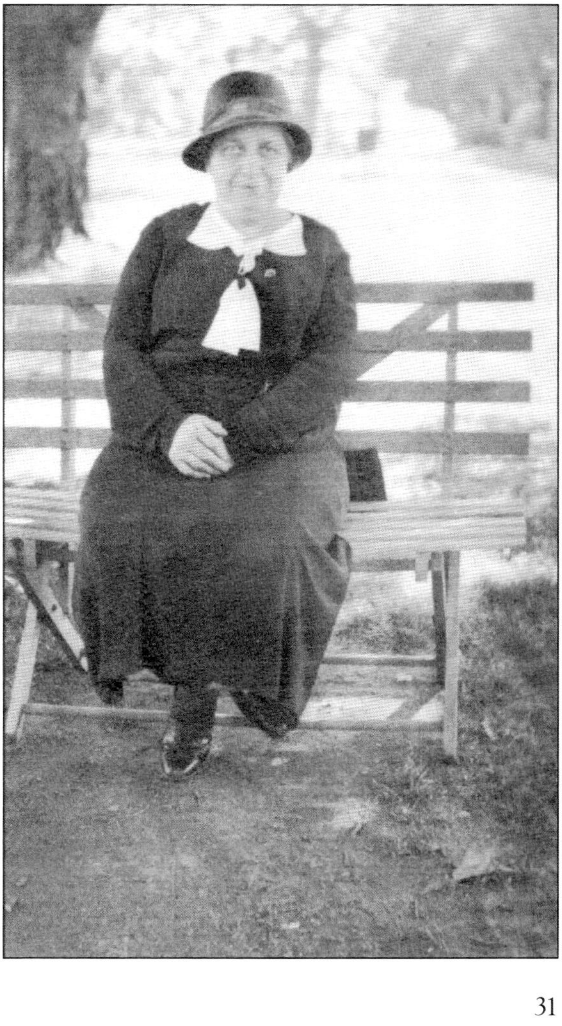

This picture, taken in Greenwich, is labeled "Clara Potter, help for mother."

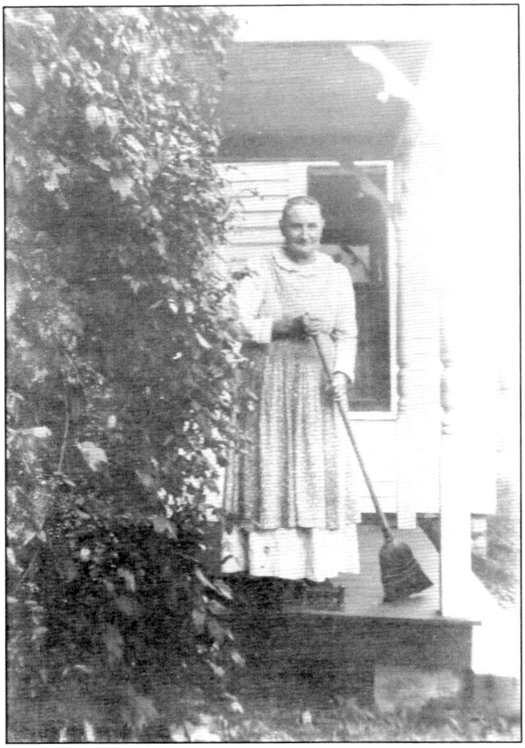

This lady is Martha Fewell, sister of Burt V. Brooks, painter and photographer of Greenwich. Housekeeping was done with none of the modern amenities.

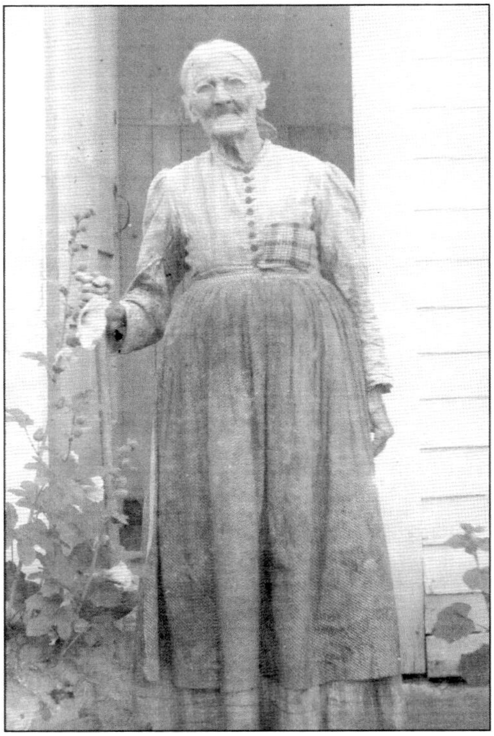

This photograph of "Grandma Morse" was taken by photographer Burt Brooks of Greenwich. An apron was always worn to protect the clothing. It could also be used to gather eggs or produce from the garden. A more formal picture of Mrs. Morse is found on page 68.

This soldier, W.W. Thomas, fought in the Civil War in 1864. He was wounded and died of his injuries. Note his uniform and the length of the gun.

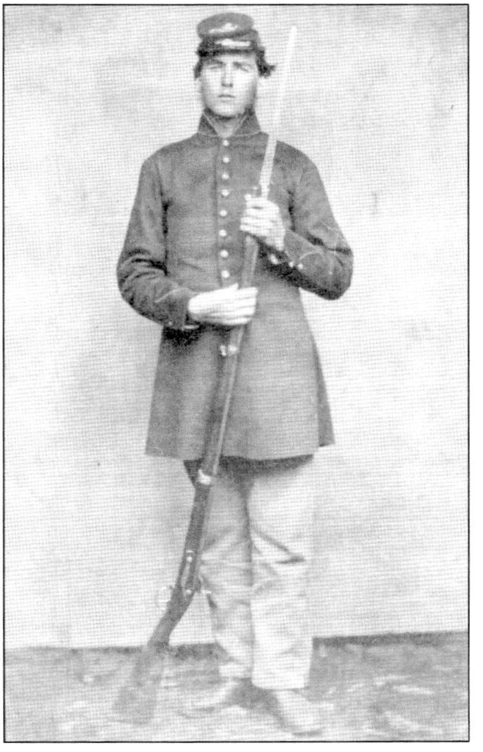

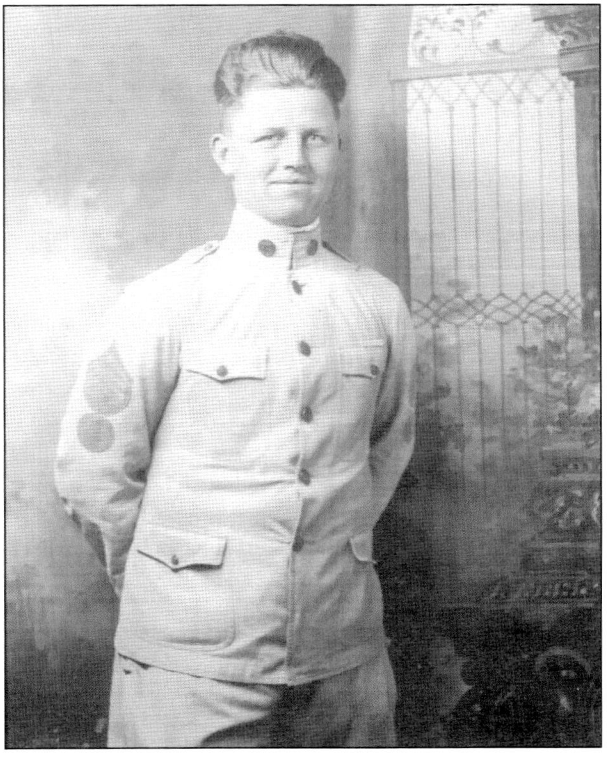

This is Clifford Hobart wearing the uniform of World War I in 1918.

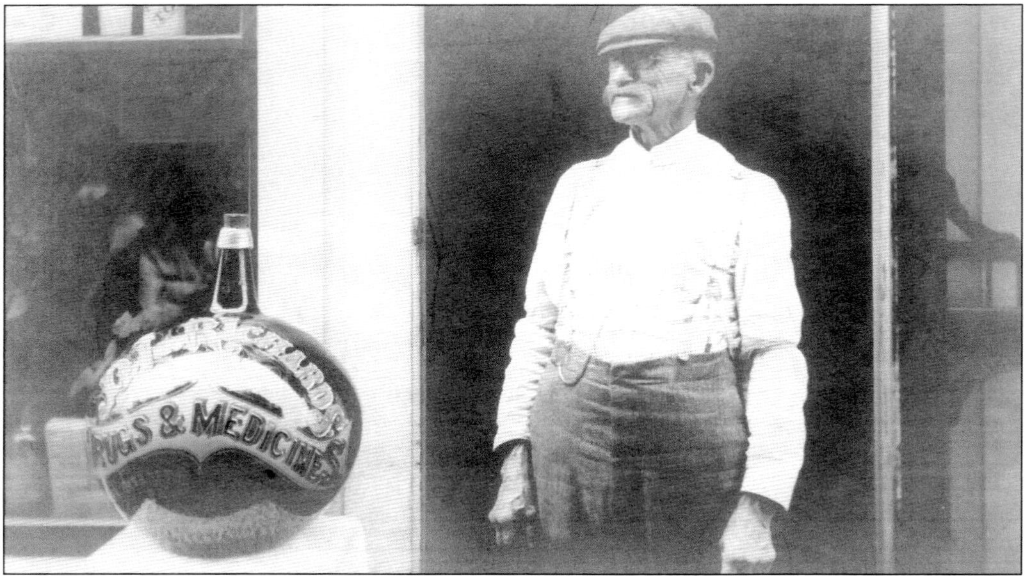

Mr. Richards stands in the doorway of his store, which advertises "drugs and medicines." His clothing, typical of the day, includes sleeve guards and suspenders. The pocket watch on a chain preceded the wrist watch. The cap became popular in 1900.

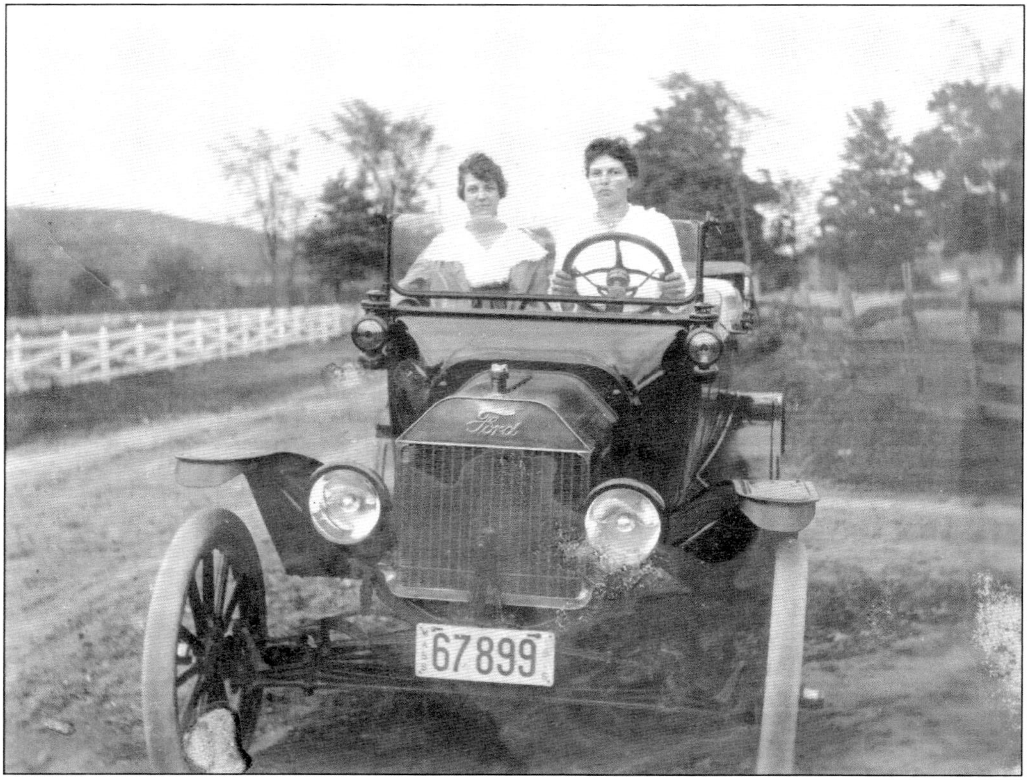

By the expression on the face of Annie Laplante, she is having a driving lesson. Theo Gould is the instructor. Note how narrow the tires are.

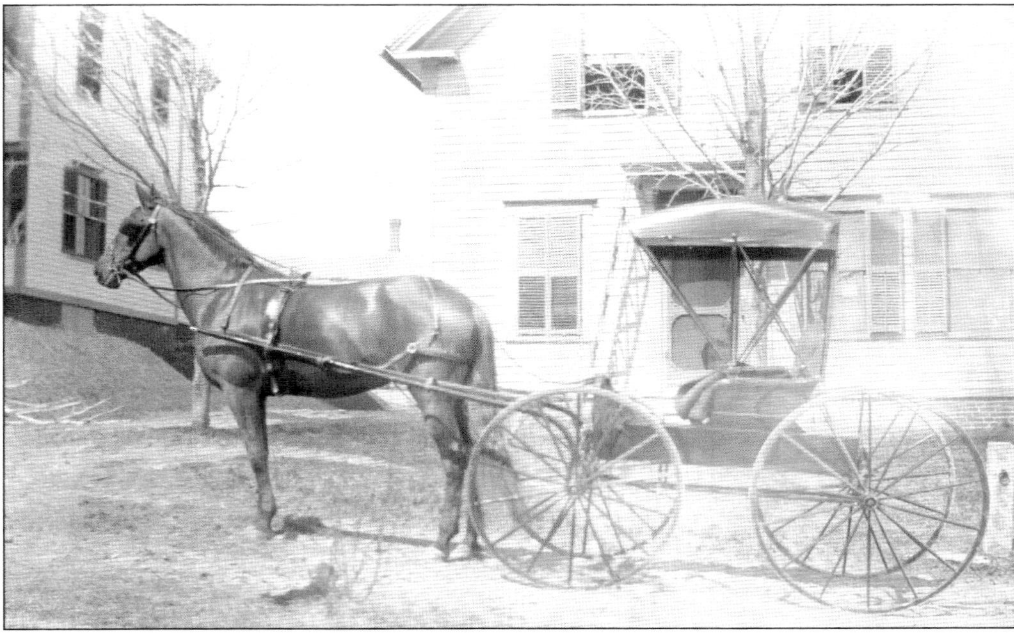

Every man's prized treasure was his horse and carriage. This one belonged to C. Eugene Coolidge, a woodworker whose many talents included making violins and baseball bats.

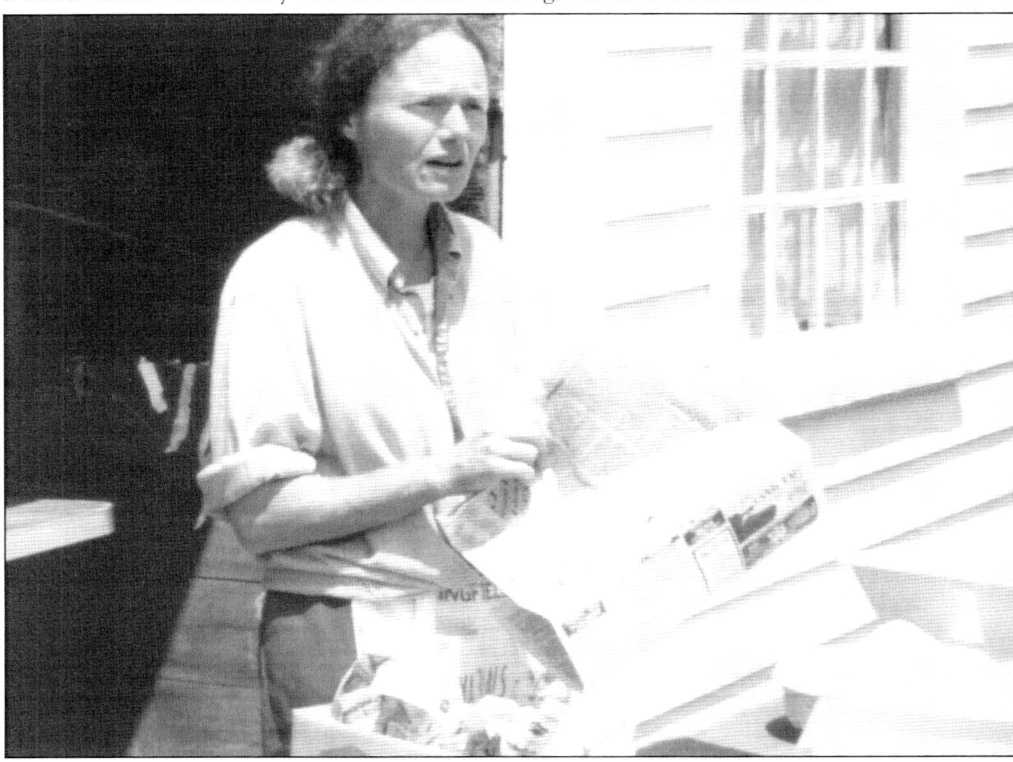

Sharon Young, an energetic fundraiser, is unpacking treasures for a tag sale on a sunny Saturday at the Swift River Valley Historical Society.

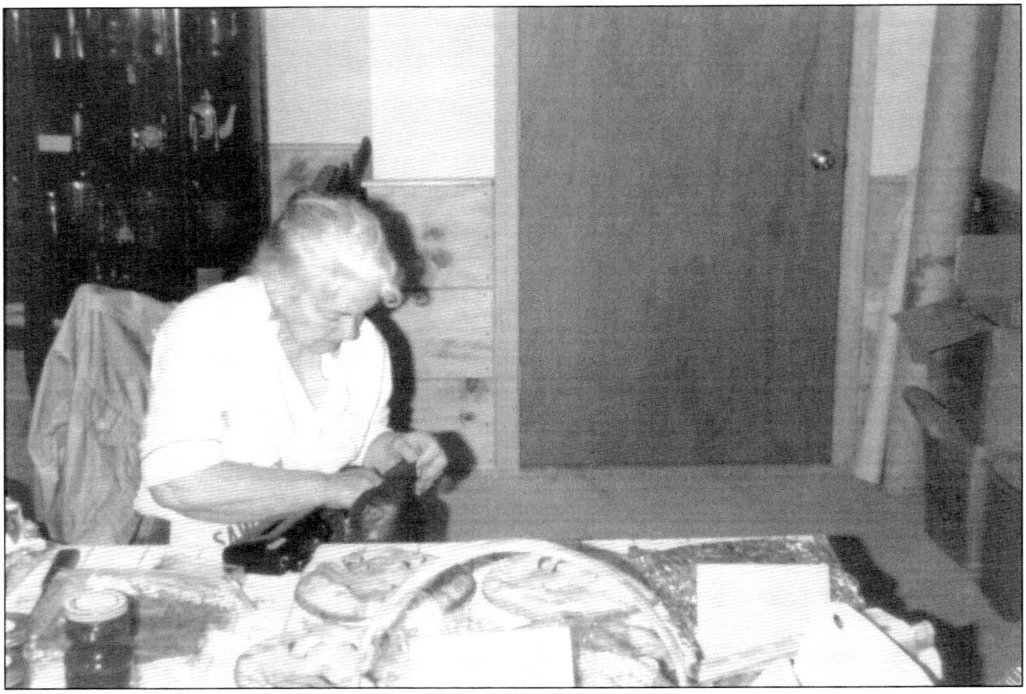

Fundraising, always a necessity, occurs at the Swift River Valley Historical Society on a regular basis. Here, Lois Barnes oversees a delicious assortment of pies and other goodies.

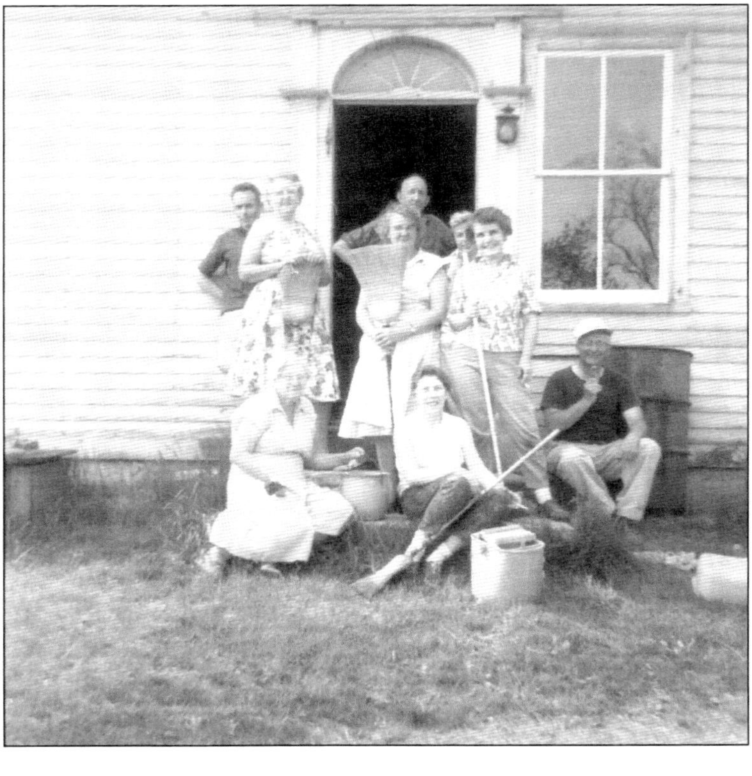

This picture shows the crew that worked long and hard to ready this house to become the Swift River Valley Historical Society in 1964. Work continues even today to maintain and preserve the artifacts and memories of the valley.

Two

PLAYING

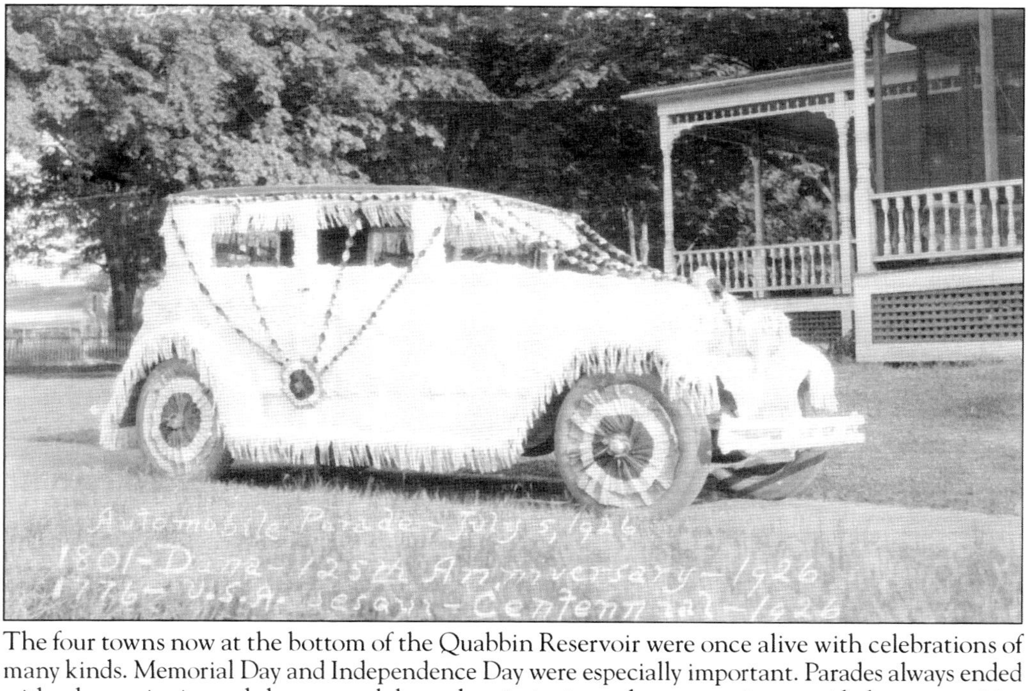

The four towns now at the bottom of the Quabbin Reservoir were once alive with celebrations of many kinds. Memorial Day and Independence Day were especially important. Parades always ended with a huge picnic, and the many clubs and societies in each community provided opportunities for socialization and pleasure. The people knew how to make a good time, and the following pictures are proof of it.

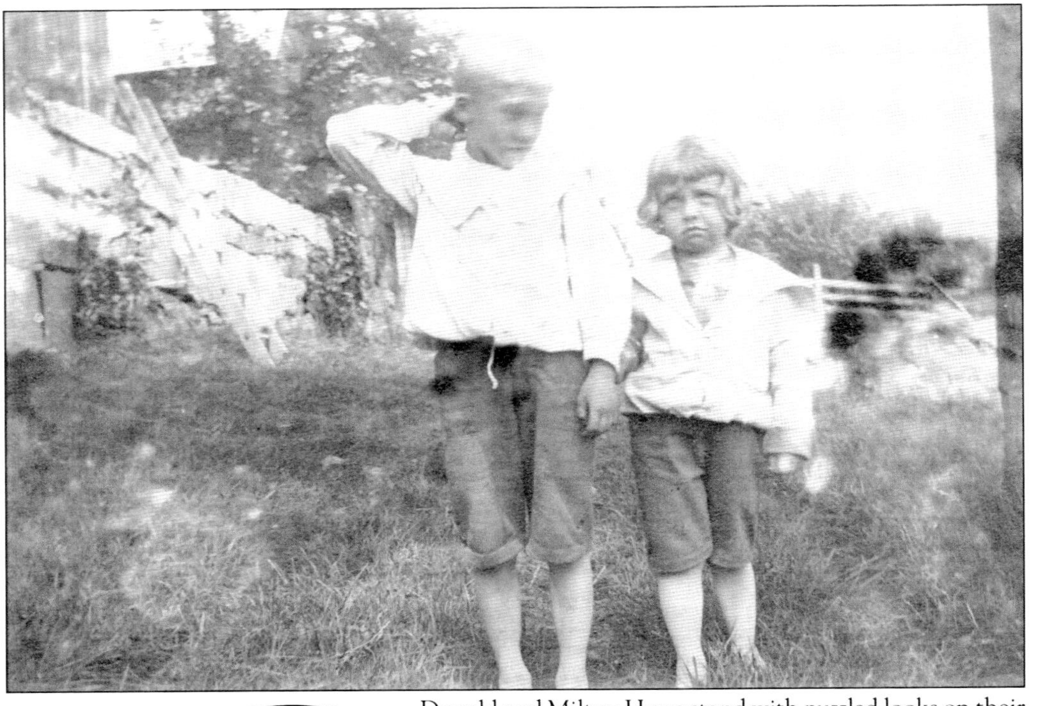

Donald and Milton Howe stand with puzzled looks on their faces. Perhaps it is the first day of summer vacation and they are trying to decide what to do first.

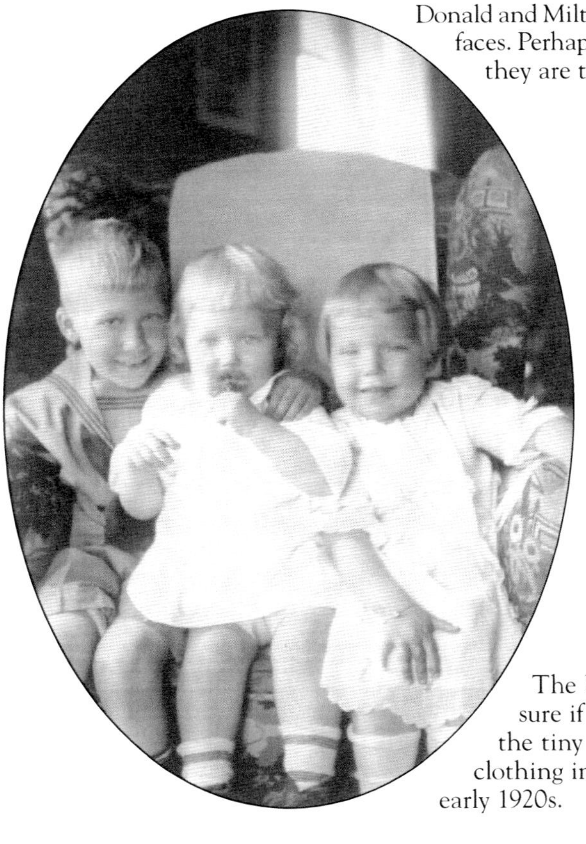

The baby sister in this photograph is not too sure if she likes having her picture taken. Note the tiny bracelet on the big sister. The children's clothing indicates that this image was taken in the early 1920s.

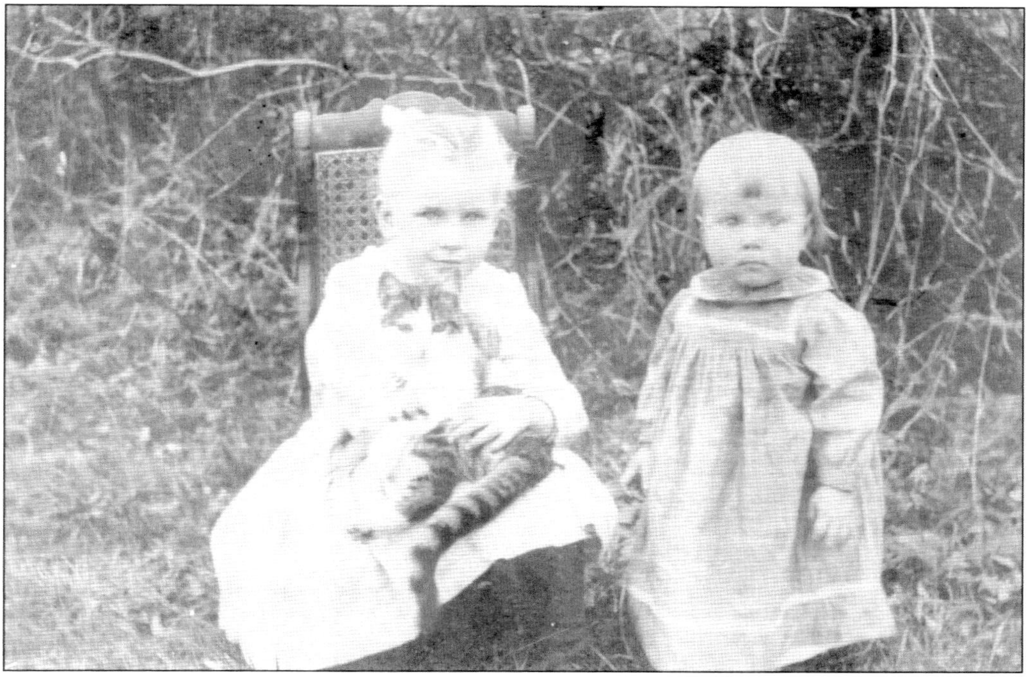

Iola and Eunice Mitchell enjoy a sunny day along with their tabby cat.

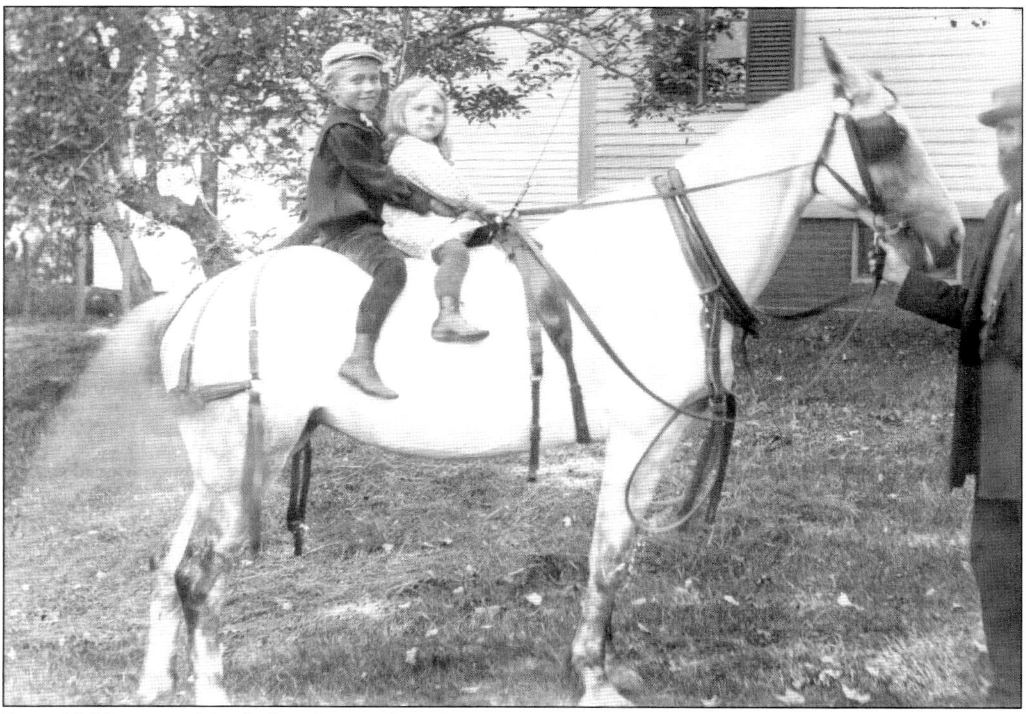

Donald Howe and little brother Milton Freeman Howe enjoy a quick ride with Edwin Henry Howe, their father, holding the horse. The Howe family was the oldest and most active in the 200-year history of Enfield.

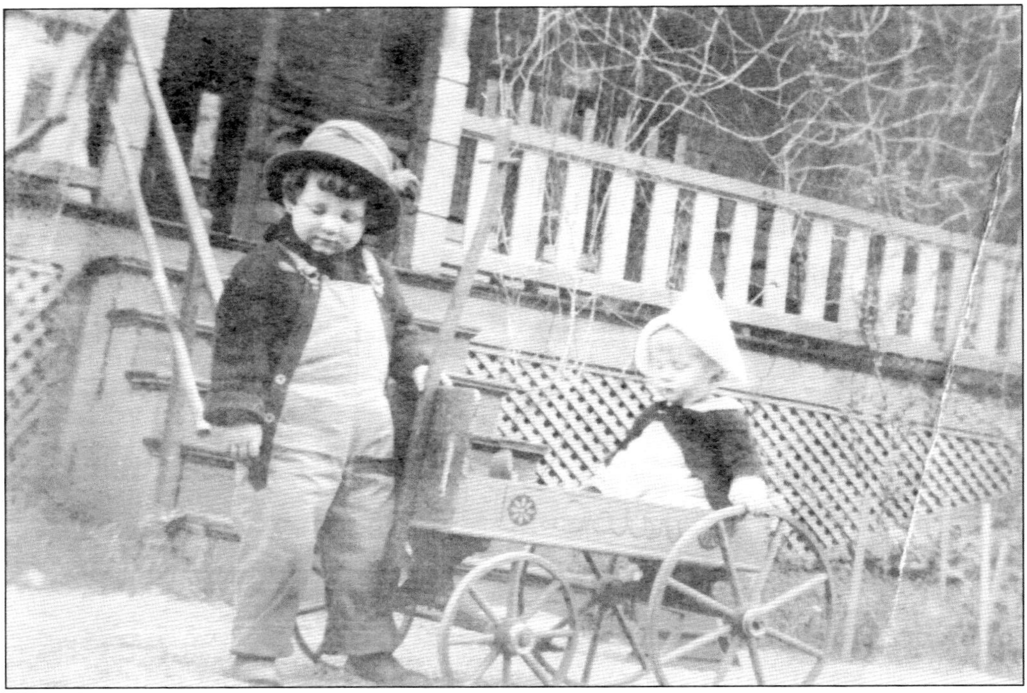

This little chap is all set to give his passenger a ride in the little wagon. The name on the side identifies it as a Daisy wagon.

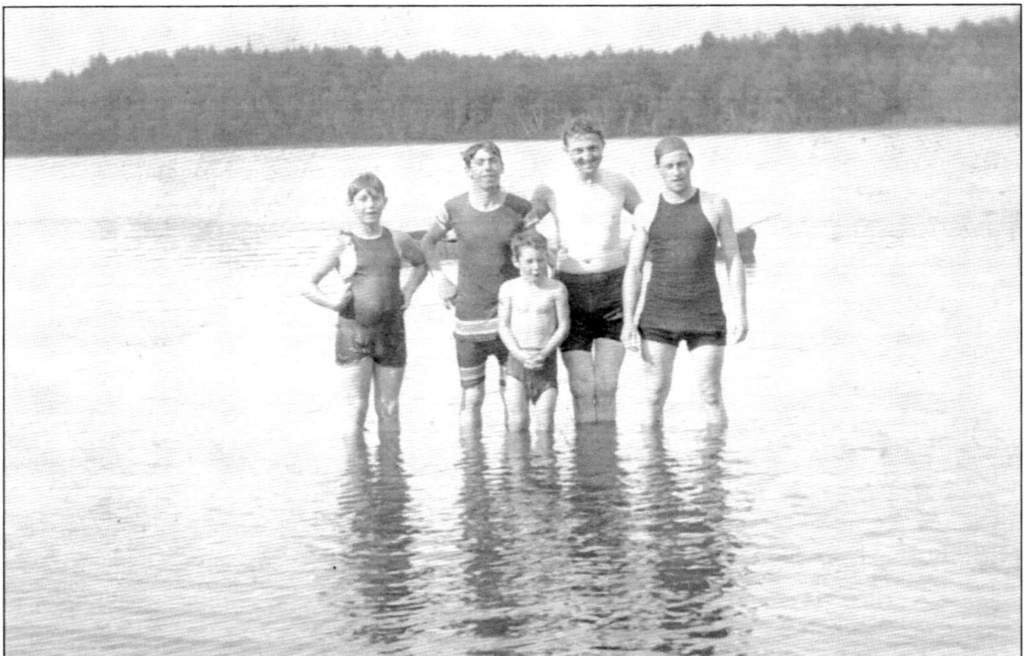

This family group enjoys a sunny day at one of the many lakes in Greenwich. The classy bathing suits are woolen and very itchy when wet.

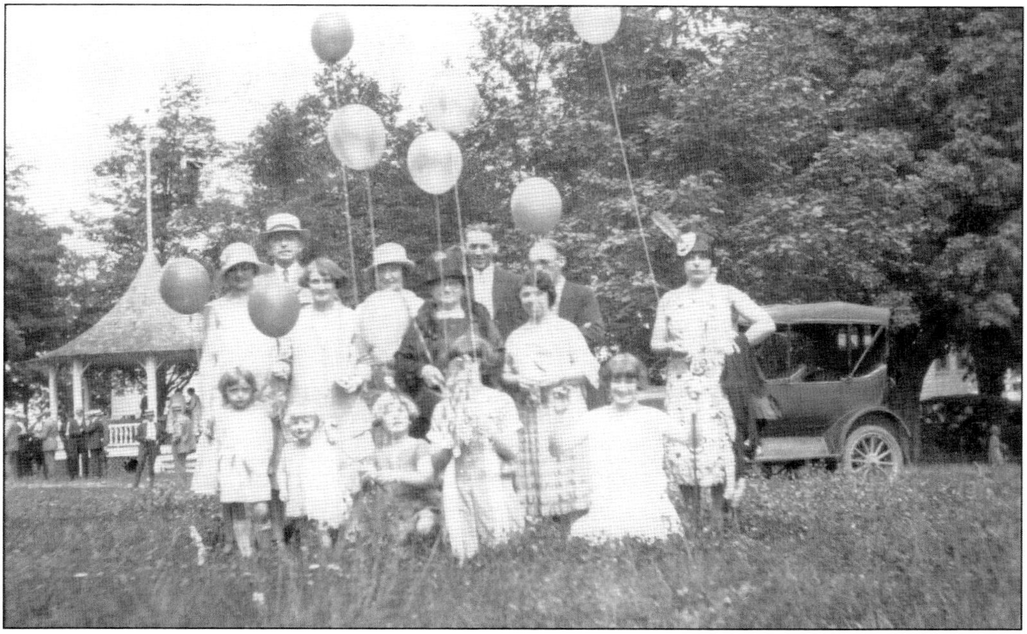

This is Reunion Day at the New Salem Academy in 1926. There were speakers, suppers, band concerts, and lots of visiting. These reunions are still happening today. The academy opened in 1795 and remained an institution of learning until 1954. Note the bandstand at the left; it was burned in an act of vandalism in about 1945 and was never rebuilt.

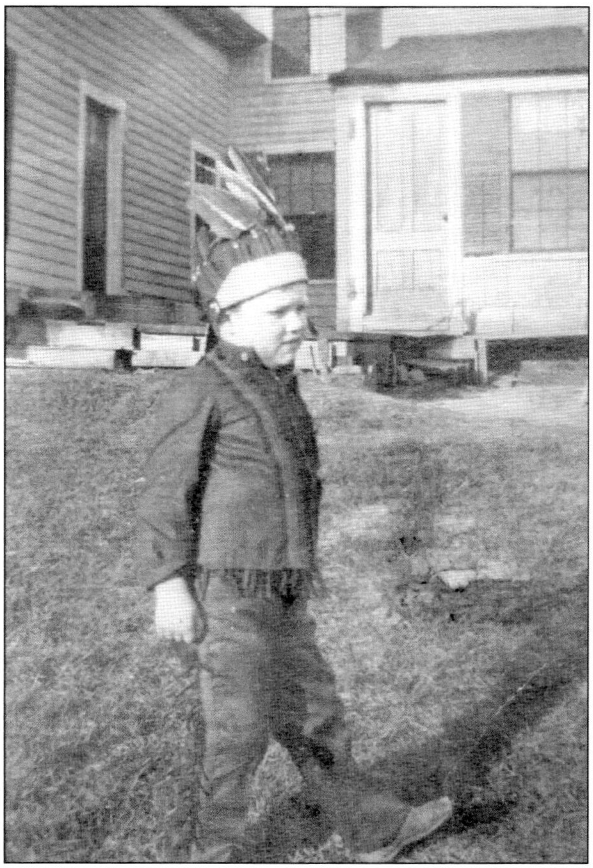

Every little boy can become an Indian if he can entice his mother to fashion him a headdress of chicken feathers.

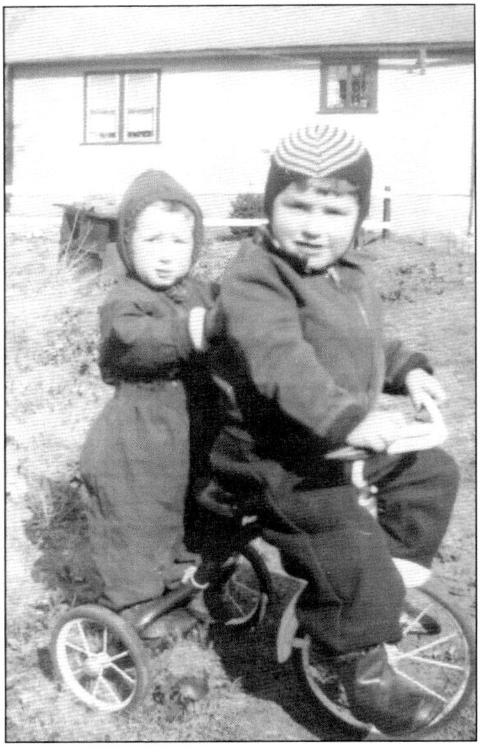

These unidentified little boys are enjoying a shiny new tricycle.

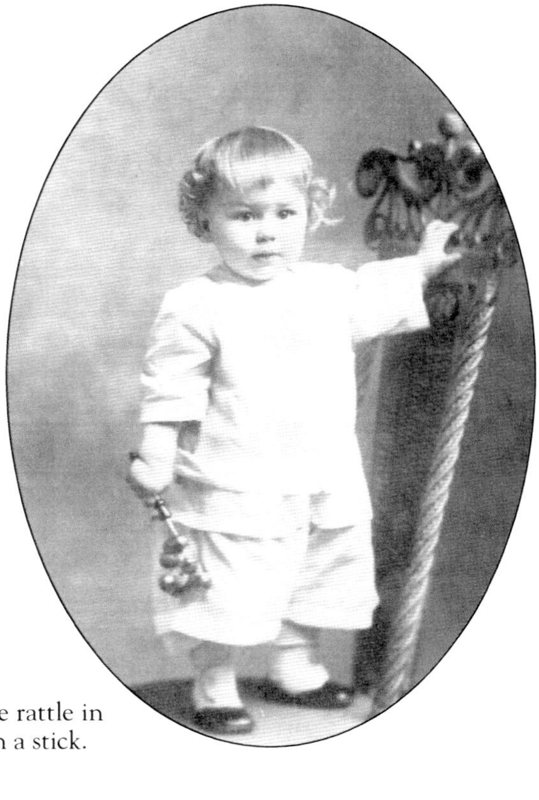

This beautiful little child is unidentified. The rattle in his hand appears to be a collection of bells on a stick.

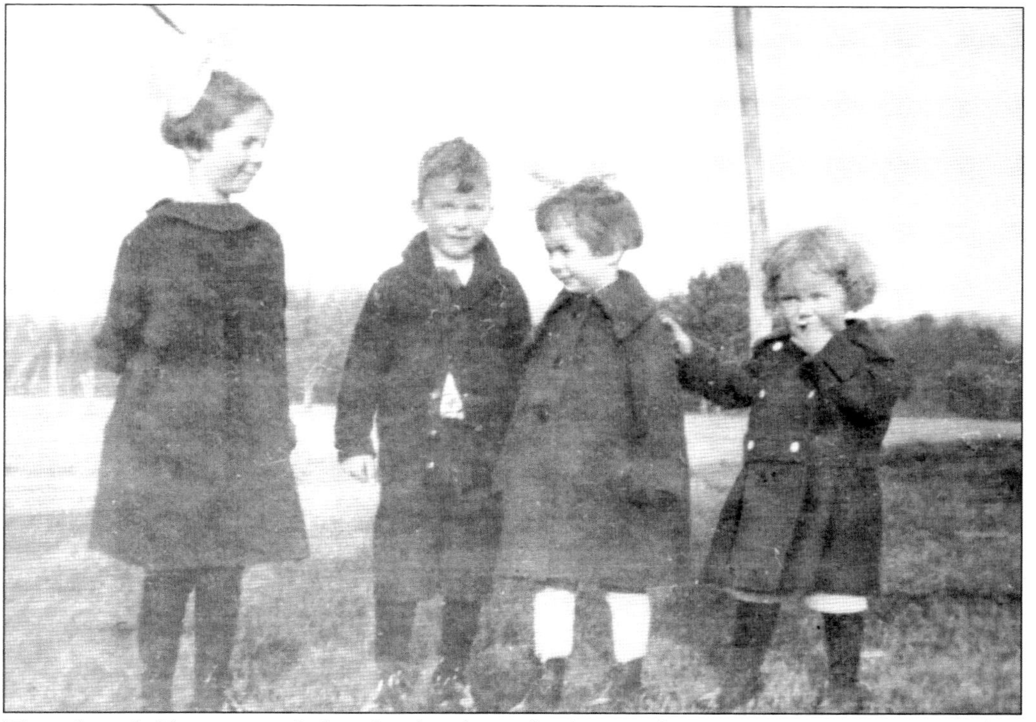

These four children are ready for school and wait for their mother to snap a picture to remember. Note the huge bows the girls wear on their short hair. Pictured, from left to right, are Thelma, Lawrence, Marion, and Clarence Bachelder.

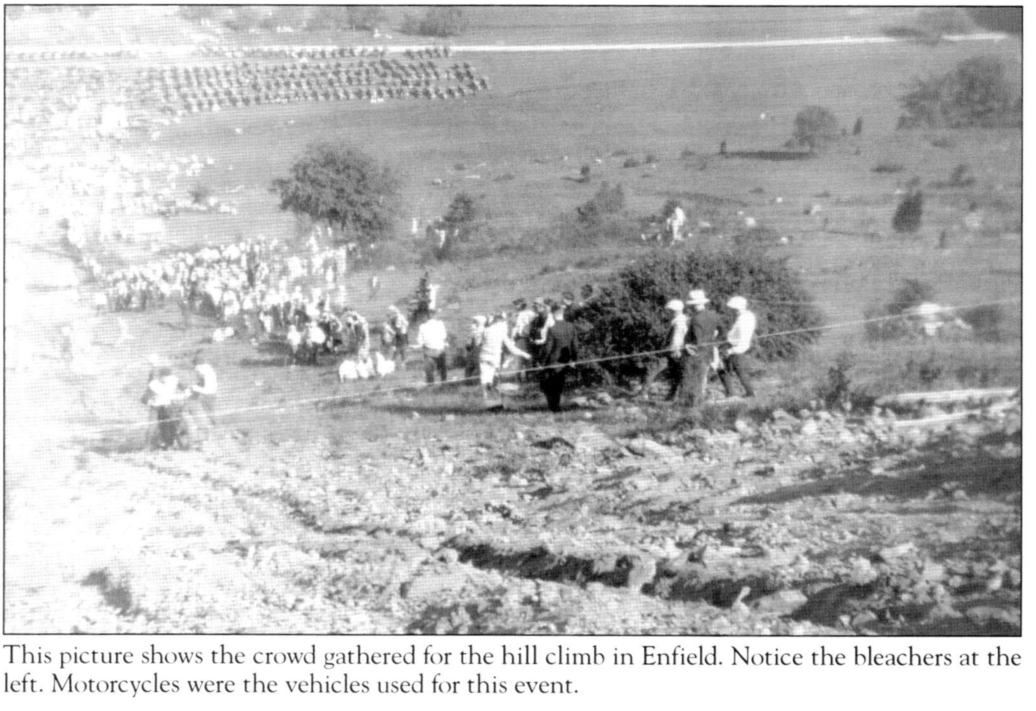

This picture shows the crowd gathered for the hill climb in Enfield. Notice the bleachers at the left. Motorcycles were the vehicles used for this event.

Little Blanche Ellsworth has found the perfect place to pose for a picture.

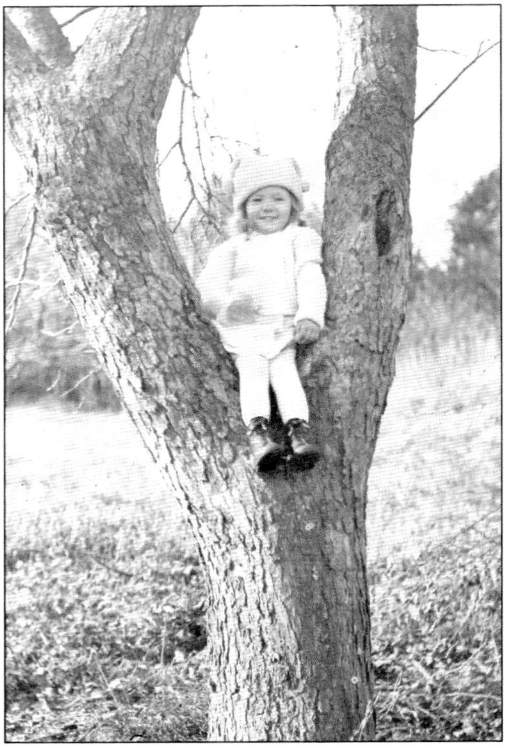

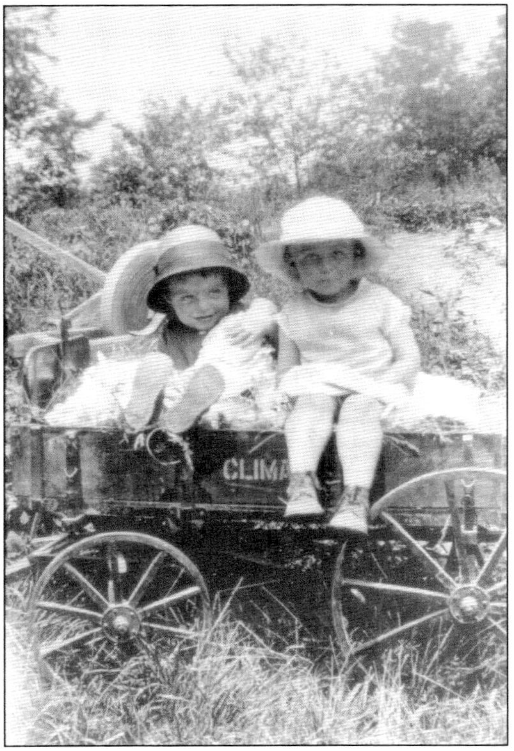

This picture was taken in Enfield in 1927. Marguerite Dyer (left) holds her doll tightly as she share a wagon ride with brother Robert Theodore Dyer Jr.

This picture shows what can be done with a lot of snow. Raymond Whitaker of New Salem looks on admiringly.

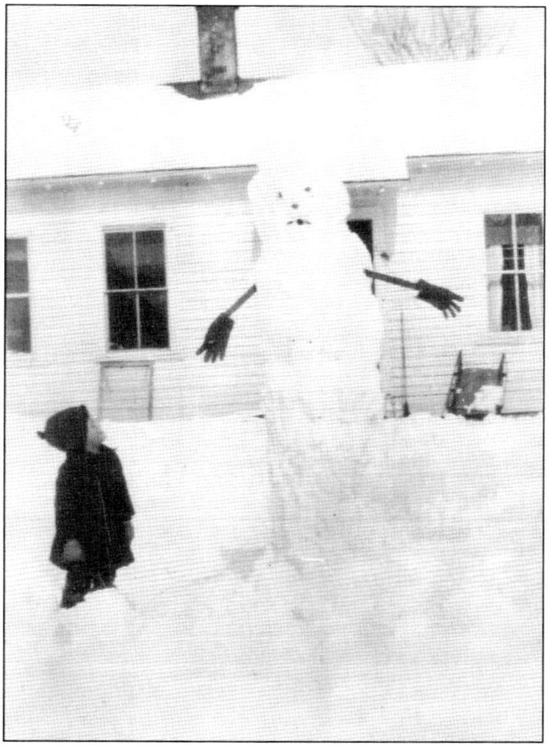

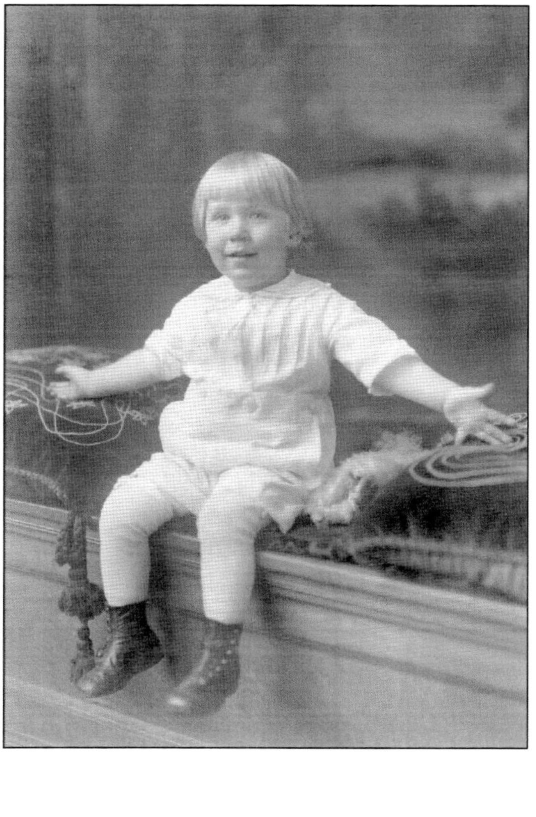

This darling little boy is unidentified; all that is known is that he is from Enfield. The caption for this picture has to be, "Look ma, no hands."

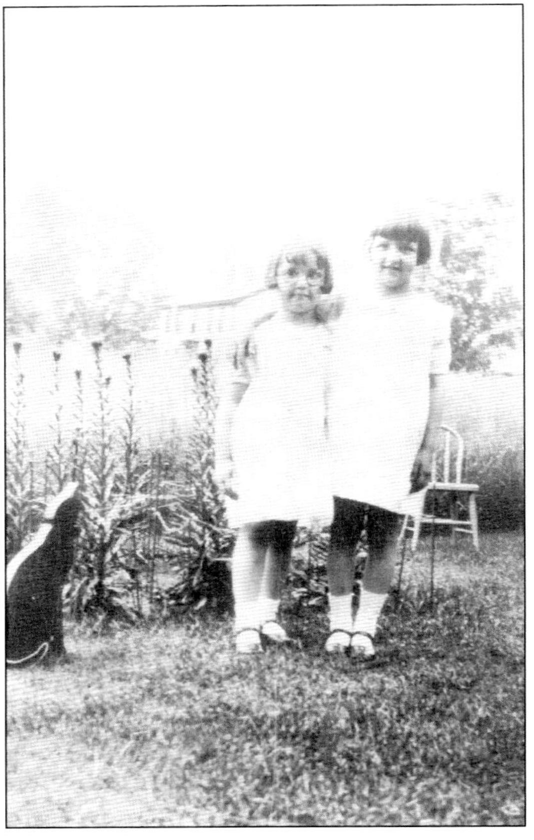

These sisters are ready for the first day of school. The younger one is wearing glasses.

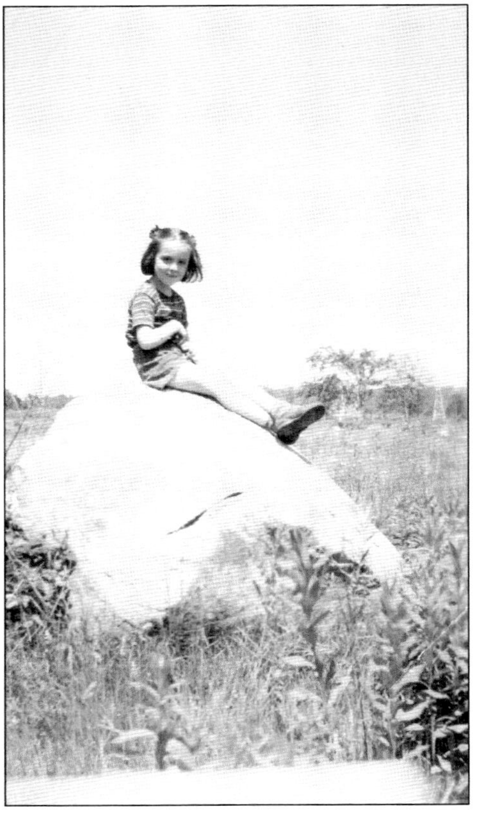

This little girl probably feels like she is sitting on top of the world, and wondering how she can get down safely.

These Greenwich boys are camping out, just like the older men do. The date is 1927.

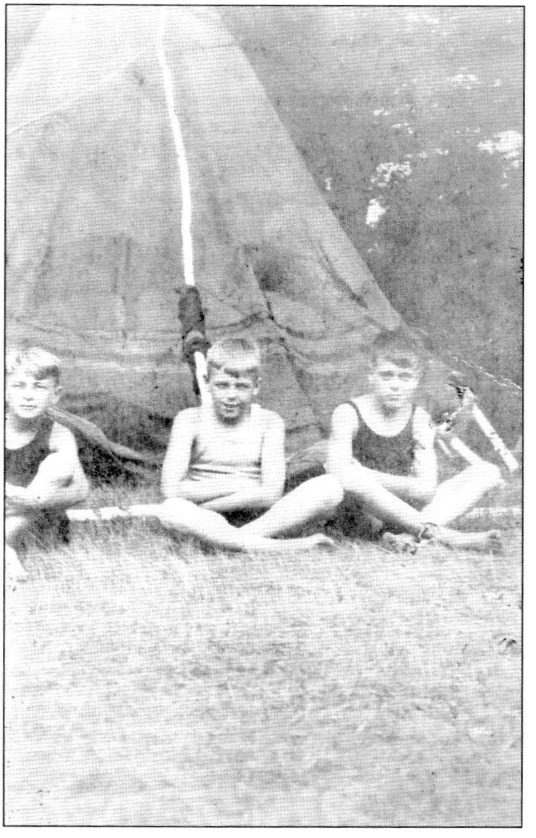

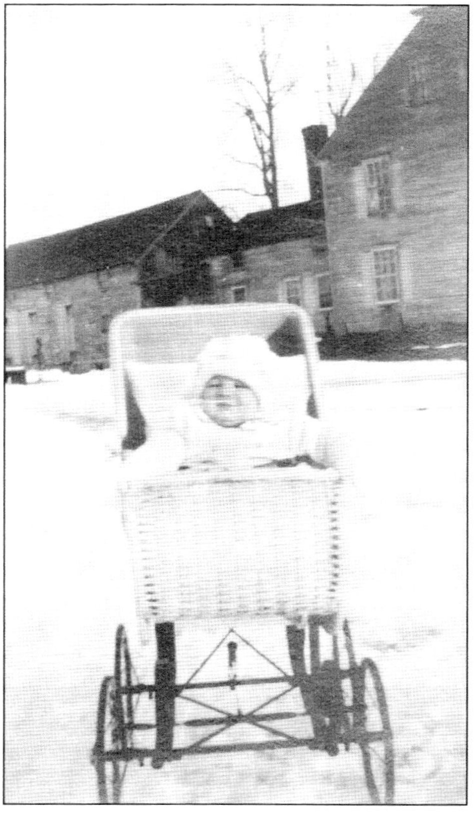

Robert Batchelder is ready for an outing. He is one year and eight months old. Today, he would be in a stroller with more freedom to move around.

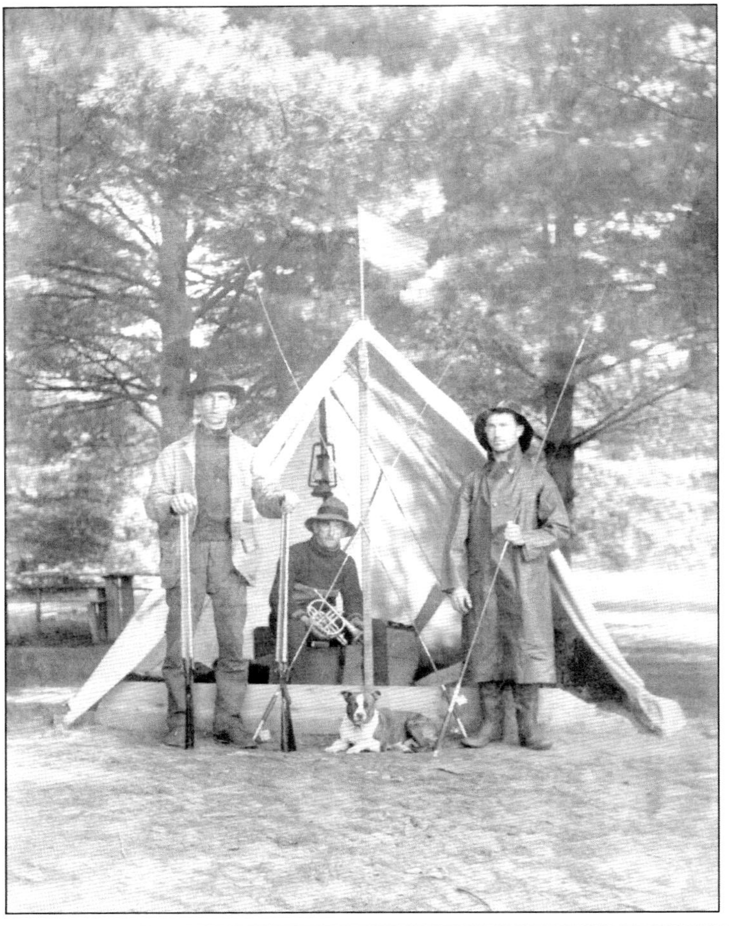

These fishermen are on a camping trip. They are, from left to right, Harry Lindner, Henry Ensminger, and Robert Metcalf. The location is somewhere in Smith's Village in Enfield.

A doll carriage was a prized possession for the little girl in the family. Knickers were the accepted pants for boys and were usually worn with a white shirt.

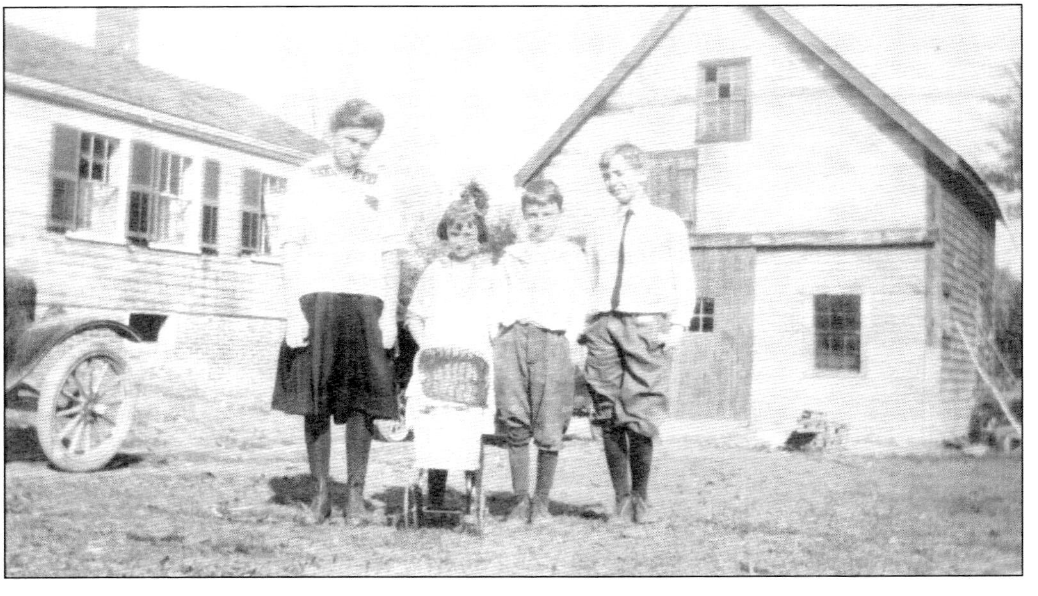

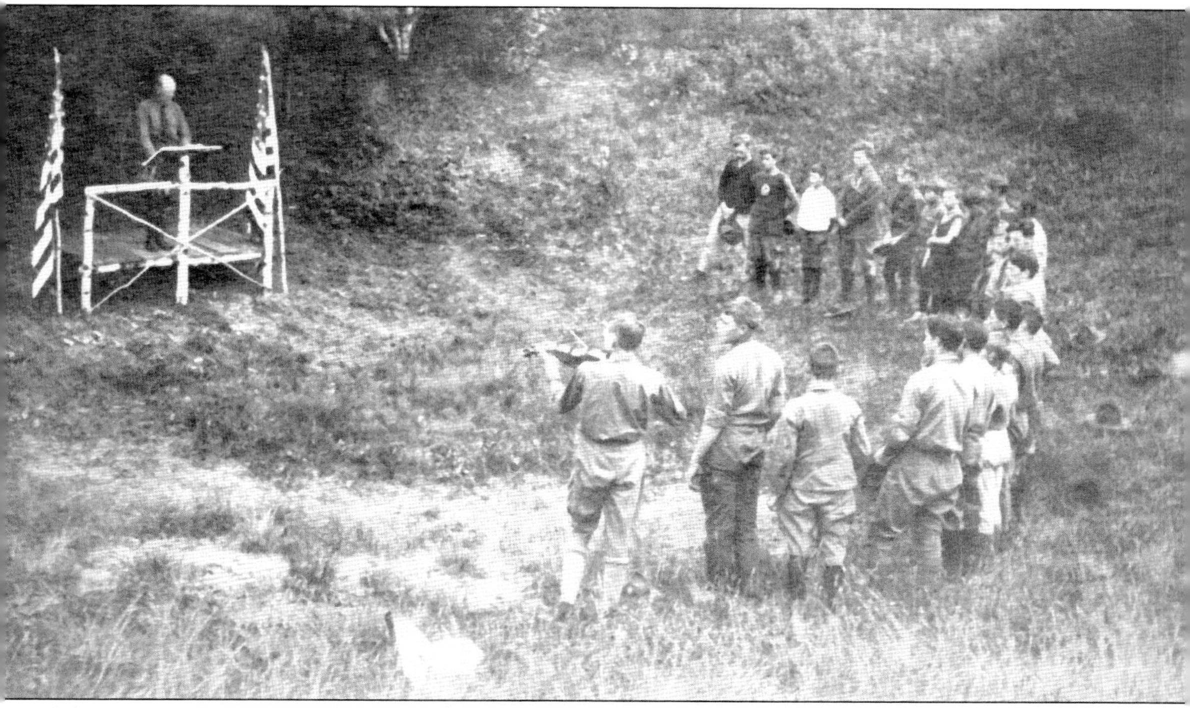

Morning prayers are in progress in this picture taken at the Boy Scout camp situated on Lake Nesseponsett in North Dana.

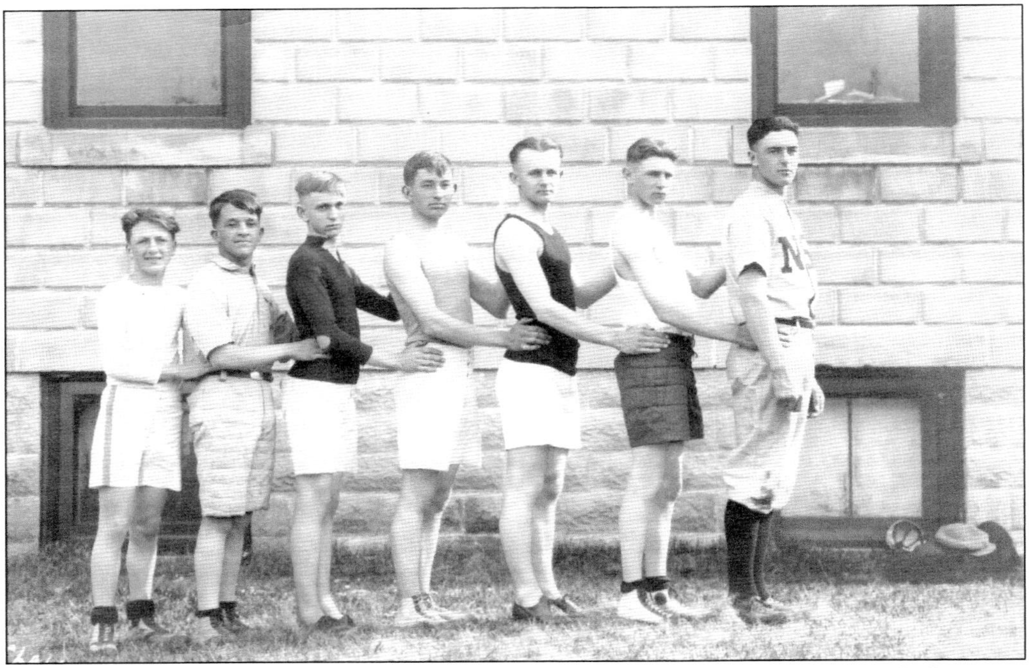

Basketball and baseball were popular sports in the Quabbin Valley. Here is the baseball team at New Salem Academy in 1922. Pictured, from left to right, are Donald McKay, Bob Goodnow, Ted Weaver, Albert Goodnow, Bob Shattuck, Albert Graves, and Robert Mitchell.

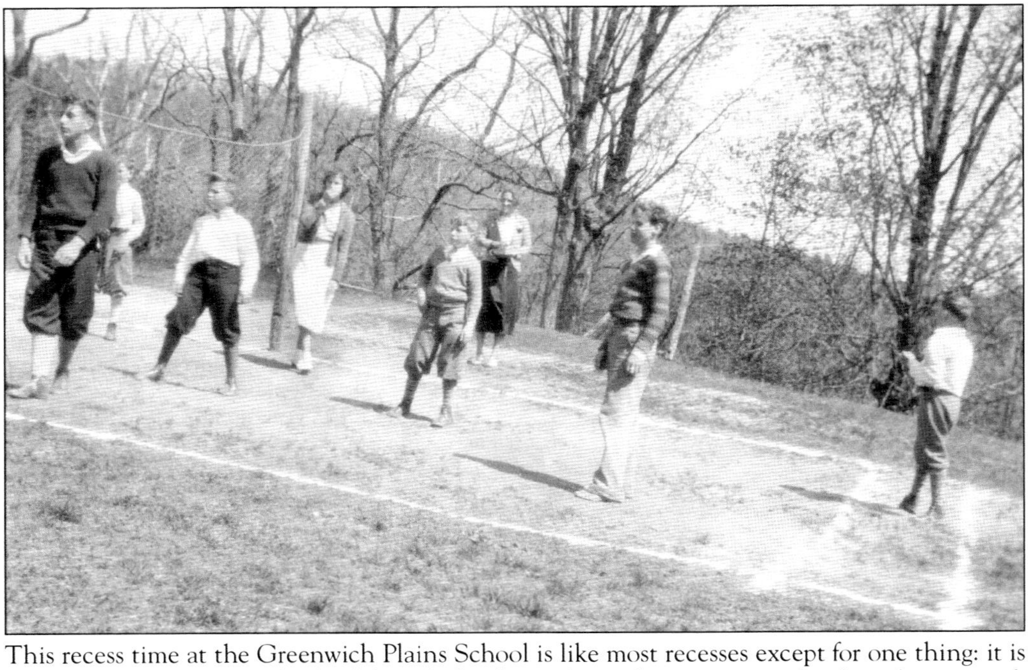

This recess time at the Greenwich Plains School is like most recesses except for one thing: it is the last one ever. This is the final day of school in 1938, and evacuation orders have been issued. Greenwich will be at the bottom of the great Quabbin Reservoir, and three of these boys will be graduating from eighth grade and entering high school somewhere else.

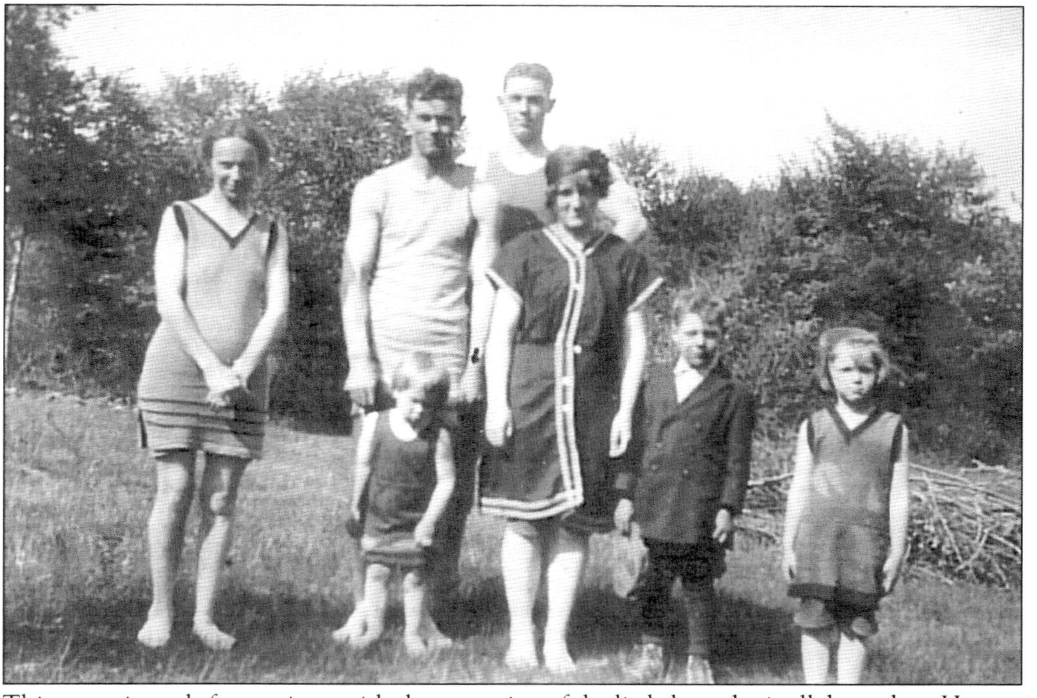

This group is ready for a swim—with the exception of the little boy who is all dressed up. He may have been visiting and did not bring his swimsuit.

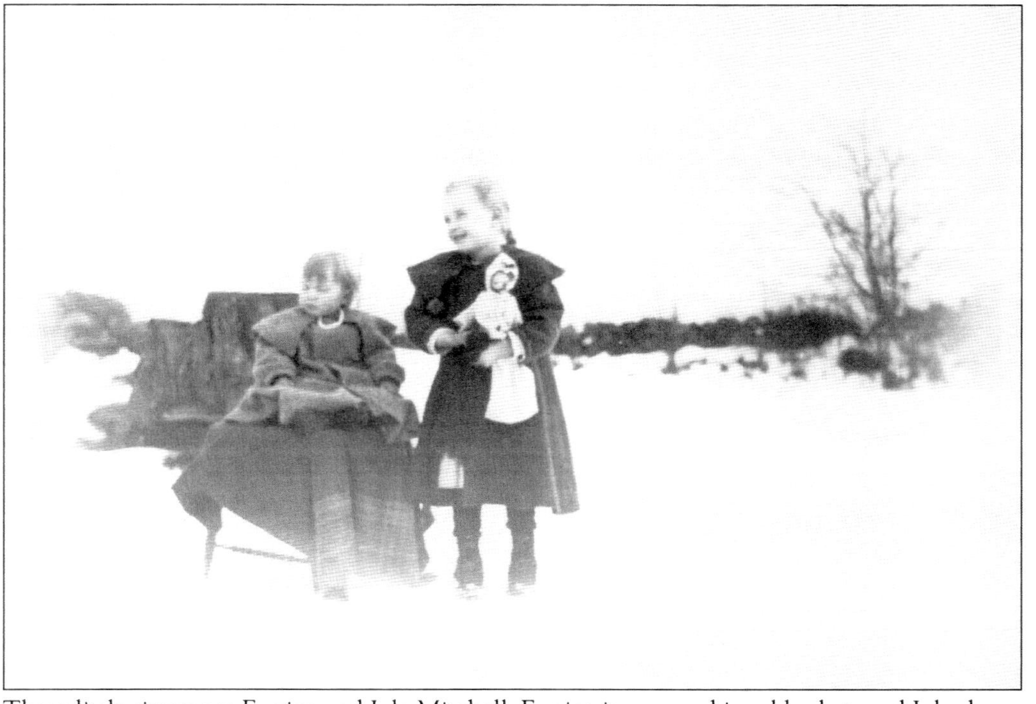

These little sisters are Eunice and Iola Mitchell. Eunice is wrapped in a blanket, and Iola shows off her doll, also dressed for a snowy day.

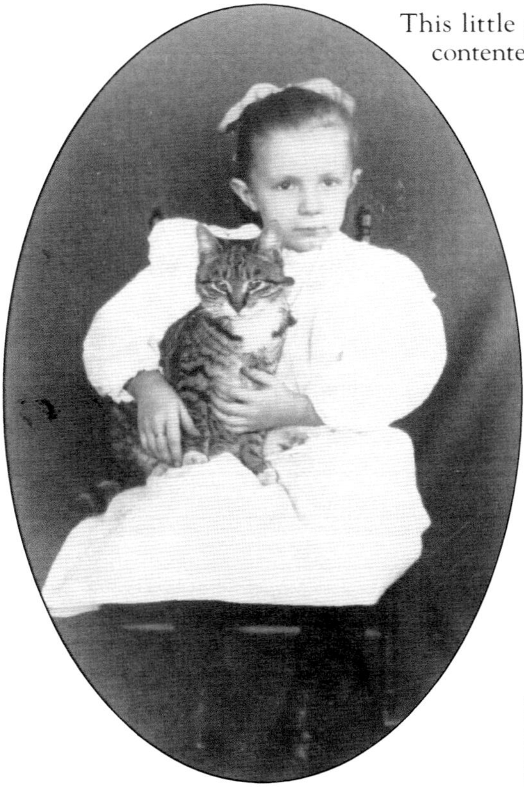

This little girl is identified only as Hazel. The cat sits contentedly, her best friend.

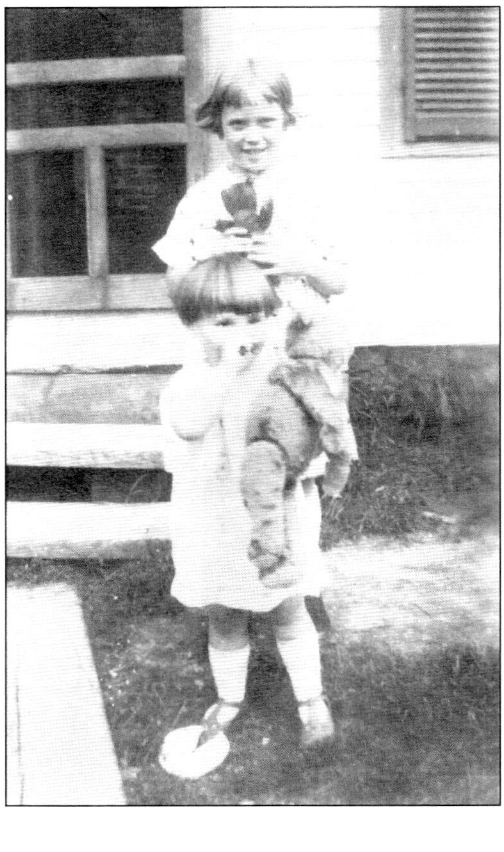

These unidentified children are both holding teddy bears. The smaller child seems more interested in his or her thumb than in having a picture taken. Toys were not as plentiful as they are today, and many a grandmother spent time making stuffed animals and doll clothes for the little ones.

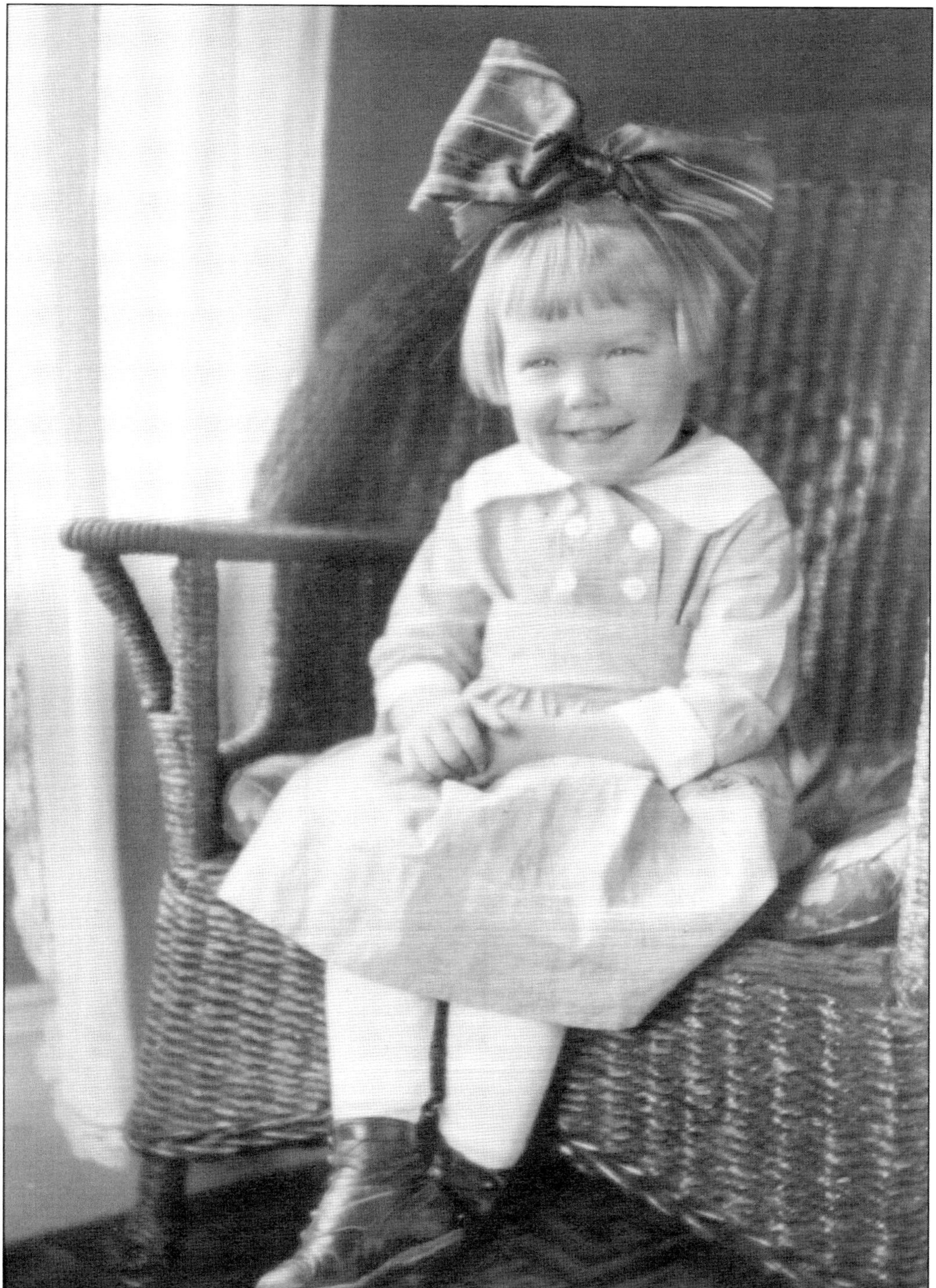

This little girl is all dressed up in her best for a picture. How did the mother attach that huge bow to her hair?

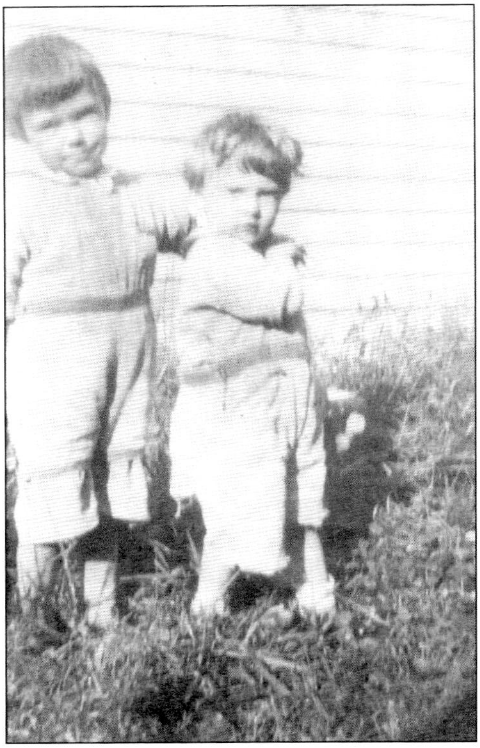

Few things are cuter than two little children.

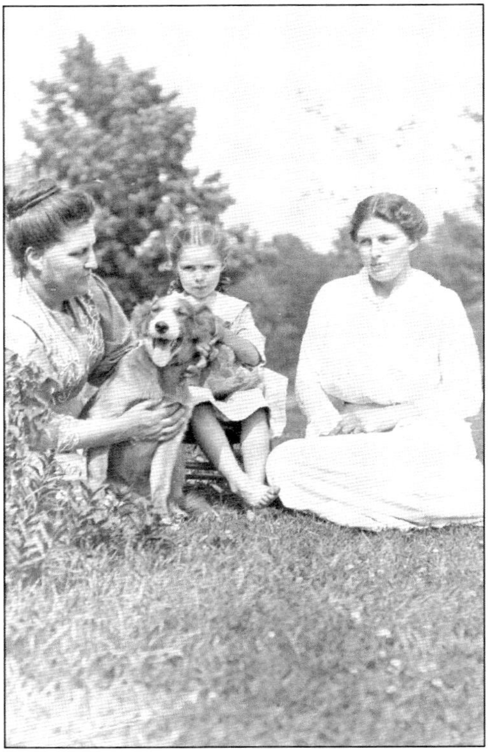

Lilian Gross, Annis Laplante, and Vera Laplante pose with their dog, who seems more anxious to run.

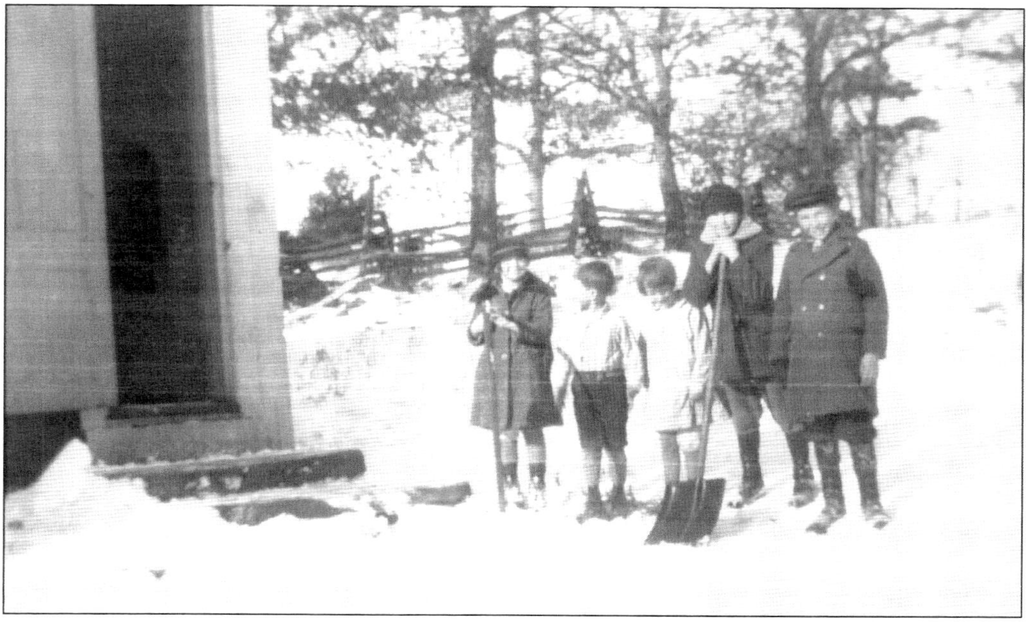

In the days of the one-room schools, everyone shared in the janitorial work. Some carried in the wood; some carried the water. In this picture, the children have just finished clearing a path to the door. This is the No. 2 School in Prescott. Pictured, from left to right, are Beulah ?, Elwyn and Lois Doubleday, Ernest ?, and Roger Doubleday.

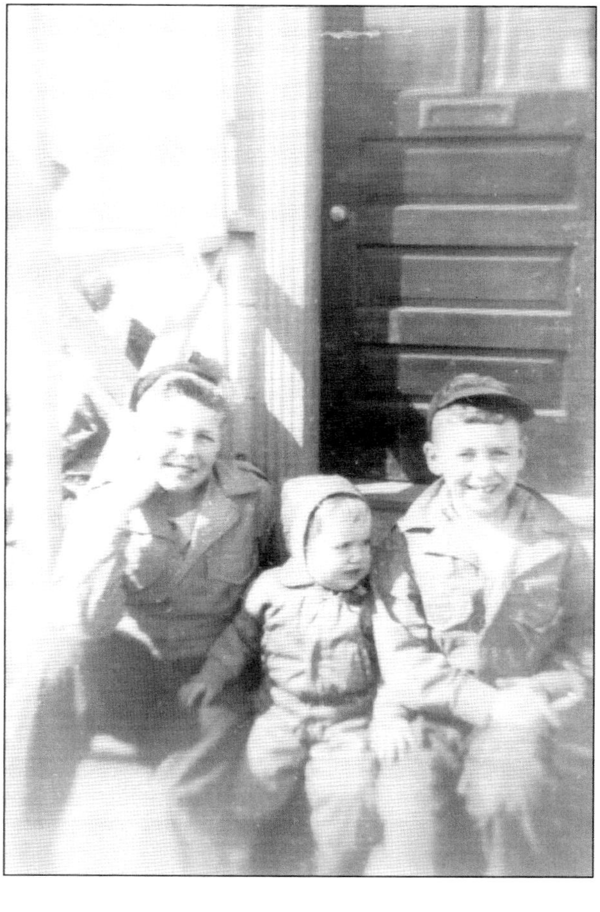

Eric, Eddy, and sister Gail (in the middle) are the children of Edward Gufstason.

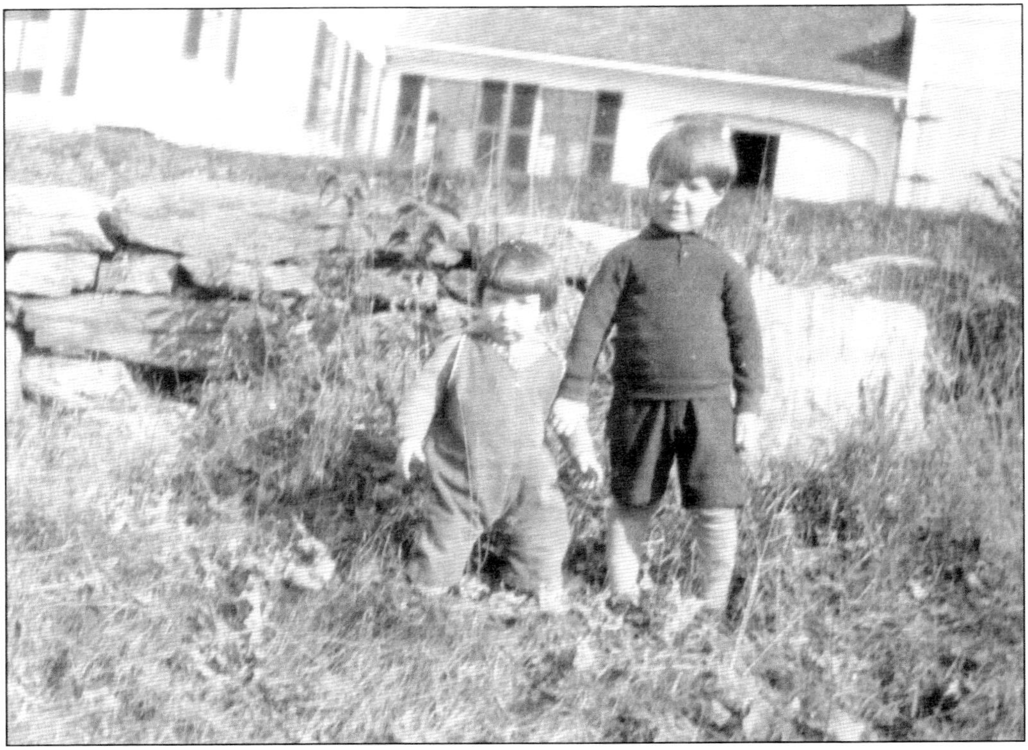

These unidentified boys—possibly brothers—are out for a walk on a sunny day.

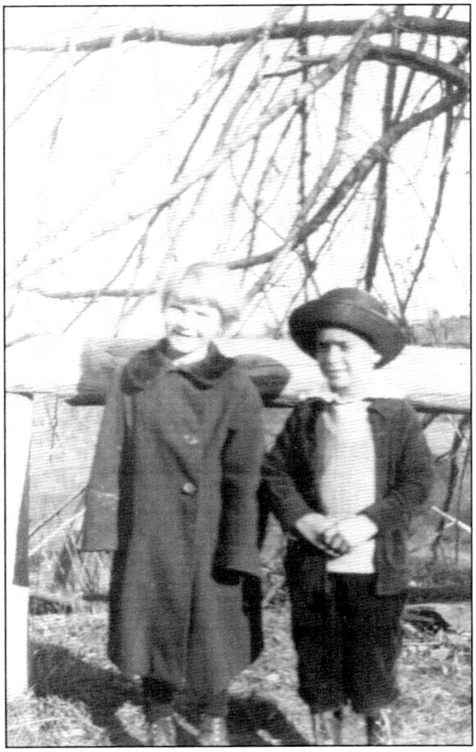

These children were students at the No. 3 School in Prescott in 1925.

These children are looking for four-leaf clovers. They are identified as Donny Jr., Malcolm, and Betty, children of Donald Howe, whose garage is in the background.

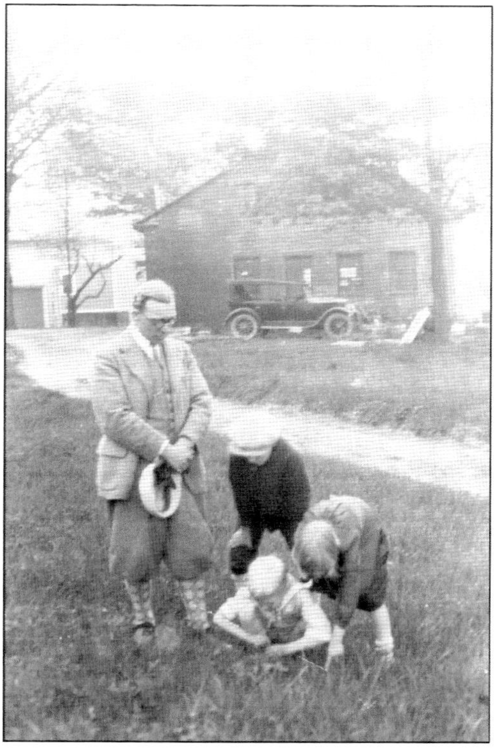

Pearl Newton lived in Millington, where her father operated a gristmill.

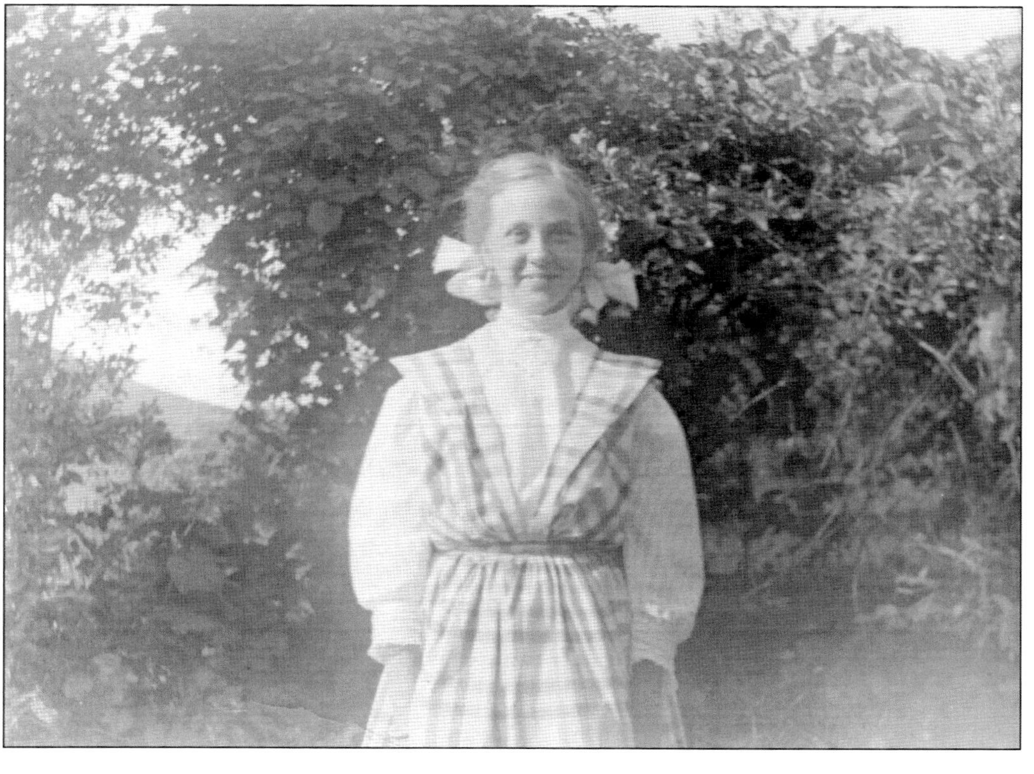

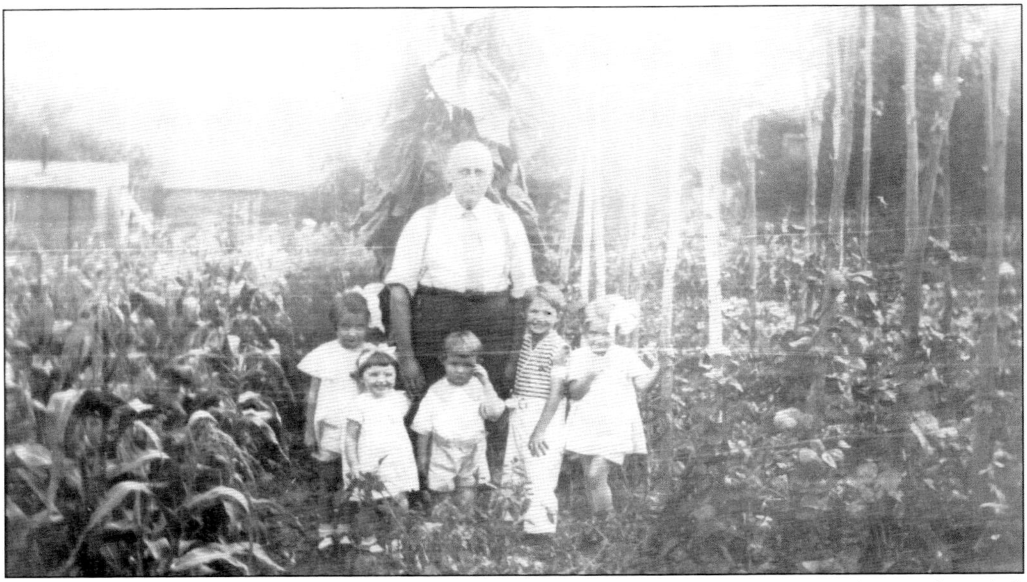

Frank Hall of Greenwich is showing his grandchildren his prized sunflowers. Shown, from left to right, are Priscilla Hayward, Betty, Ken, Ralph, and Patty.

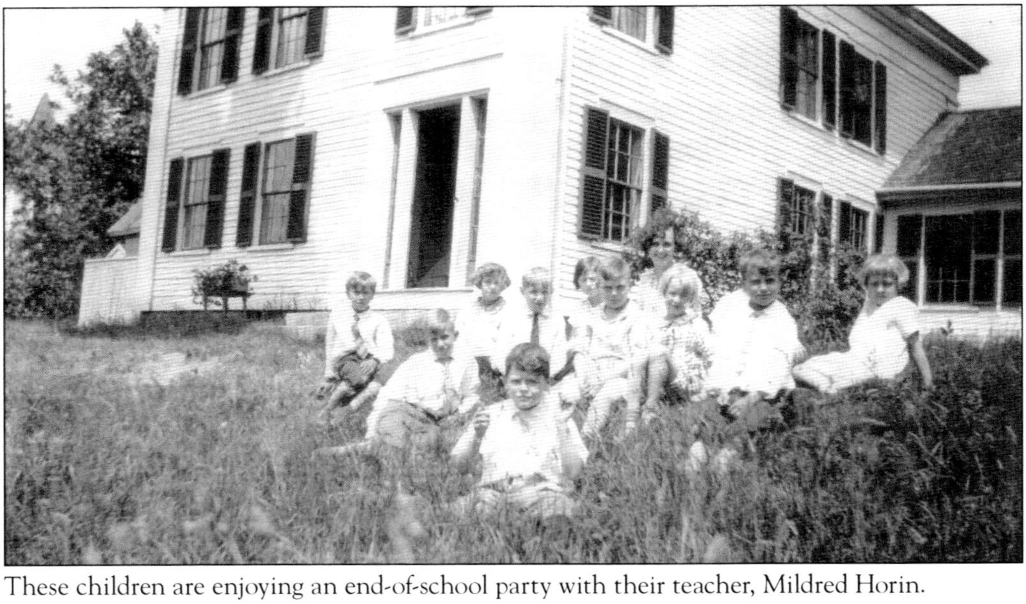

These children are enjoying an end-of-school party with their teacher, Mildred Horin.

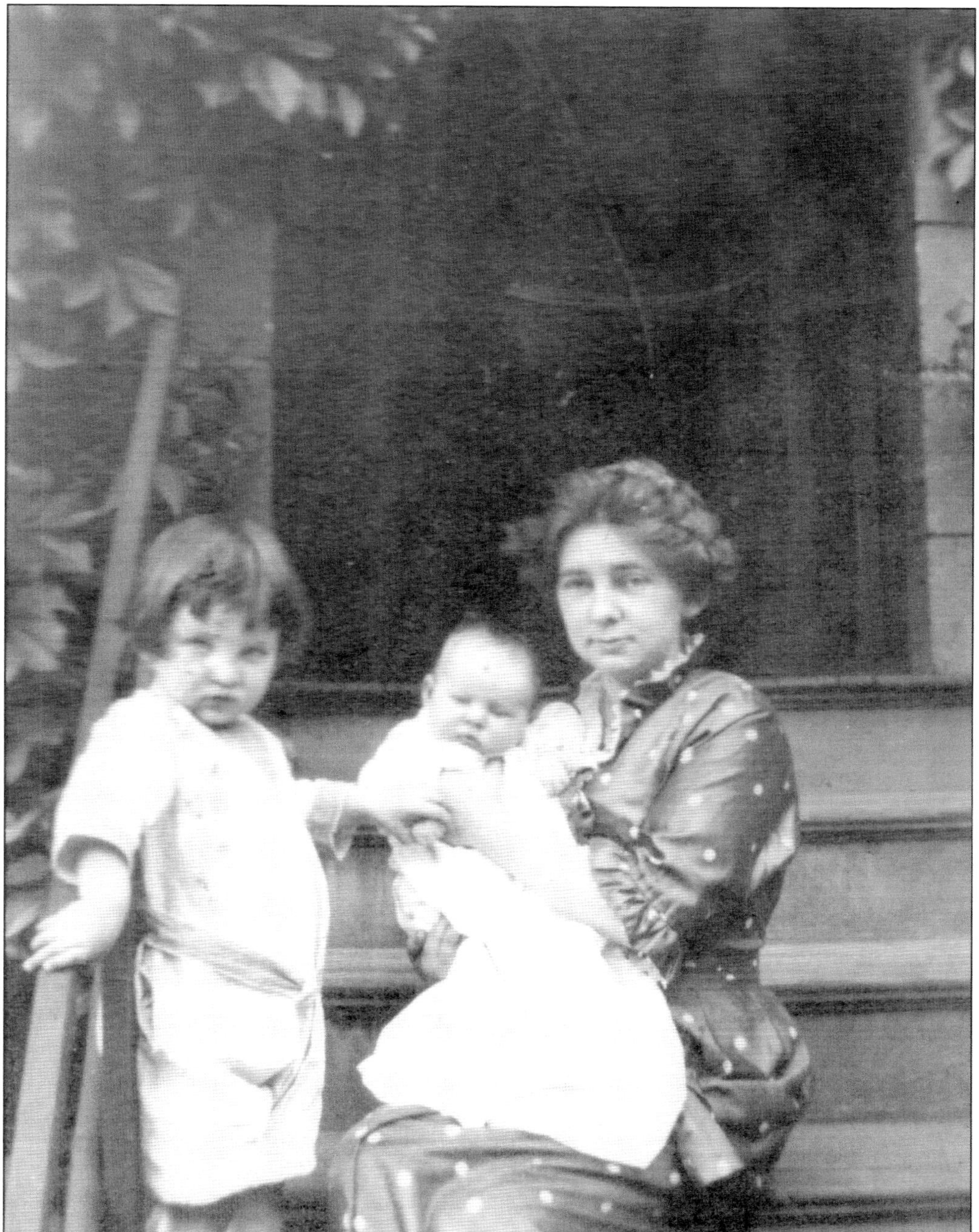

Marjorie Sinclair is posing with children Hazel and Douglas.

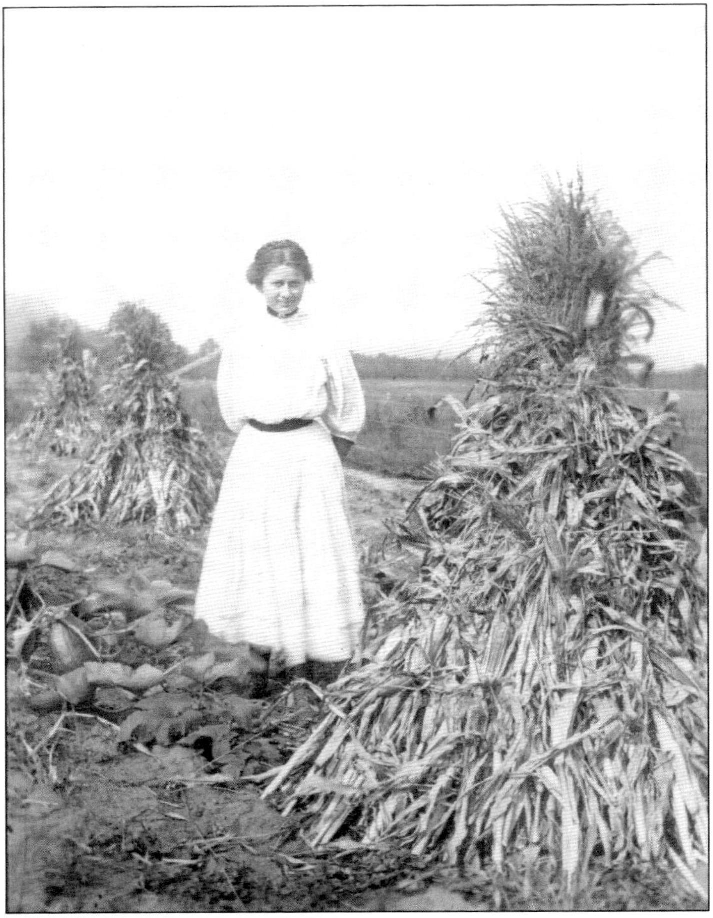

Eunice Billings admires a shock of corn on a sunny fall day. The location is in Greenwich on the road leading to Prescott.

Pictured here in 1914 is 15-year-old Warren Emory Hewett with a bicycle, a prized possession.

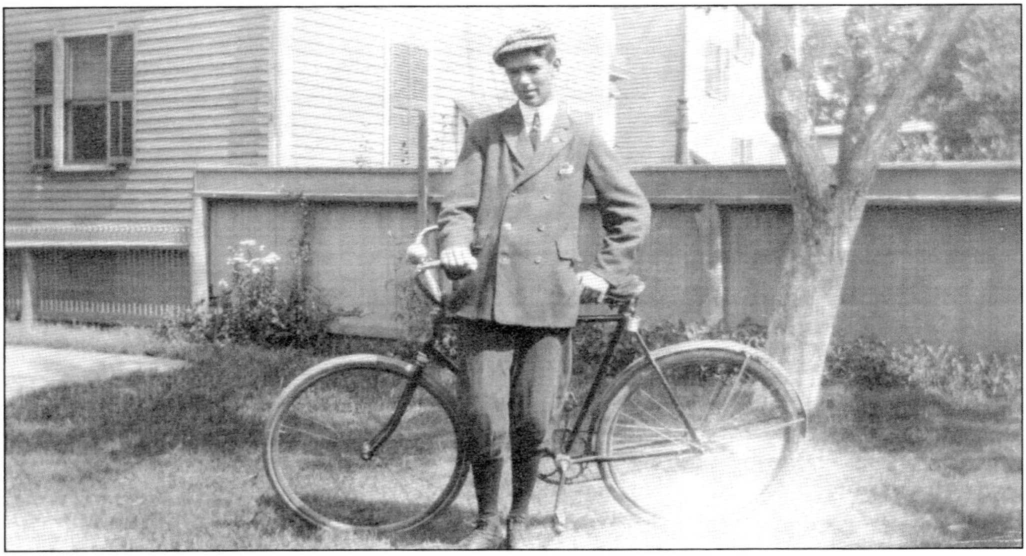

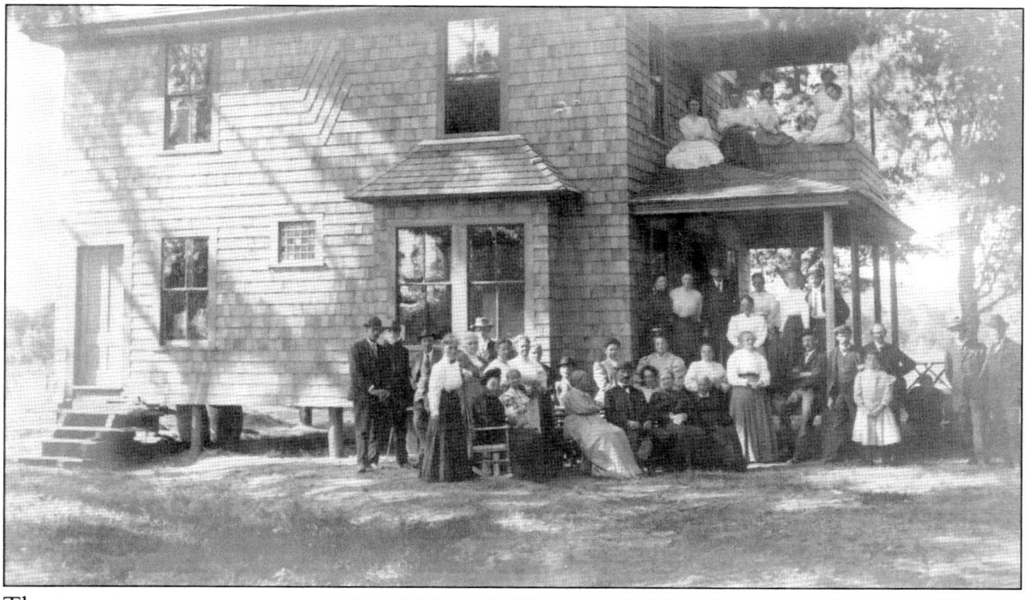

There were many camps on Greenwich Lake. Family reunions, picnics, and parties were enjoyed by the young and old. A small porch is on the second level of this cottage.

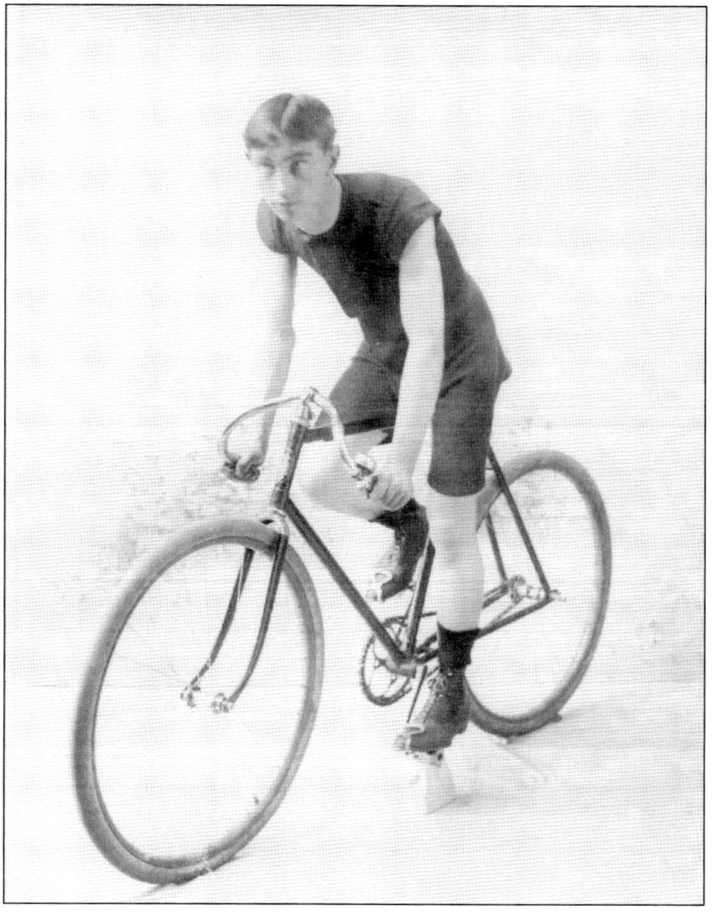

Robert Metcalf is shown here in his racing attire, ready to go when the signal is given. Bicycle races were popular in Enfield.

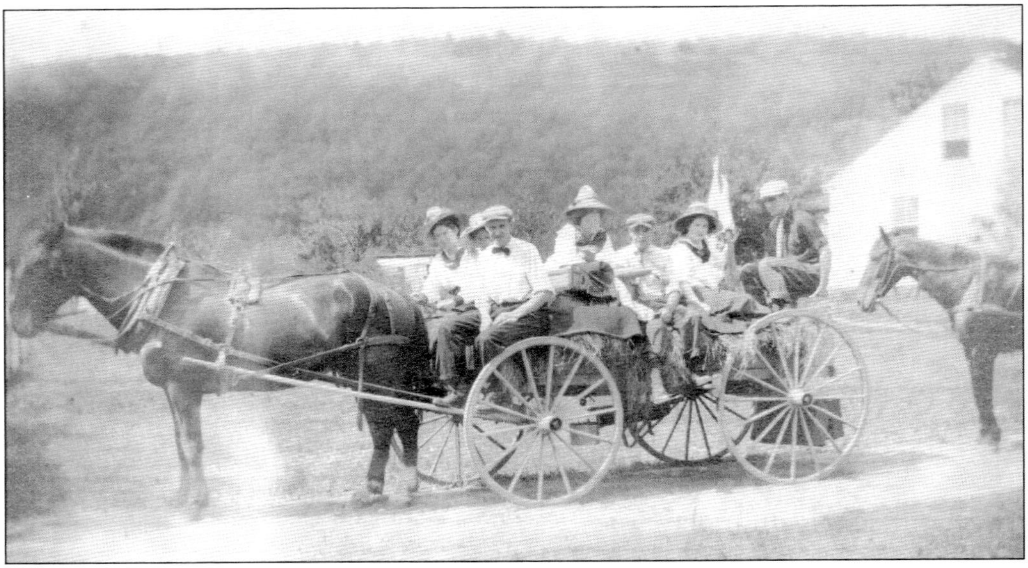

What could be more fun than a ride in a wagonload of friends?

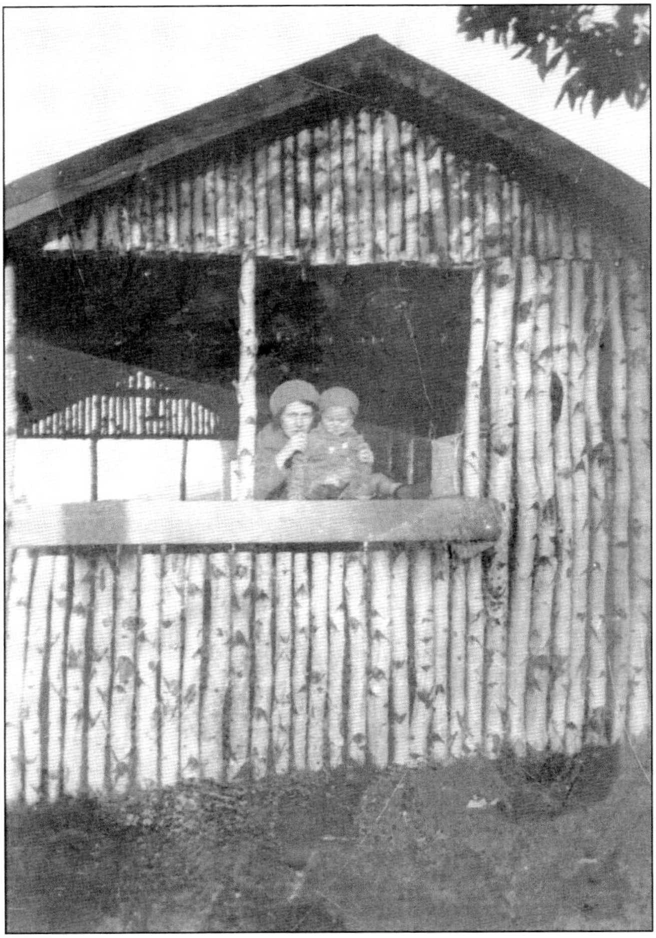

This picture shows the ice cream stand on one of the lakes in Enfield in 1930. It was known as "the Birches."

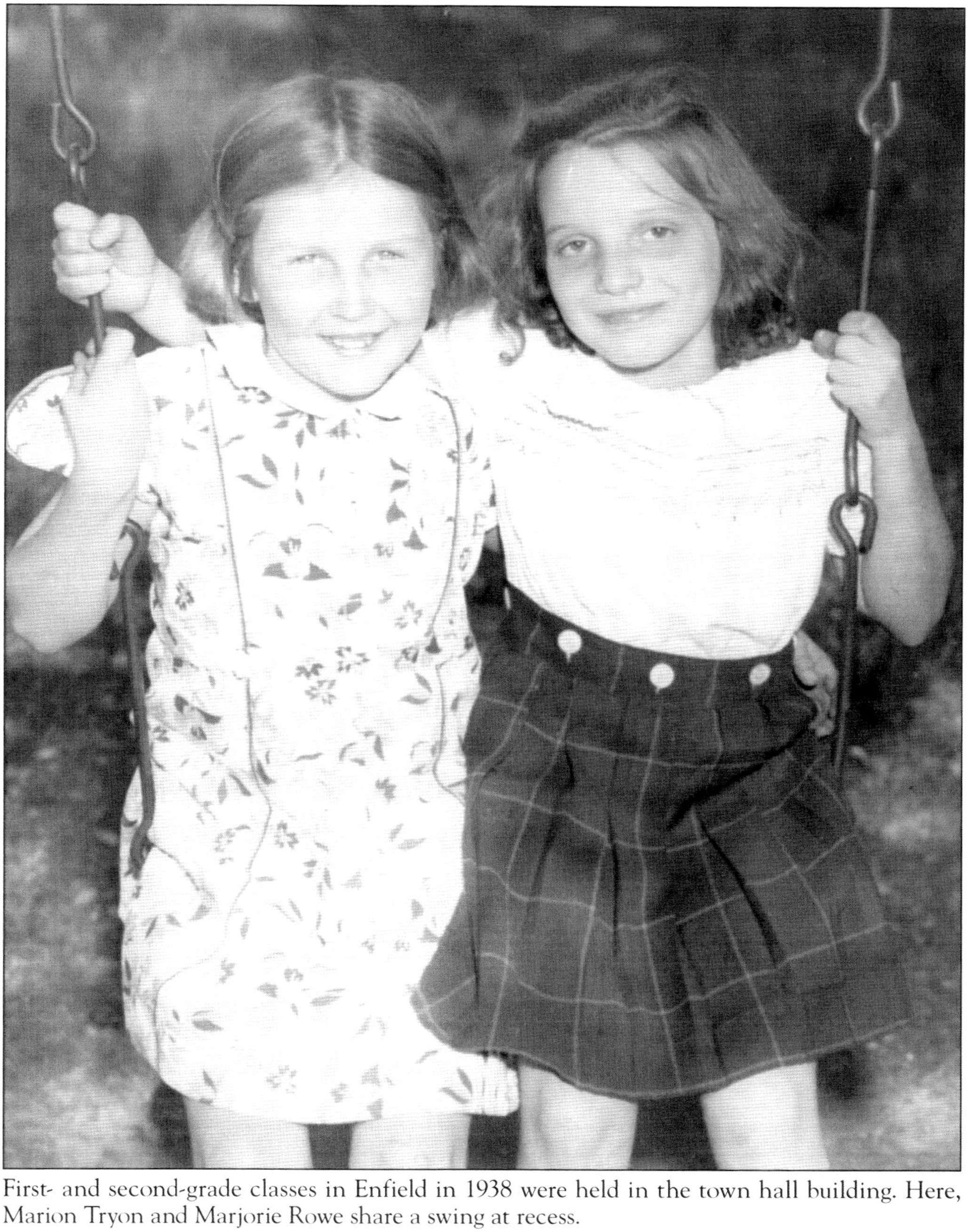

First- and second-grade classes in Enfield in 1938 were held in the town hall building. Here, Marion Tryon and Marjorie Rowe share a swing at recess.

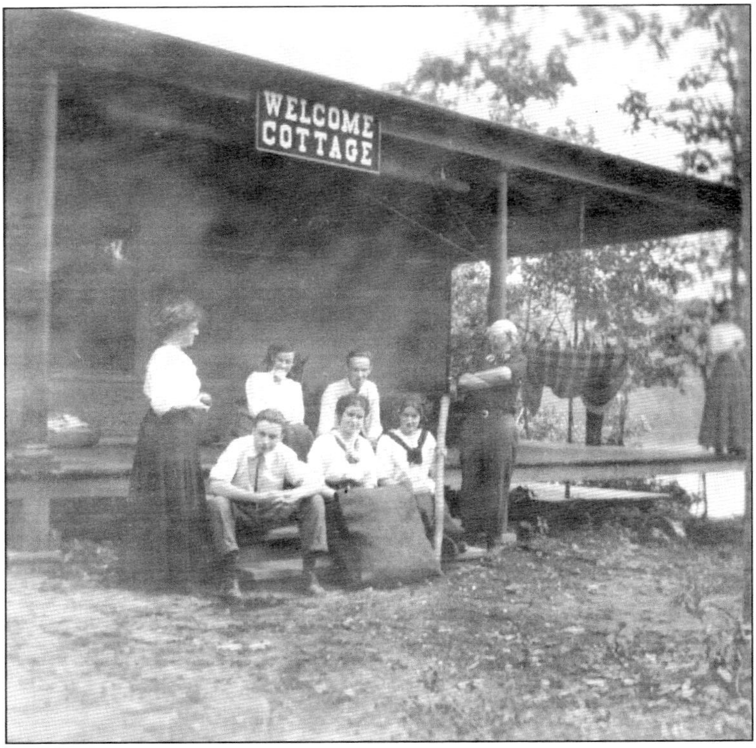

The many lakes and ponds were dotted with cottages with intriguing names. They were a magnet for large gatherings and, frequently, parties in the summer. This group may be waiting for its chaperone to arrive.

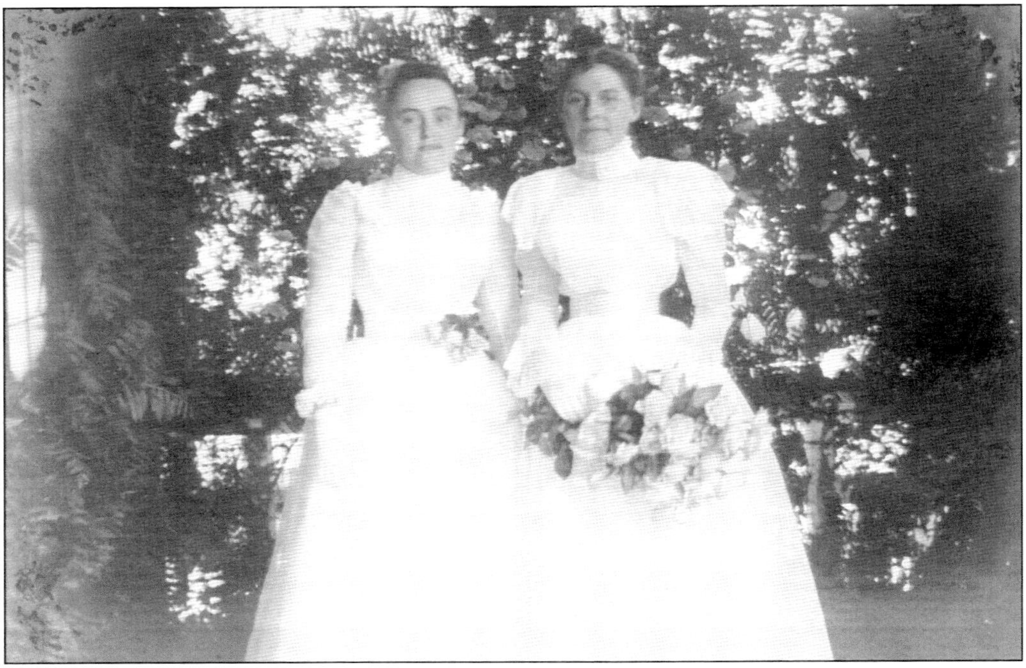

The bride in this image is Elizabeth Lannon Rogers of Enfield, and her attendant is Hattie Fairbanks. The hourglass figure was very much in style. White wedding gowns became fashionable after 1900.

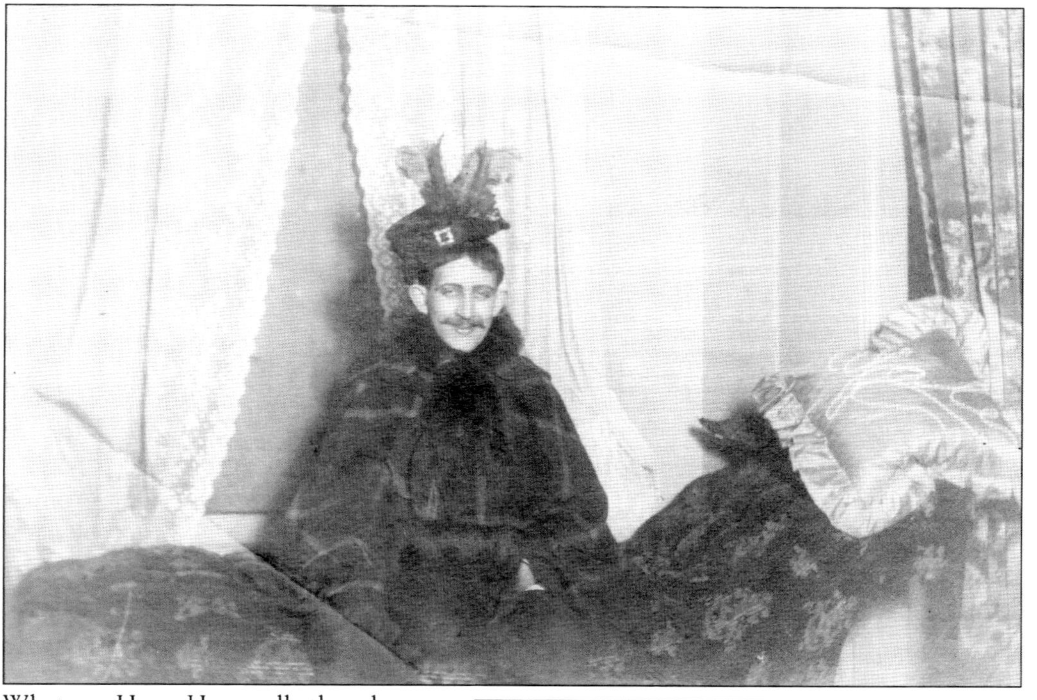

Whatever Harry Hess really thought about the hat he models here, he found it amusing to show it off. He is sitting on what was commonly known as a "fainting couch."

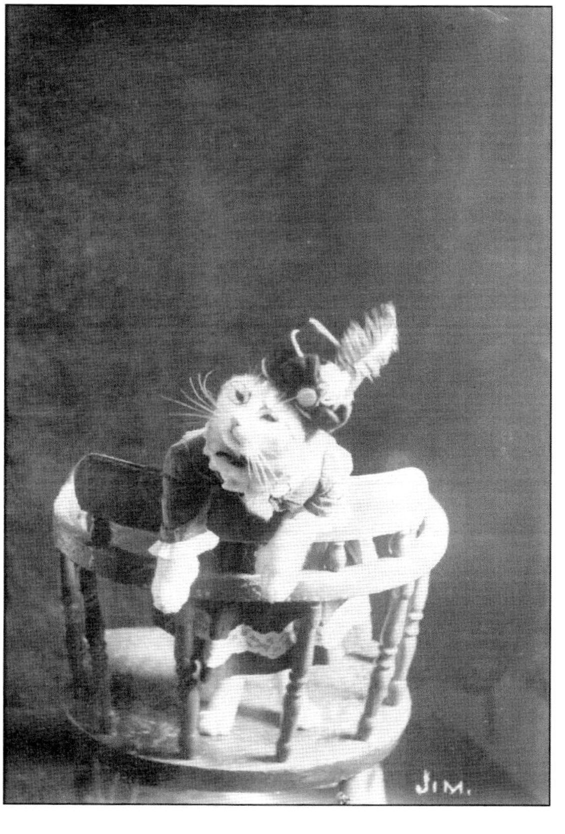

This cat was the pet of Mrs. Joseph Bishop, a resident of North Dana. She dressed him up in a red suit and a matching hat with an ostrich plume, and taught him many tricks. His name was Jim, and he lived to be 13 years old.

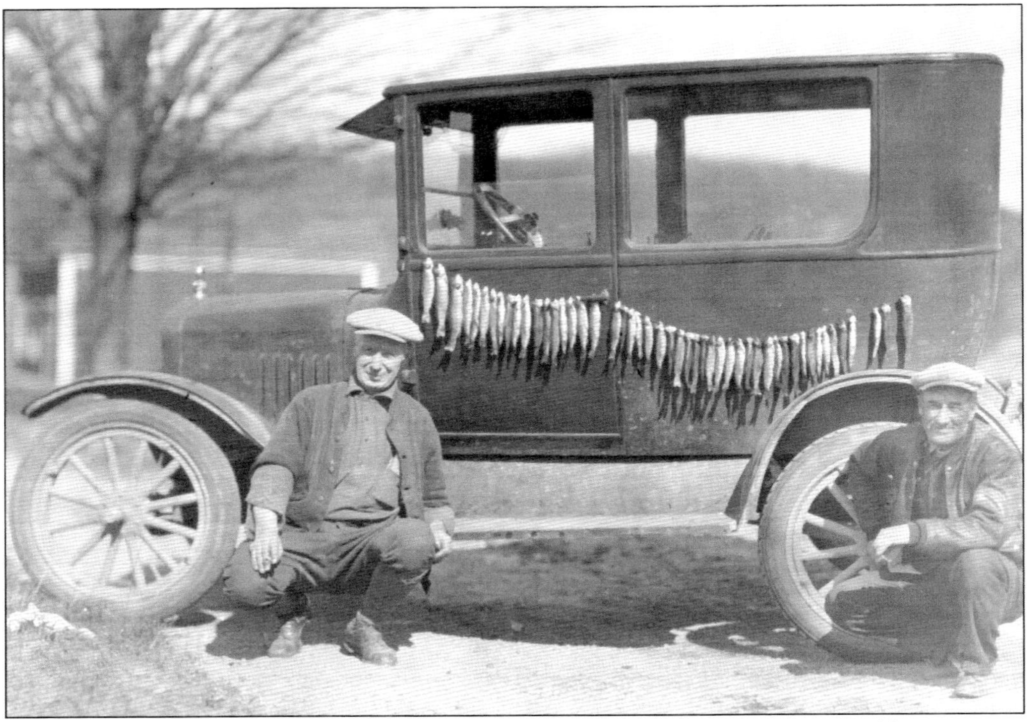

These fishermen display their catch of trout on an early-May day in 1928 in Enfield.

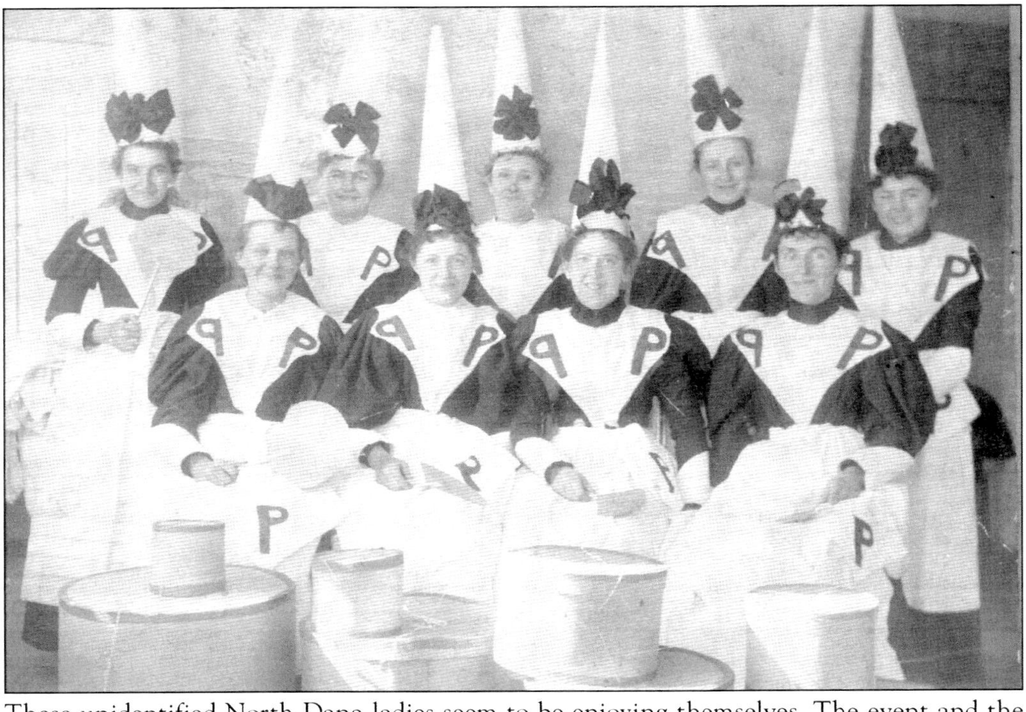

These unidentified North Dana ladies seem to be enjoying themselves. The event and the significance of the costumes and props are not known.

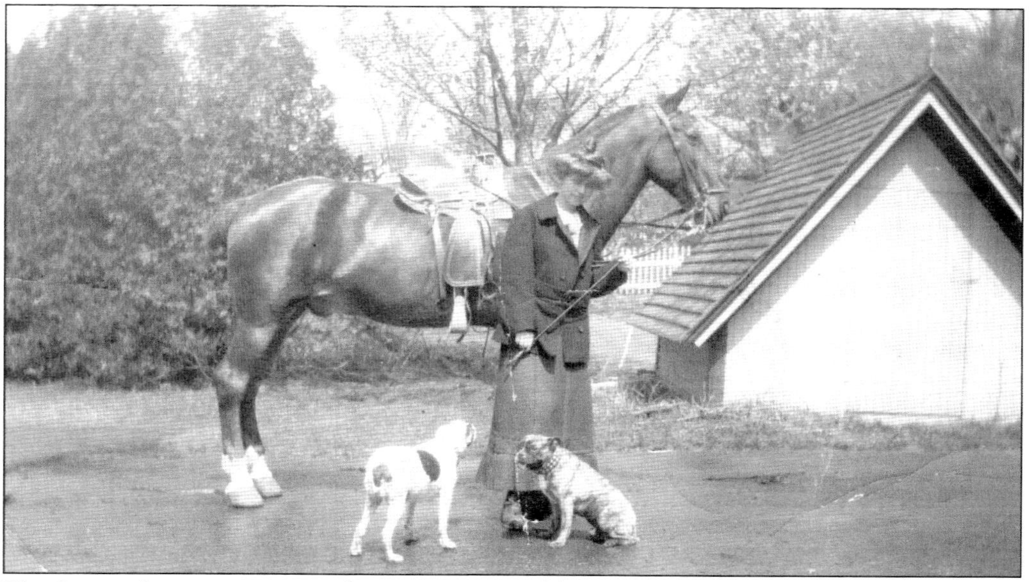

The dogs in this picture seem to be waiting to see if they can go with their mistress too. Note the horse and dogs all have bobbed tails.

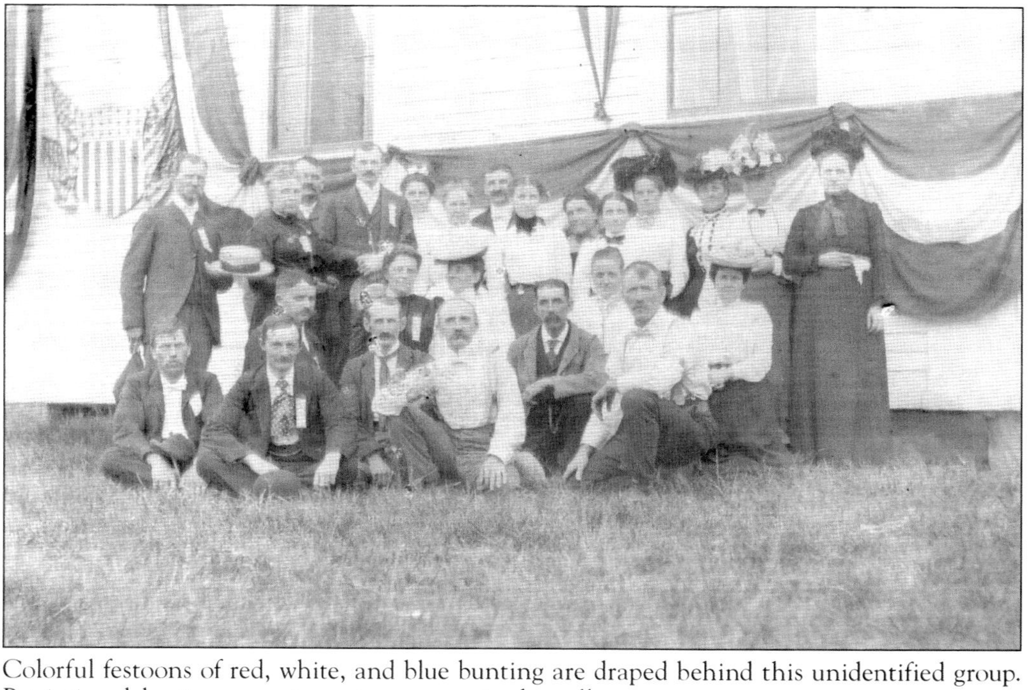

Colorful festoons of red, white, and blue bunting are draped behind this unidentified group. Patriotic celebrations were important events in the valley towns.

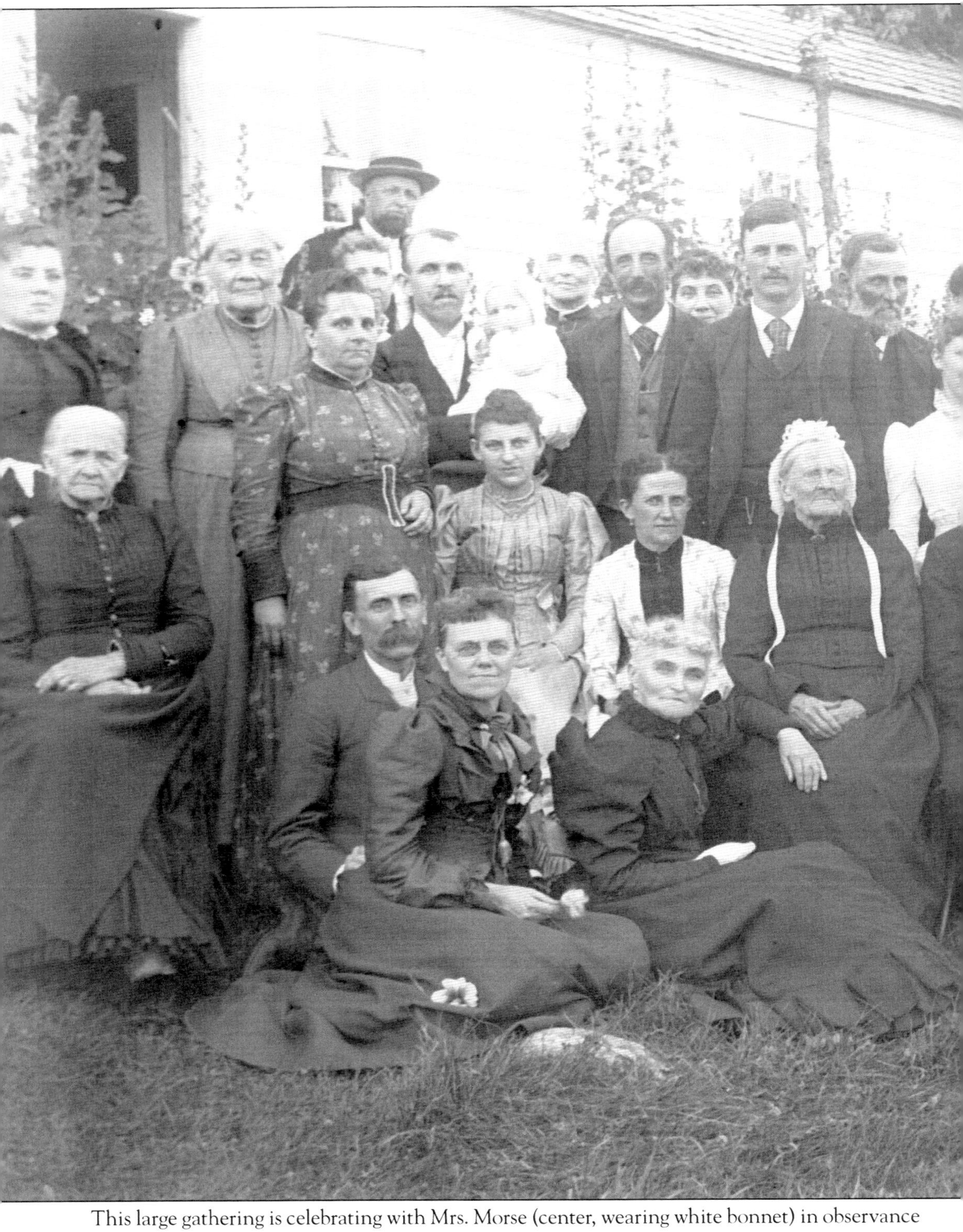

This large gathering is celebrating with Mrs. Morse (center, wearing white bonnet) in observance

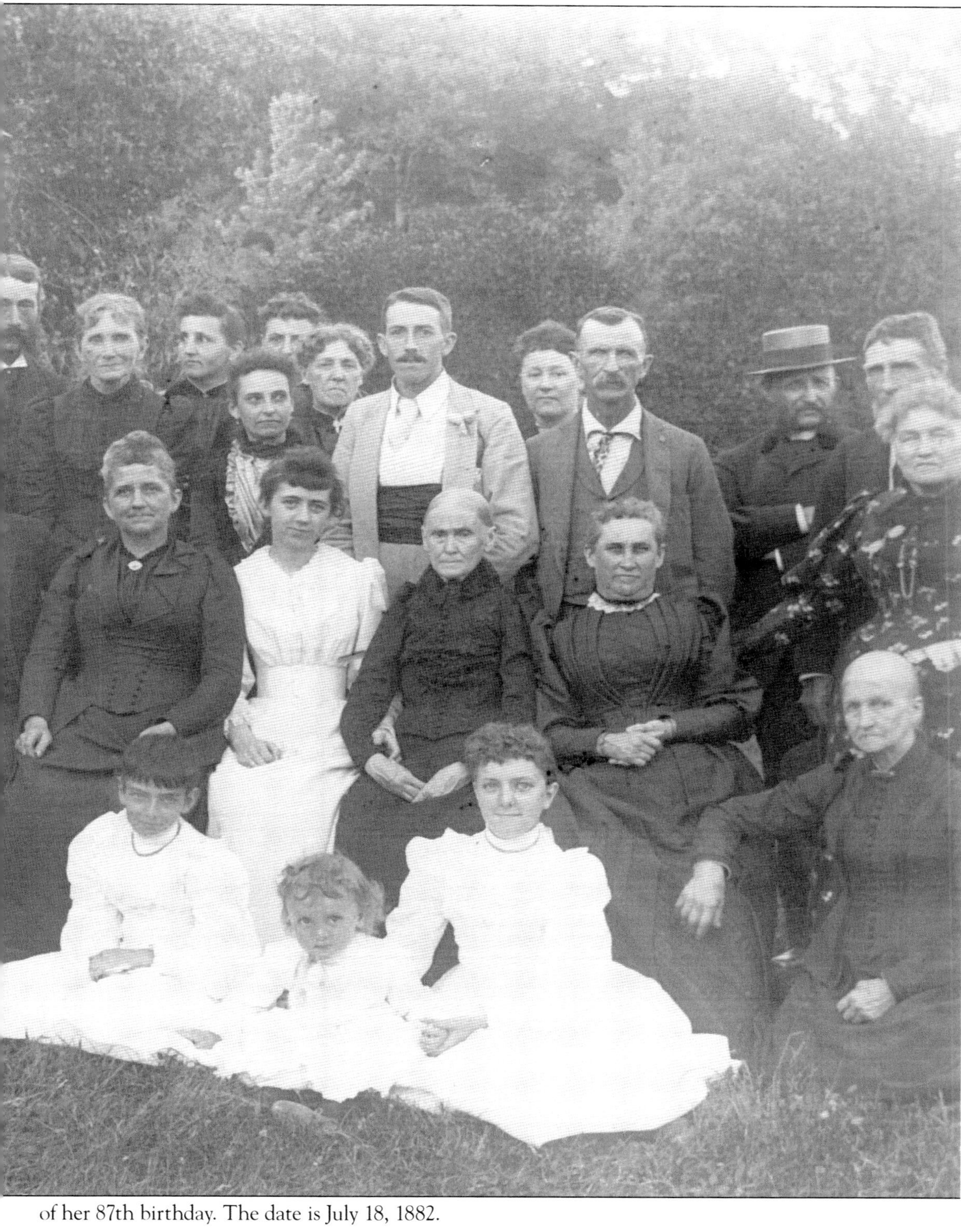

of her 87th birthday. The date is July 18, 1882.

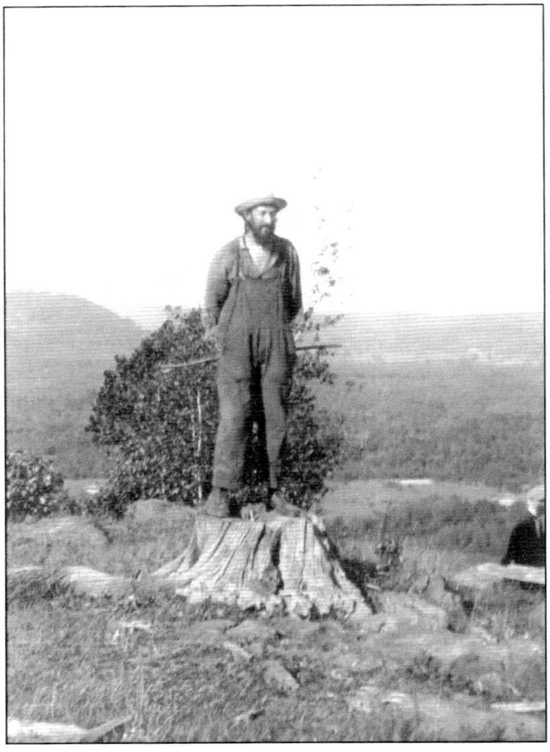

This man, known as "Whiskers," has chosen a place to stand to watch a hill climb in Enfield. These events were held frequently and attracted very large crowds.

Mrs. Edwin Matthews gathers her darling grandchildren for a picture. Edwin Matthews was known as the "singing milkman."

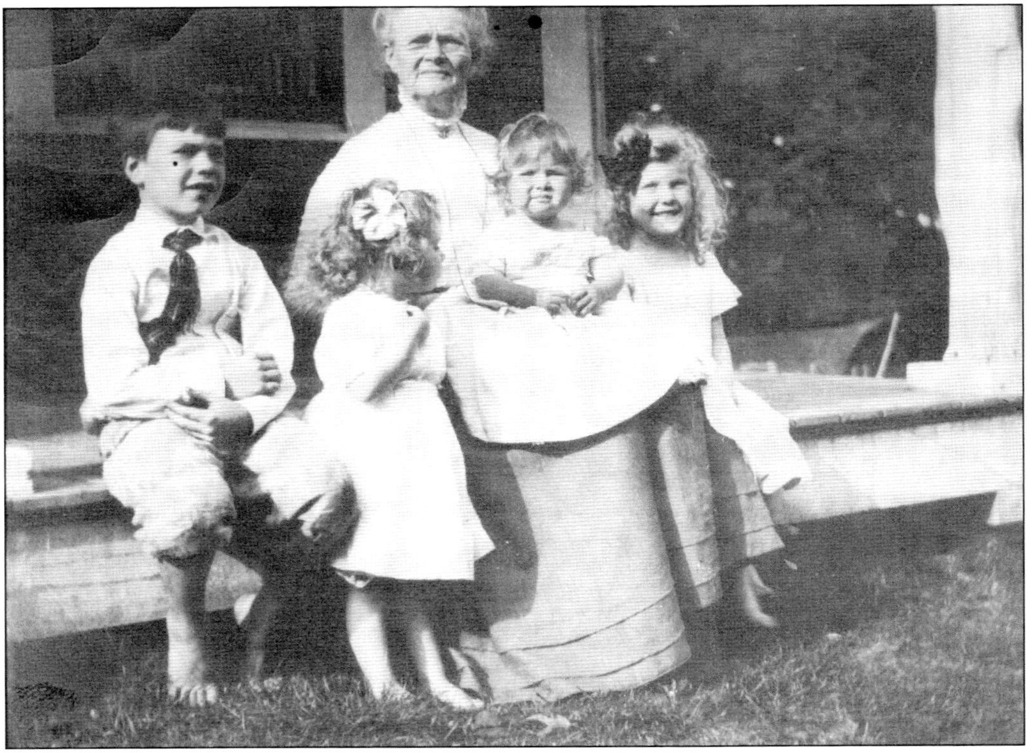

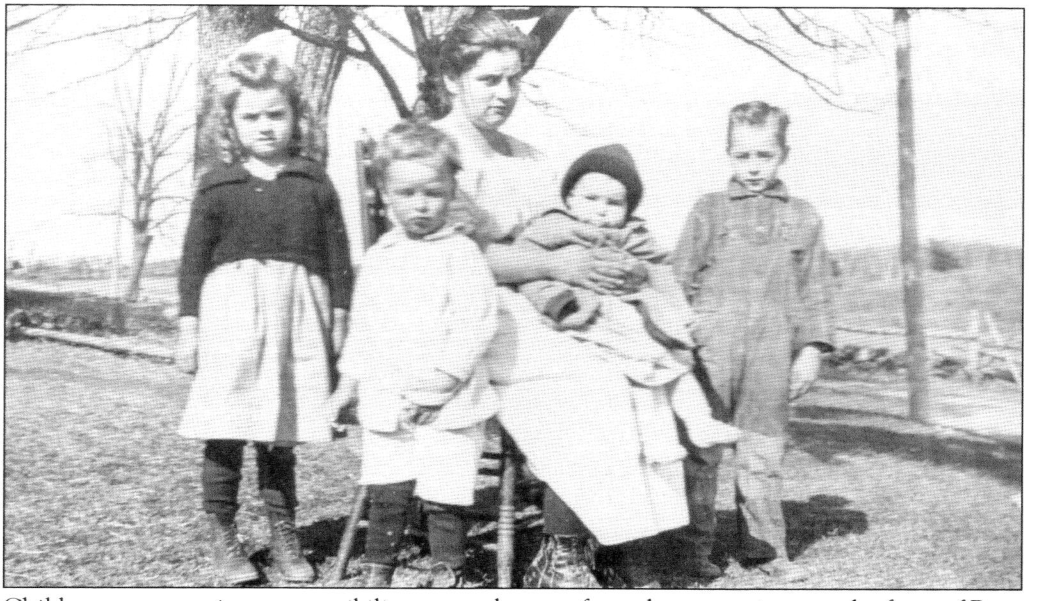

Child care was a serious responsibility, as can be seen from the expressions on the faces of Rose Currier Waugh and her children.

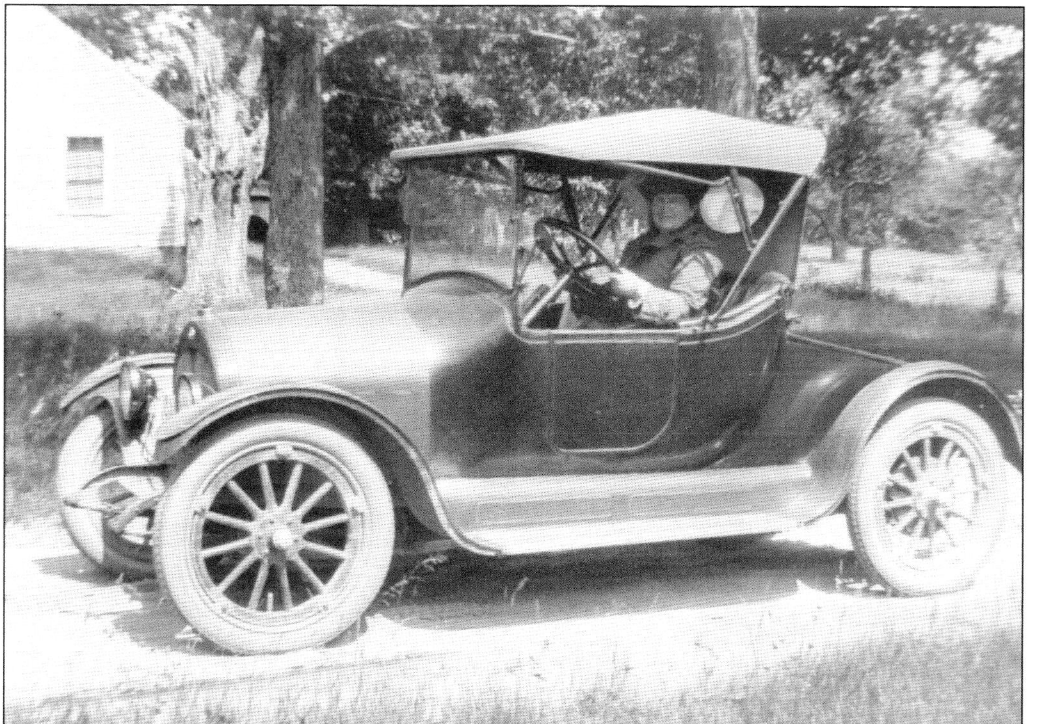

This is Martha Harrington in her 1913 Saxton automobile. Women did not have the right to vote, but they were beginning to claim their independence. Note the location of the rearview mirror above and to the left of the driver' shoulder.

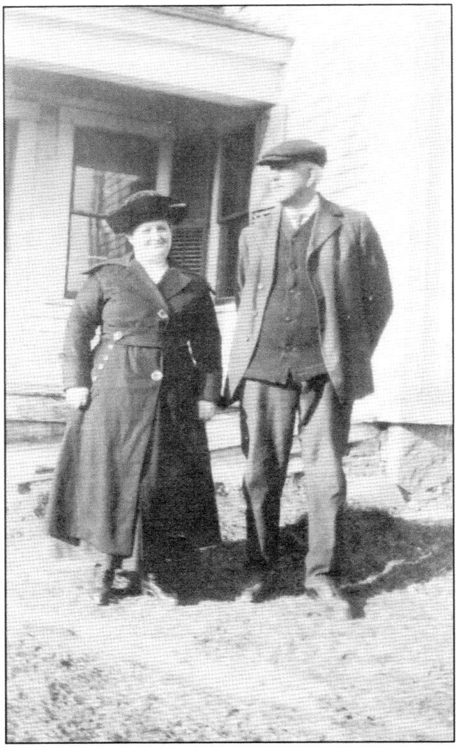

Cora and Eugene Kelley step out the door on a sunny day. They may be heading for church, to which ladies always wore hats.

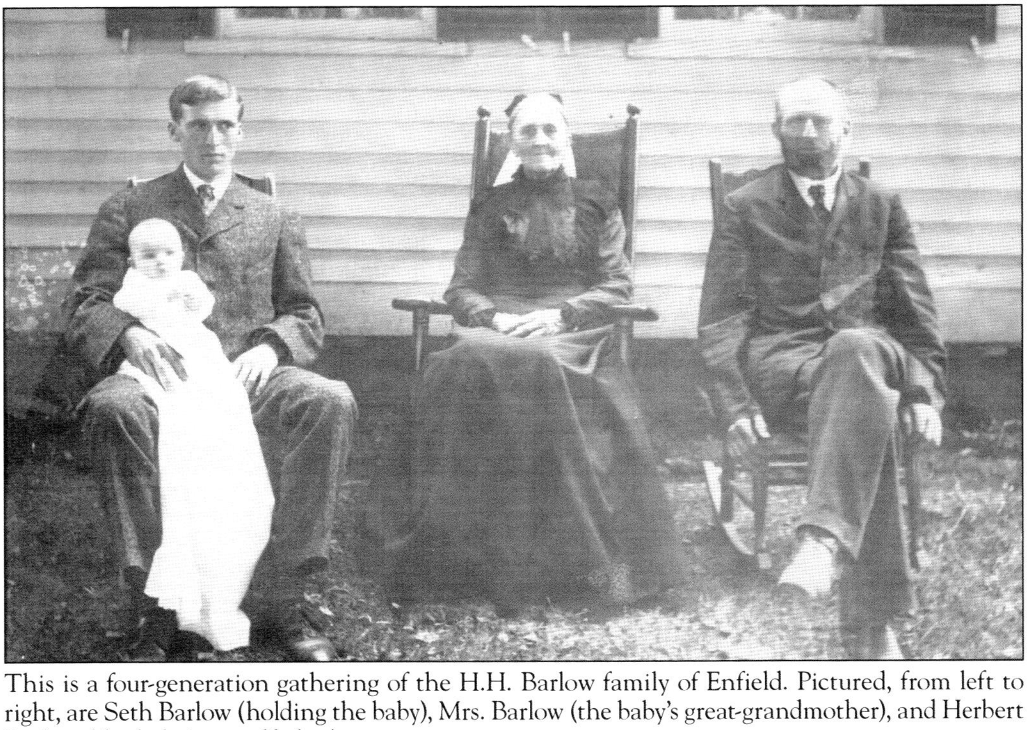

This is a four-generation gathering of the H.H. Barlow family of Enfield. Pictured, from left to right, are Seth Barlow (holding the baby), Mrs. Barlow (the baby's great-grandmother), and Herbert Barlow (the baby's grandfather).

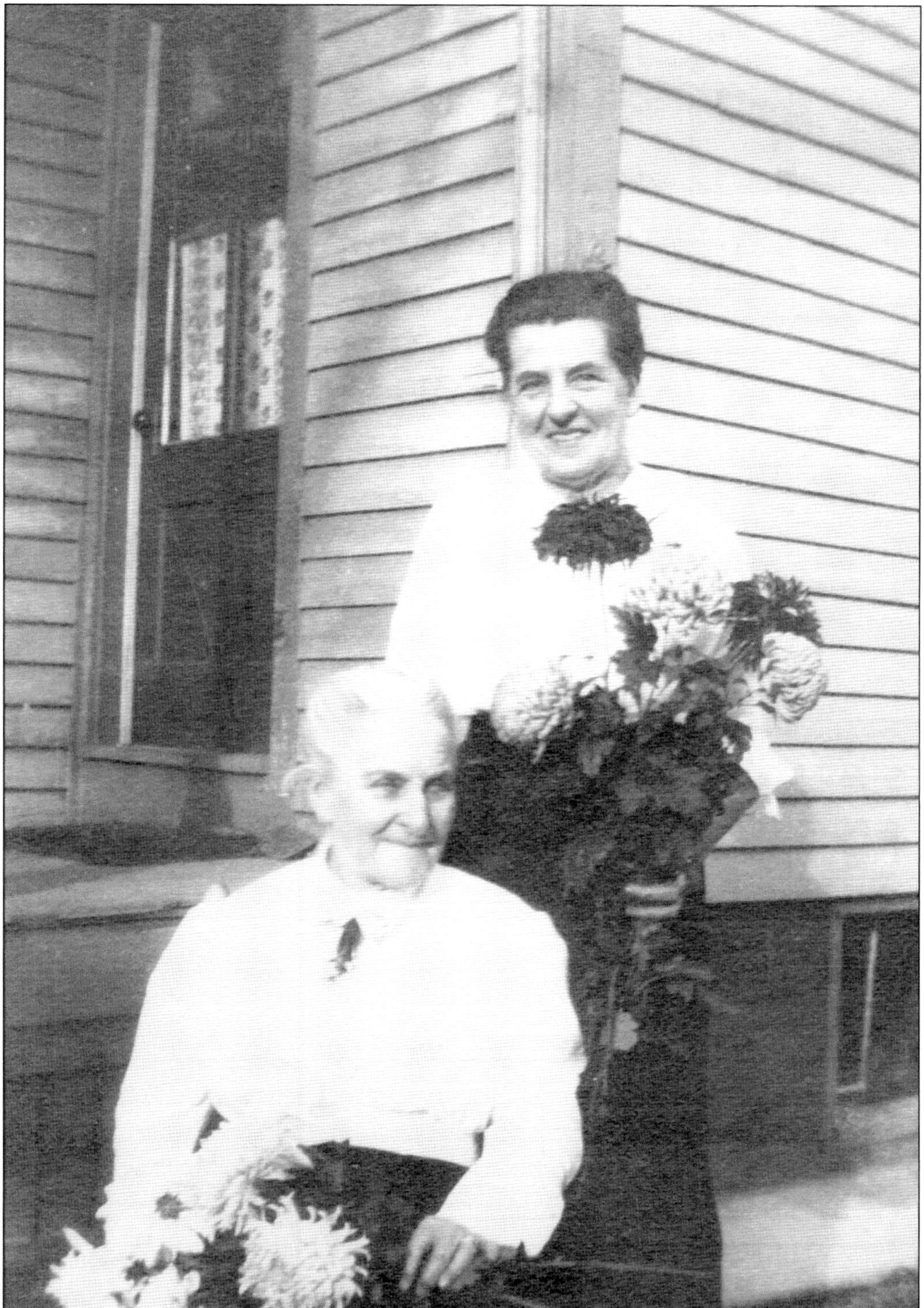

Mrs. Nevins and Mrs. Sloan are celebrating their birthdays on November 23, 1913.

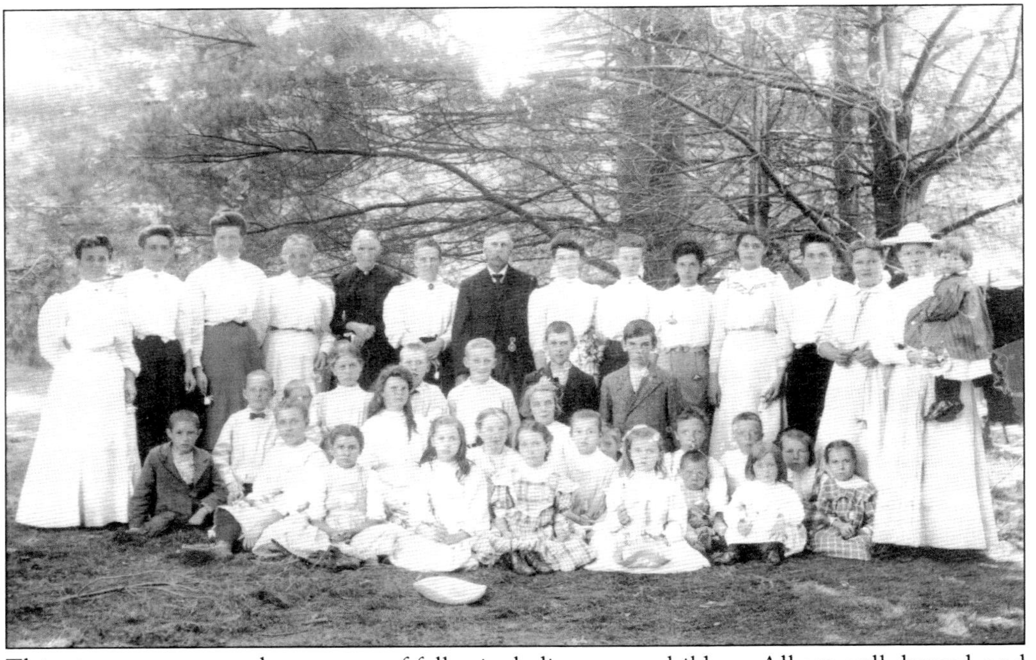

This picture portrays a large group of folks, including many children. All are well dressed, and one could speculate that this is a reunion or summer meeting.

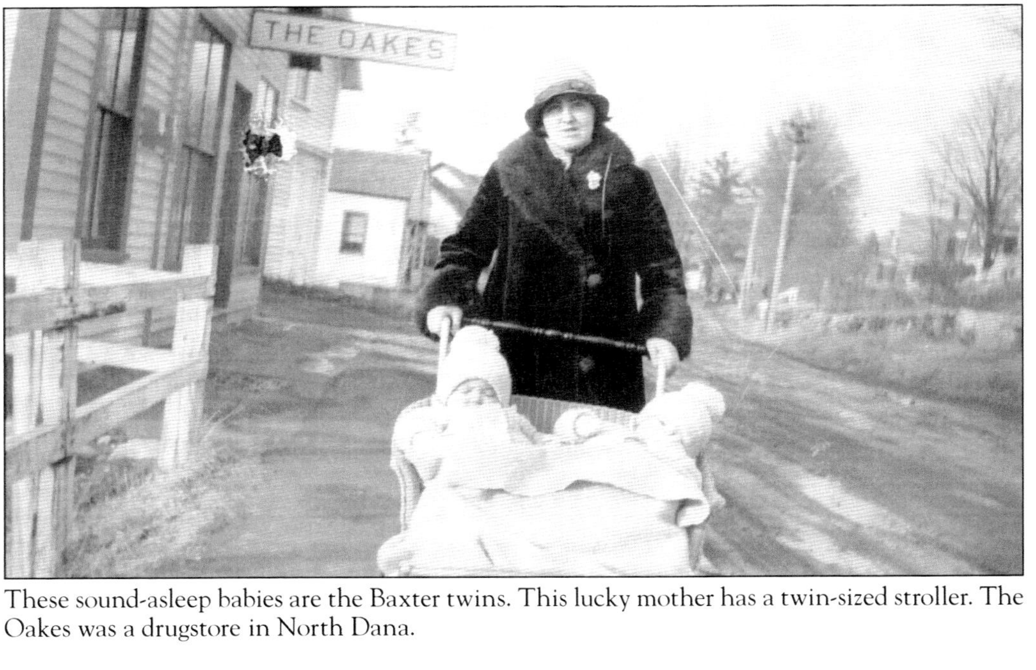

These sound-asleep babies are the Baxter twins. This lucky mother has a twin-sized stroller. The Oakes was a drugstore in North Dana.

This unidentified couple of senior citizens is enjoying a sunny morning.

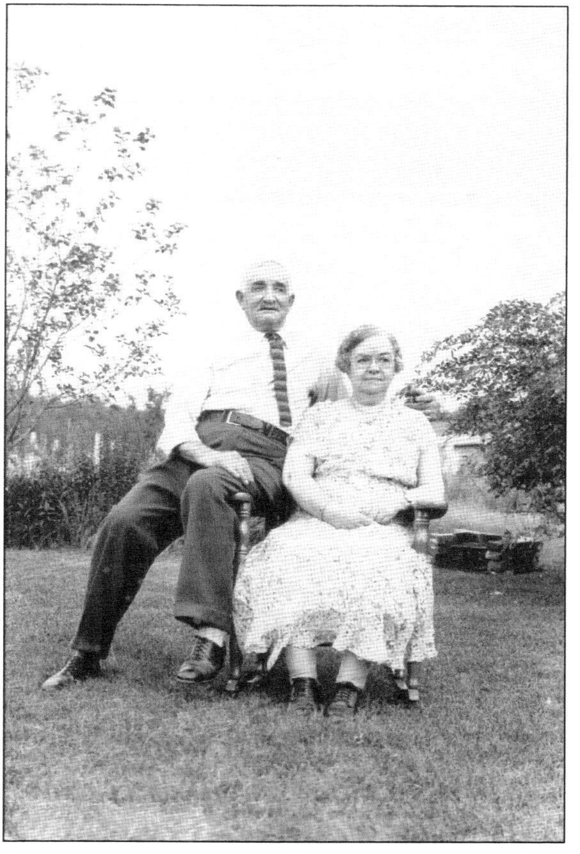

This mother and her children are ready to go somewhere. The year is 1925, and automobiles do not have the comforts that they do today. Note how warmly the family is dressed. There was no heat and no windows that could go up and down—only see-through squares at the sides. There was a crank for starting the car, a spare tire, and probably a buffalo robe to keep warm.

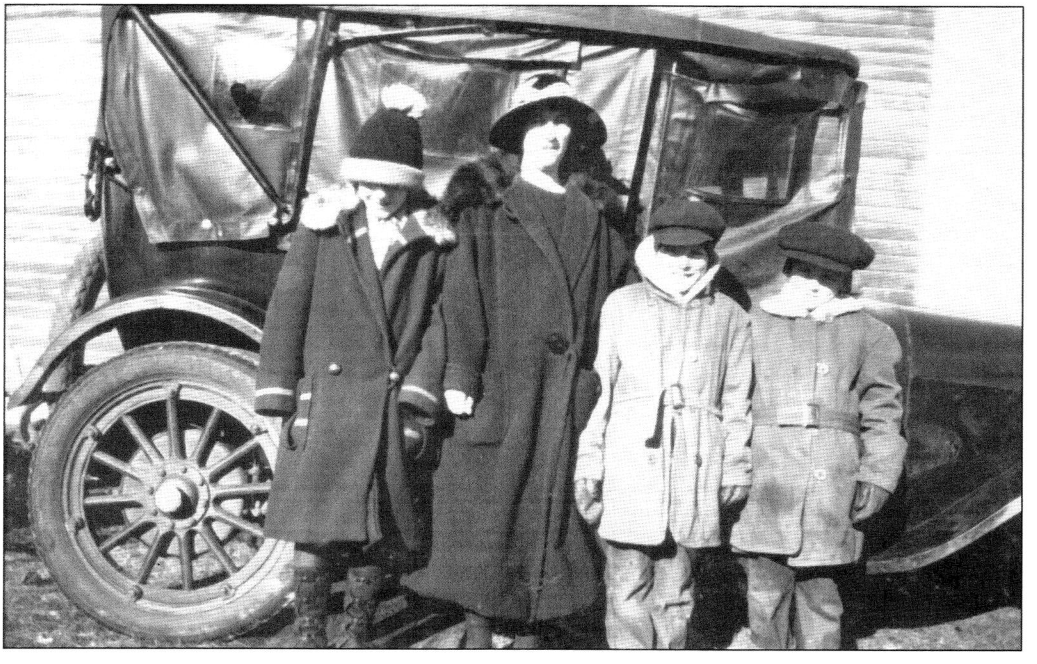

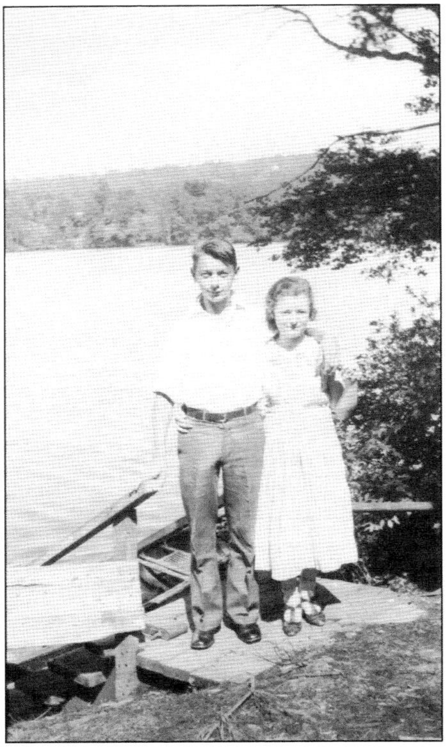

This unidentified couple spends a pleasant day at one of the many lakes in the valley.

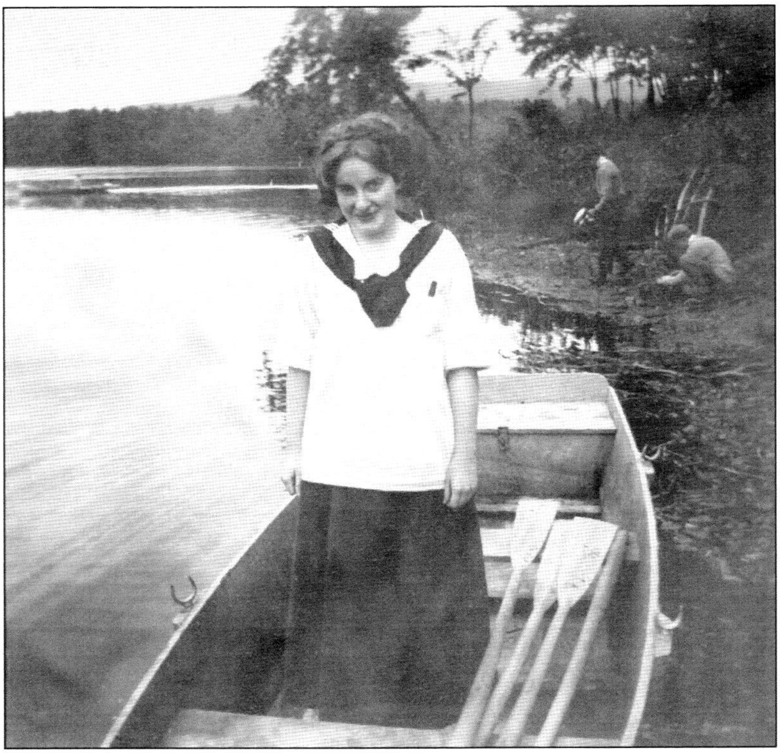

This unidentified young lady is ready to go rowing in Greenwich Lake, another of the many bodies of water in the valley.

These three, labeled "the three musketeers," are, from left to right, Elmer Thresher, Harry Thresher, and Donald Towne. They are leaning on Towne's antique car.

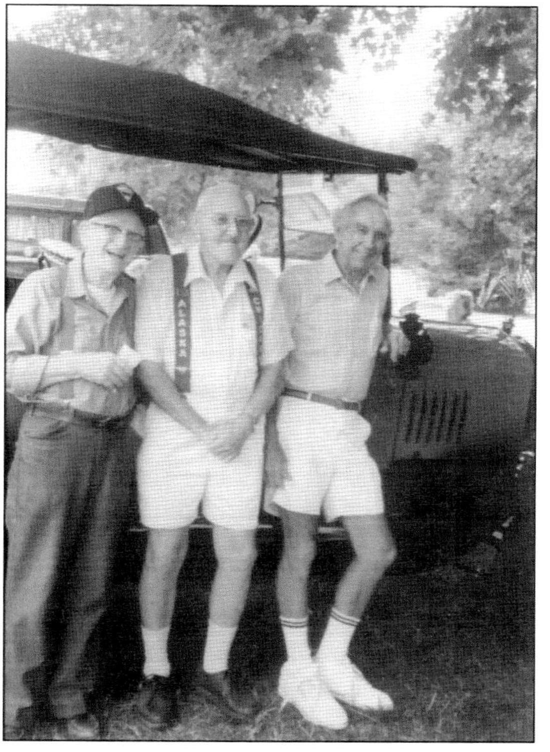

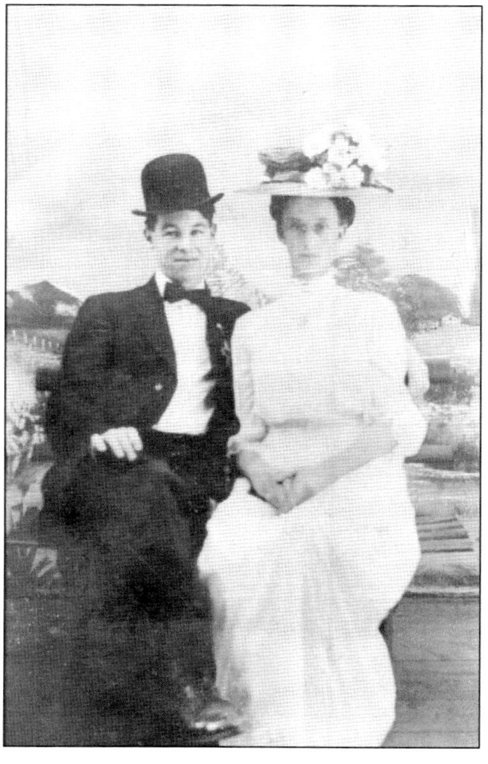

Weddings were joyous occasions. Formal portraits were carefully posed and seem to reflect a very serious side of marriage. Candid wedding shots, such as we see today, were never taken.

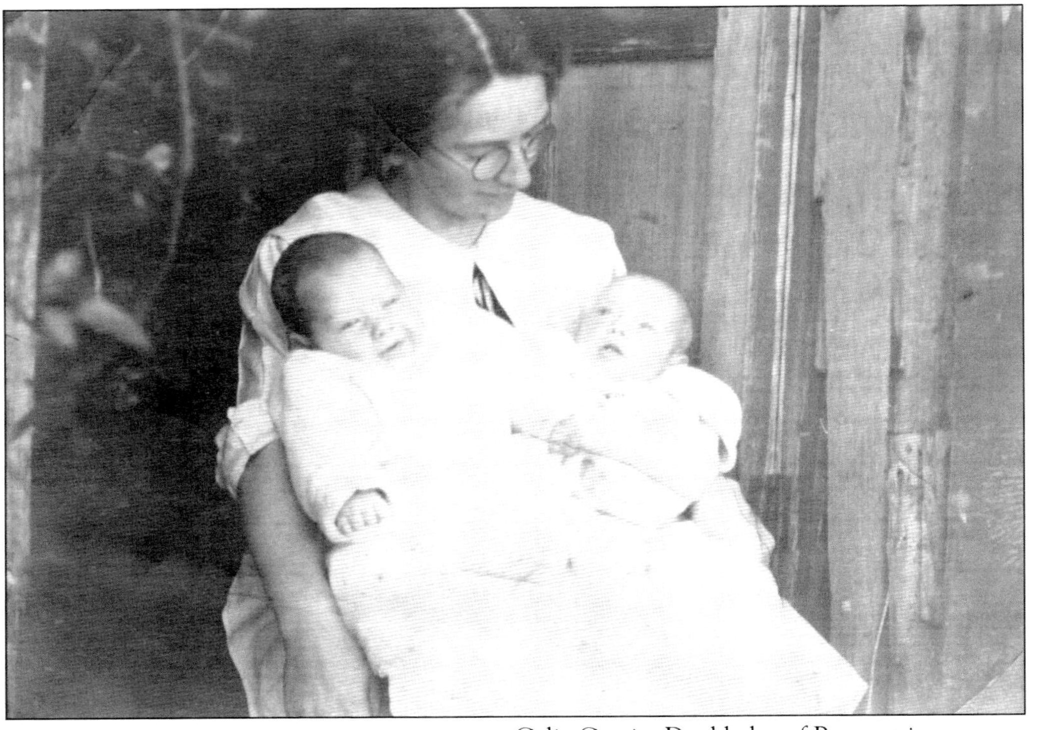

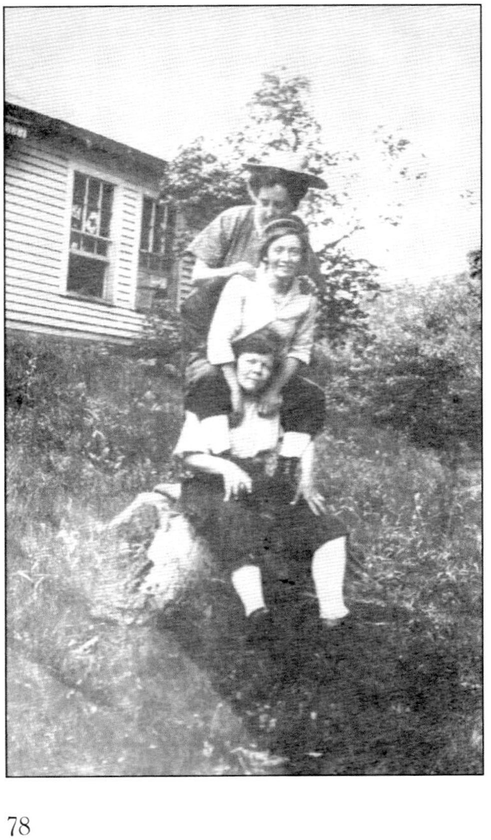

Celia Currier Doubleday of Prescott is holding twins Elwyn and Lois Doubleday. It is uncertain which is which.

How many people can pile up without a crash? These ladies from Prescott are trying to find the answer.

This little girl steps out into the morning sunshine under the watchful eyes of her mother.

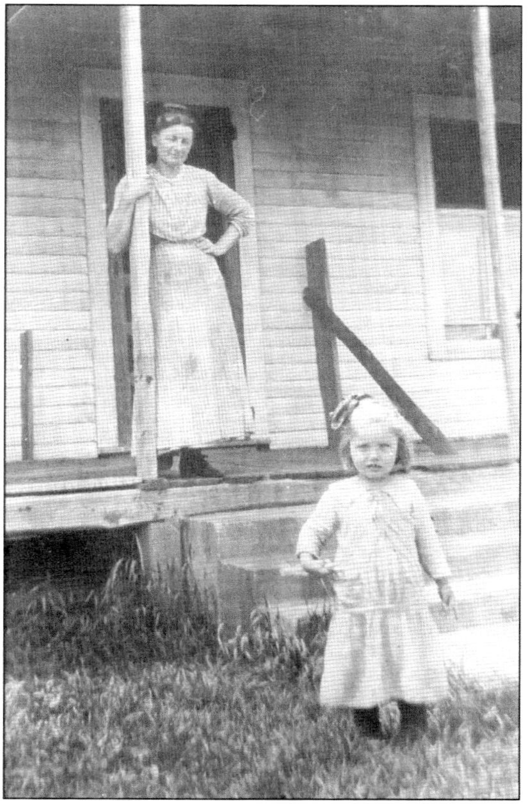

Many family reunions were held during the summer. There was always plenty of good food, lots of conversation, and a chance for cousins to play together.

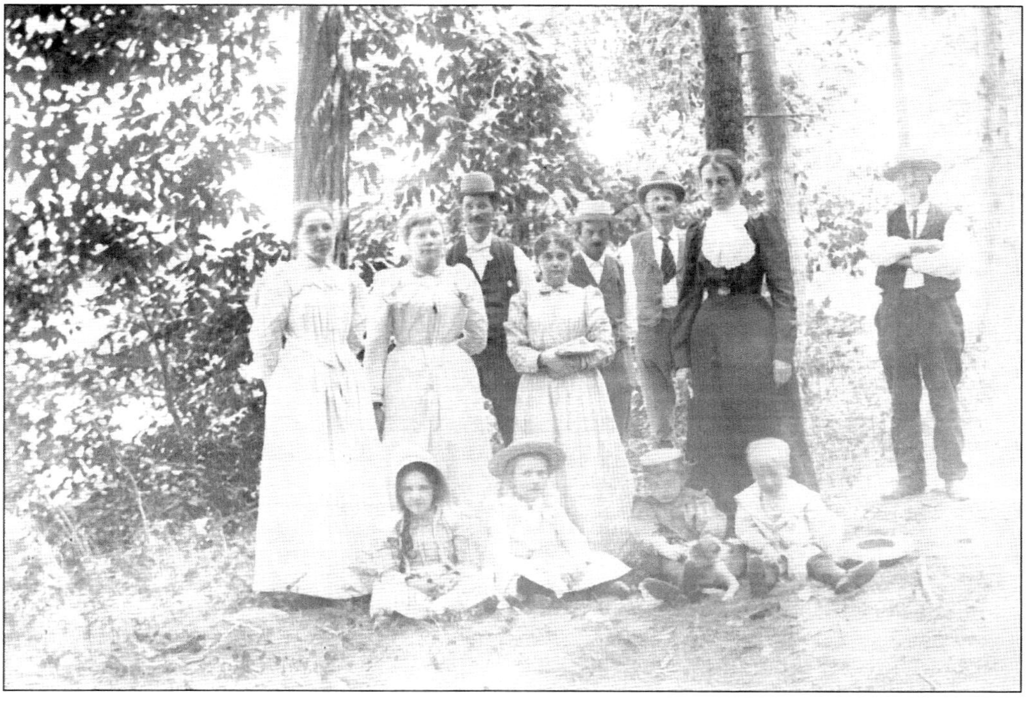

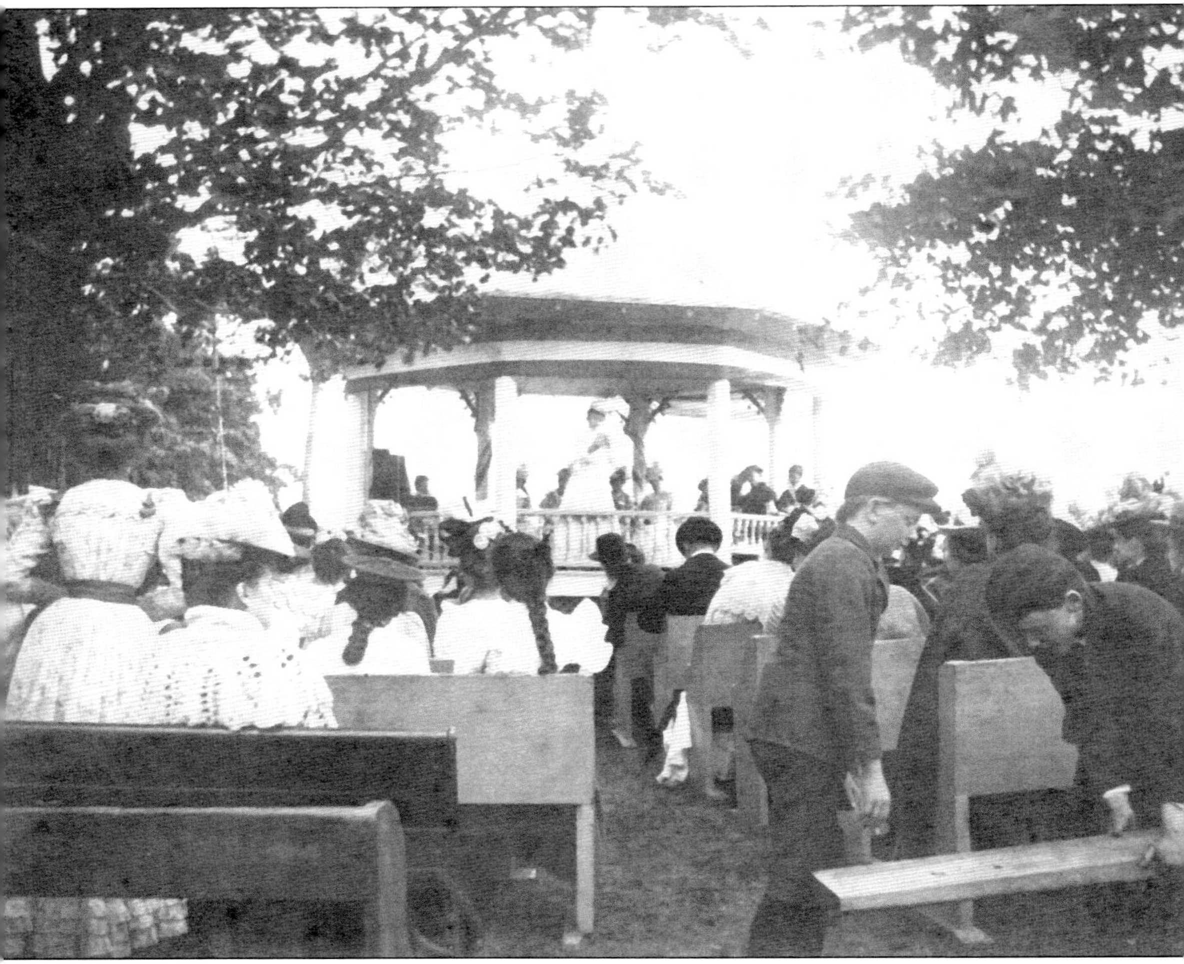

This picture shows family and friends gathered for Class Day at New Salem Academy in 1900. Hattie Paige is speaking on the bandstand.

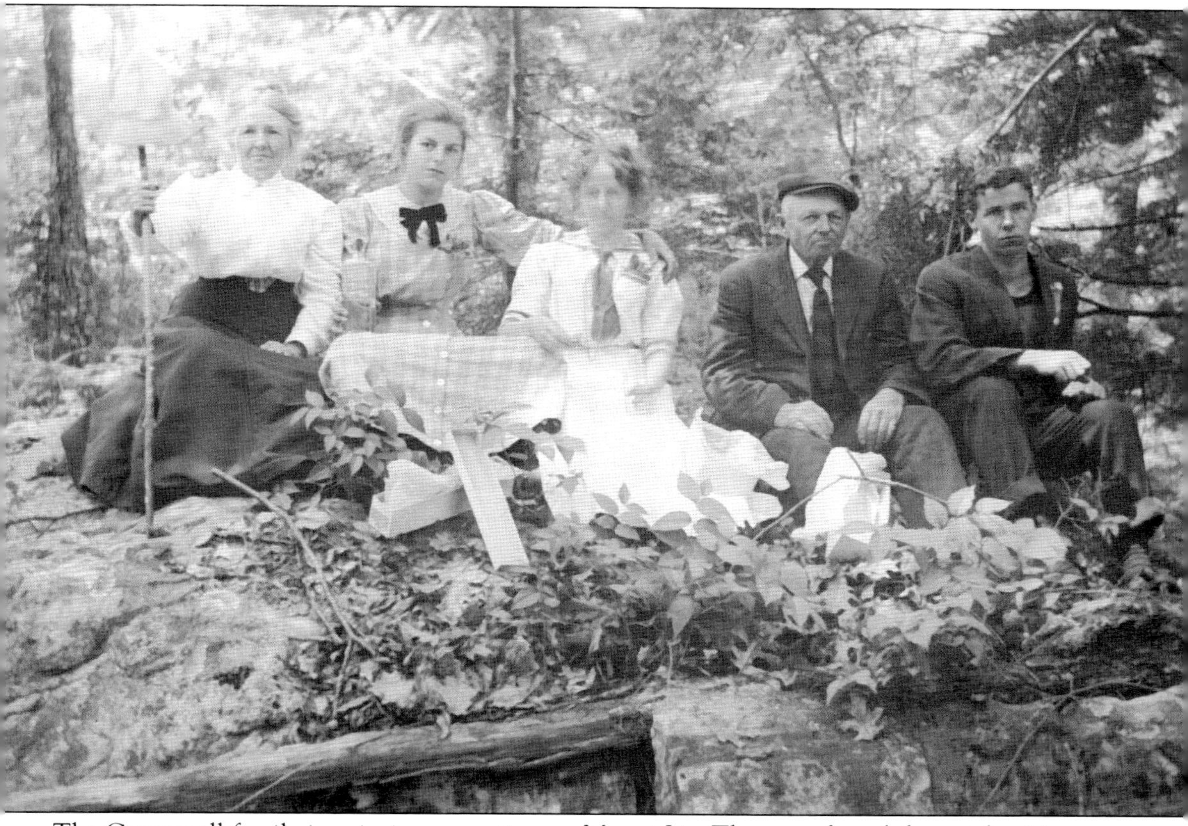

The Gammwell family is enjoying an outing on Mount Liz. They are, from left to right, Mrs. Gammwell, Mable Edson, Iris Gammwell, George Gammwell, and Clarence Lyman.

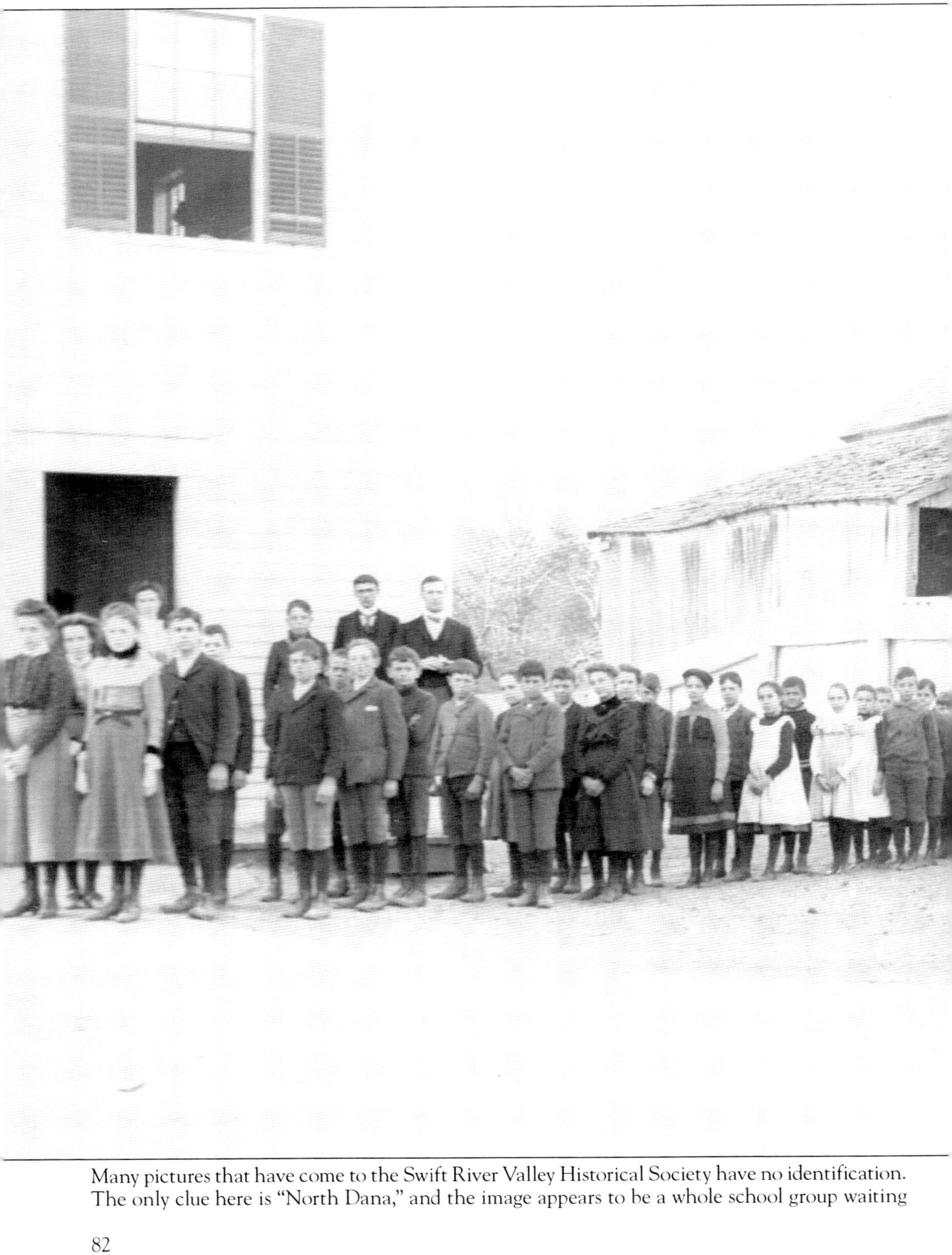

Many pictures that have come to the Swift River Valley Historical Society have no identification. The only clue here is "North Dana," and the image appears to be a whole school group waiting

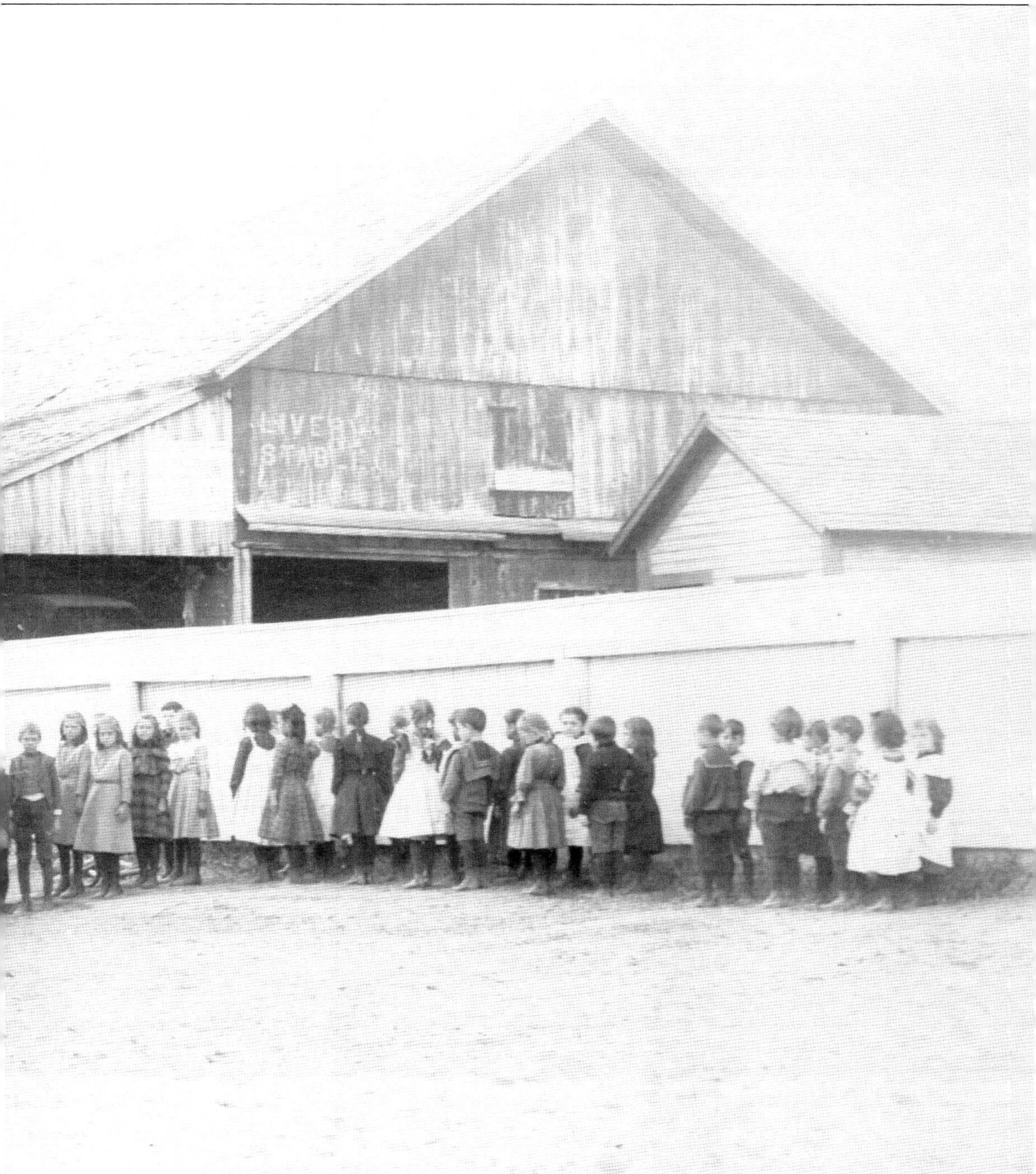

for a special event. Note how neat and well dressed they appear to be.

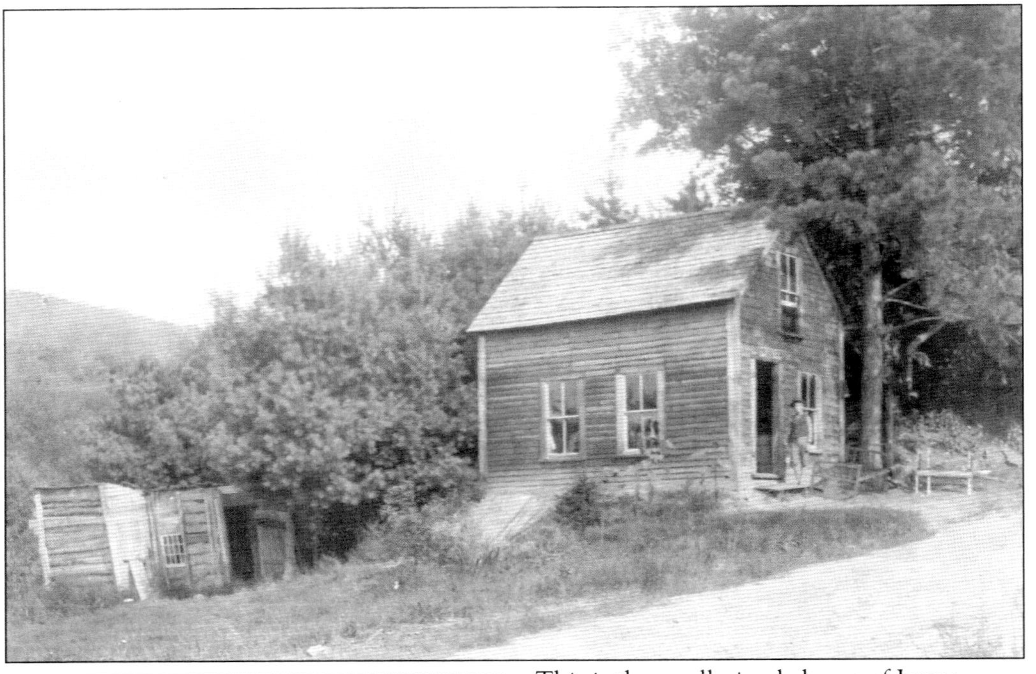

This is the small, simple home of James Thayer in Greenwich. He is standing in the doorway.

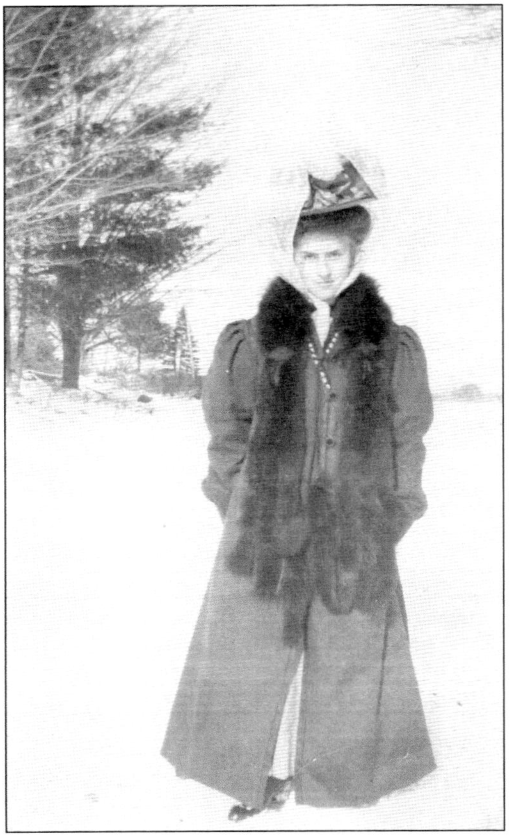

Furs were very fashionable in the 1920s. Hunting and trapping provided ladies with fur pieces from foxes and beavers.

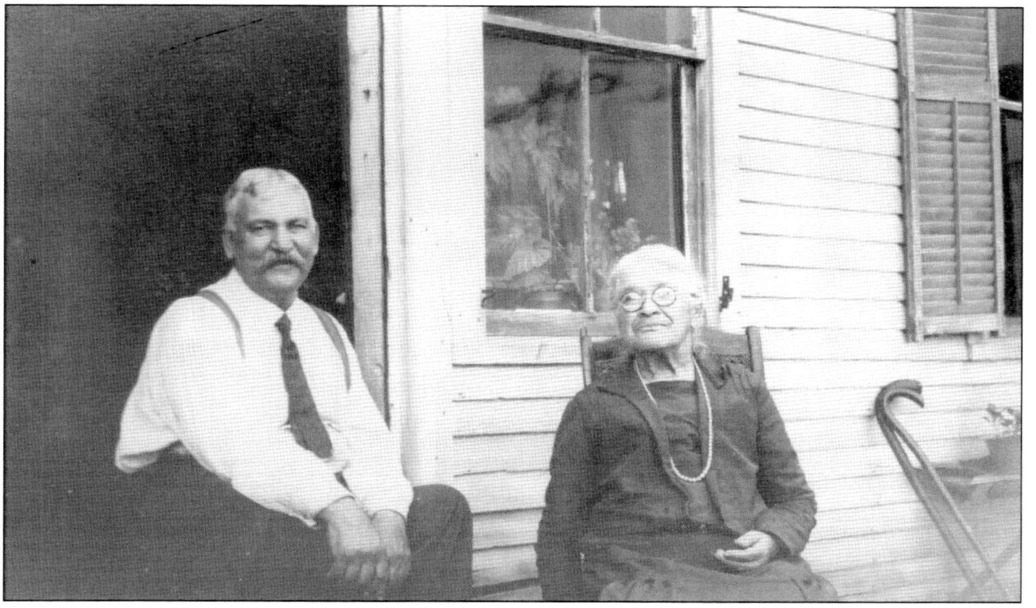

This unidentified elderly couple appears to be enjoying the sunshine. Note the canes leaning against the wall on the right.

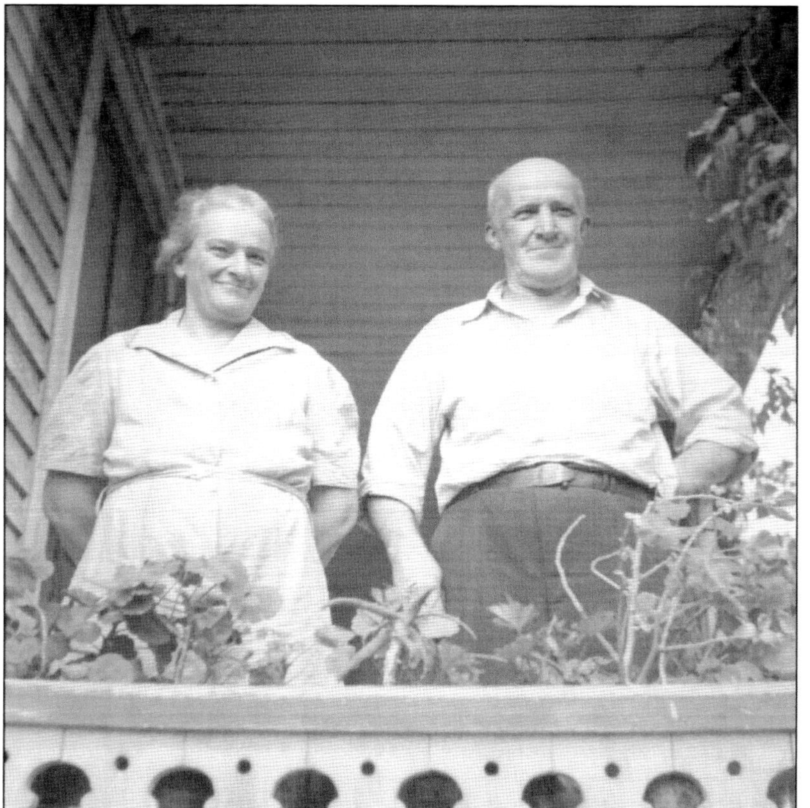

This picture shows Olive Jenny Griswold and her brother Eugene.

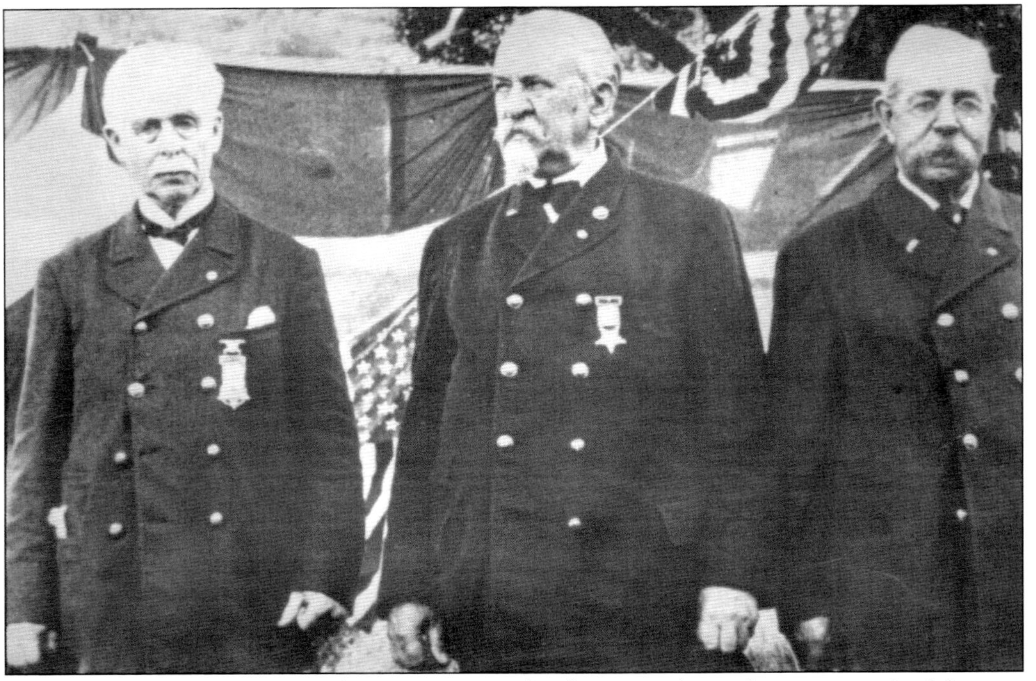

These Civil War veterans stand at attention as the flag passes by at the centennial celebration of Enfield in 1916.

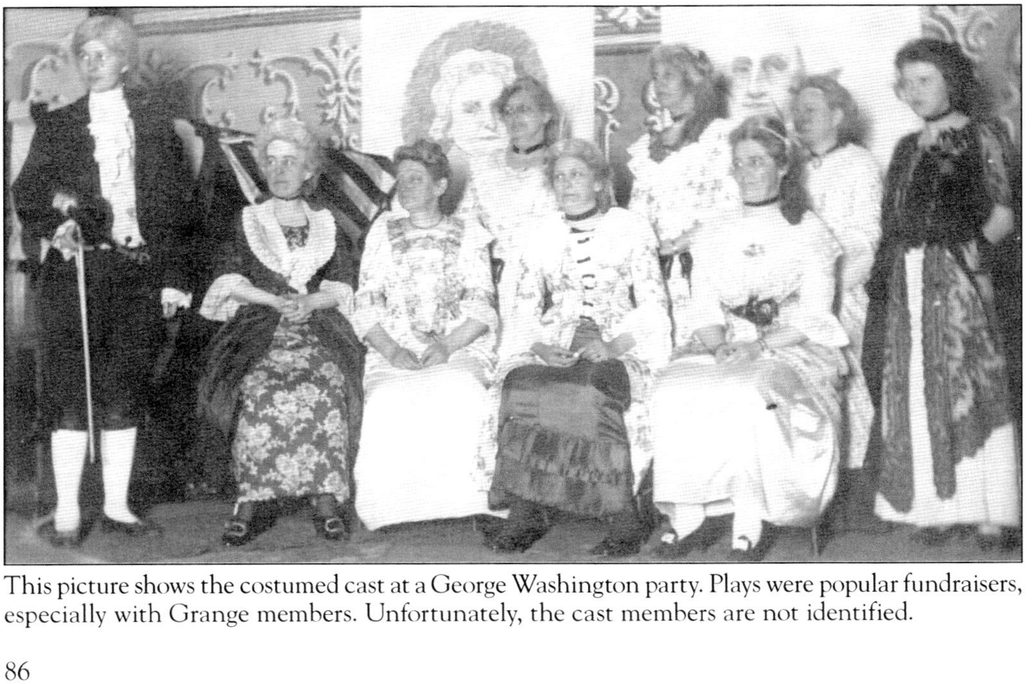

This picture shows the costumed cast at a George Washington party. Plays were popular fundraisers, especially with Grange members. Unfortunately, the cast members are not identified.

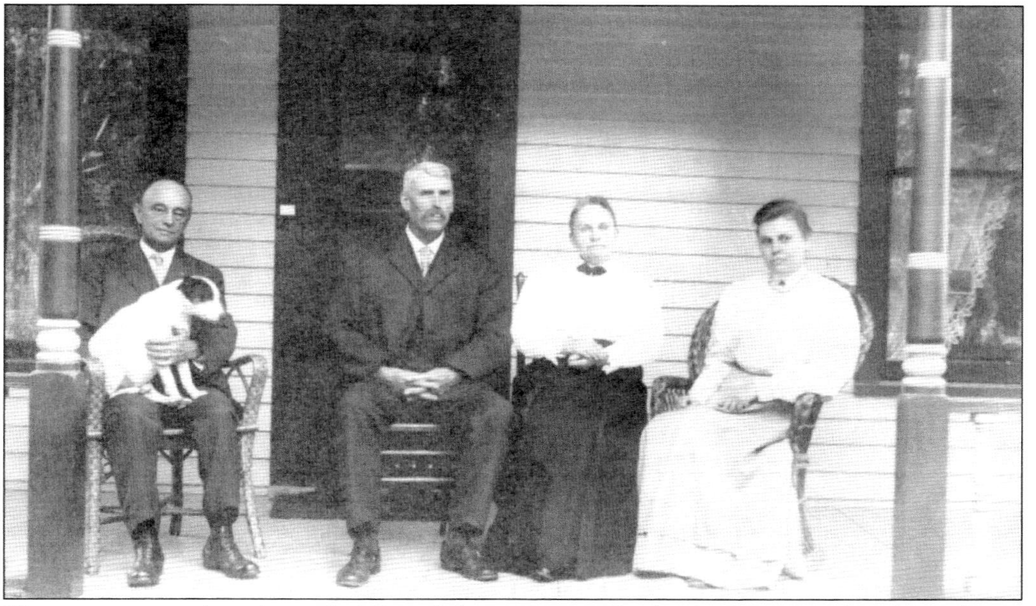

This picture was taken about 1916. From left to right are Charles A. Sloan, C. Edward Goodman, Della Doubleday Goodman, and Bertha Goodman Sloan.

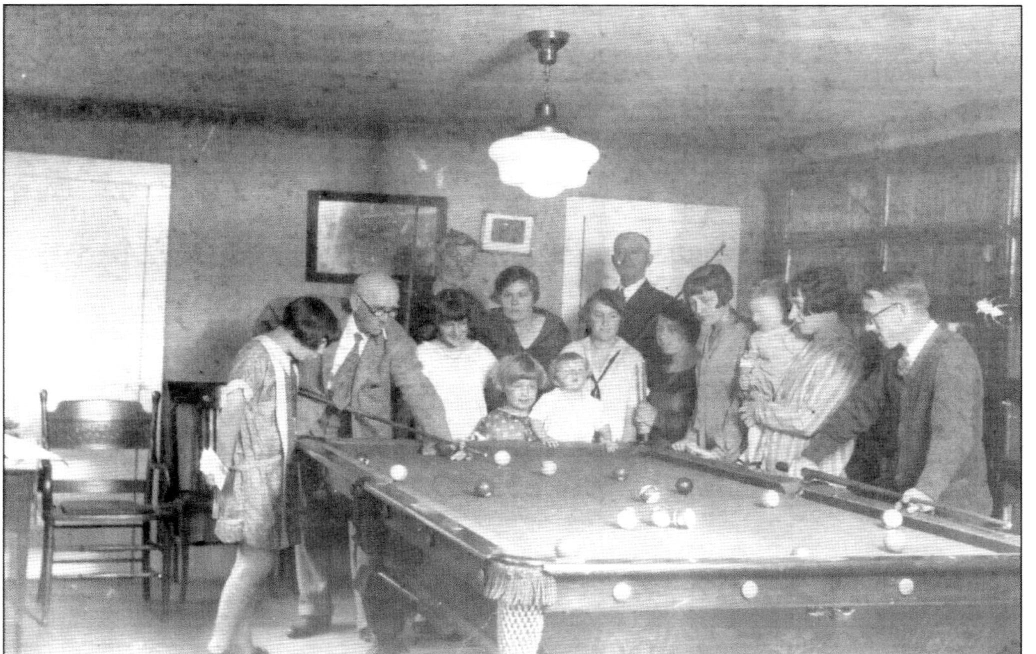

The Dorothy Dix girls were a branch of the Boston Children's Theatre. Thomas Fraser Reddy, an attorney, brought these stage children to New Salem to study, perform, and play in the summer. Reddy's summer residence in New Salem became a dormitory for the girls, complete with a housemother and all the necessary support staff. This picture shows an evening gathering in the billiard room.

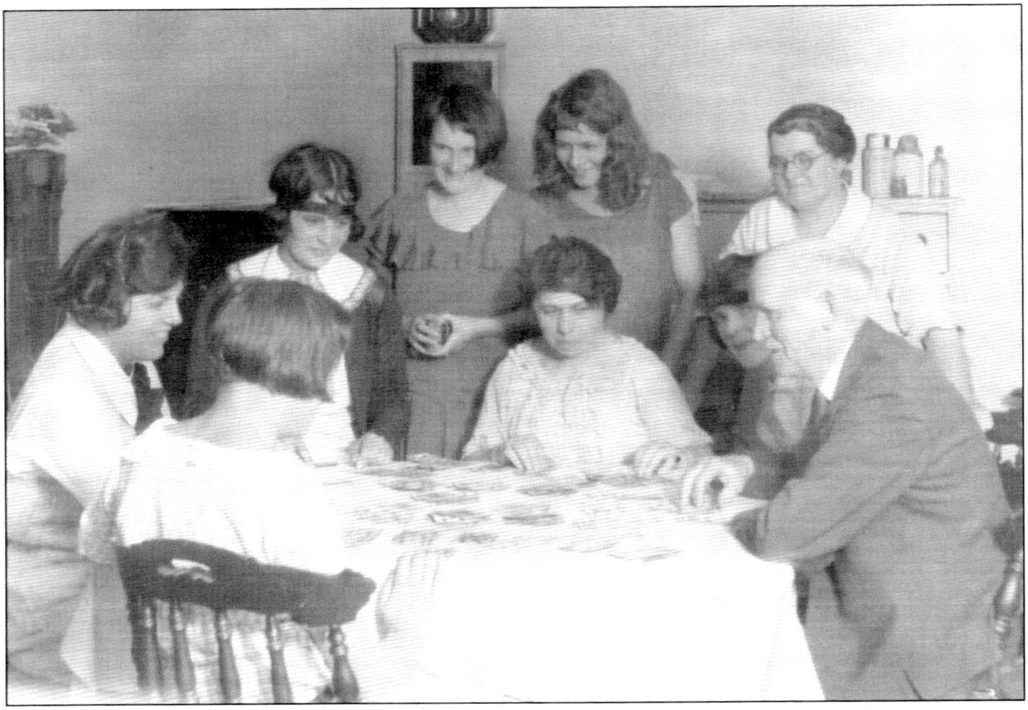

This picture shows the Dorothy Dix girls enjoying their nightly game of "Race Horse." Attorney Thomas Reddy is the gentleman at the right. The girls referred to him affectionately as "Daddy."

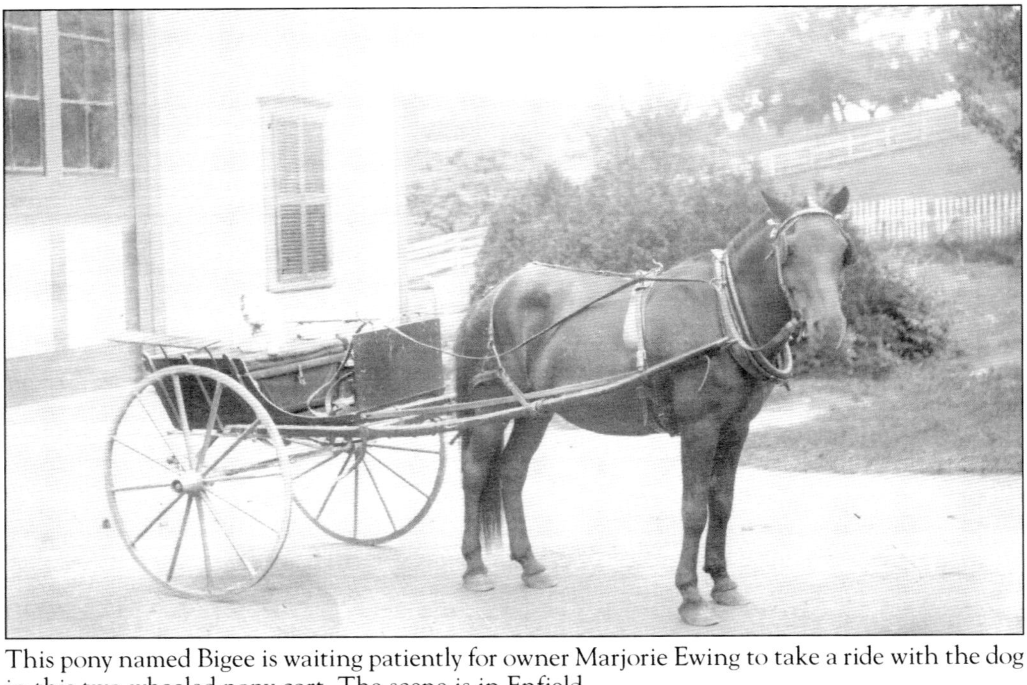

This pony named Bigee is waiting patiently for owner Marjorie Ewing to take a ride with the dog in this two-wheeled pony cart. The scene is in Enfield.

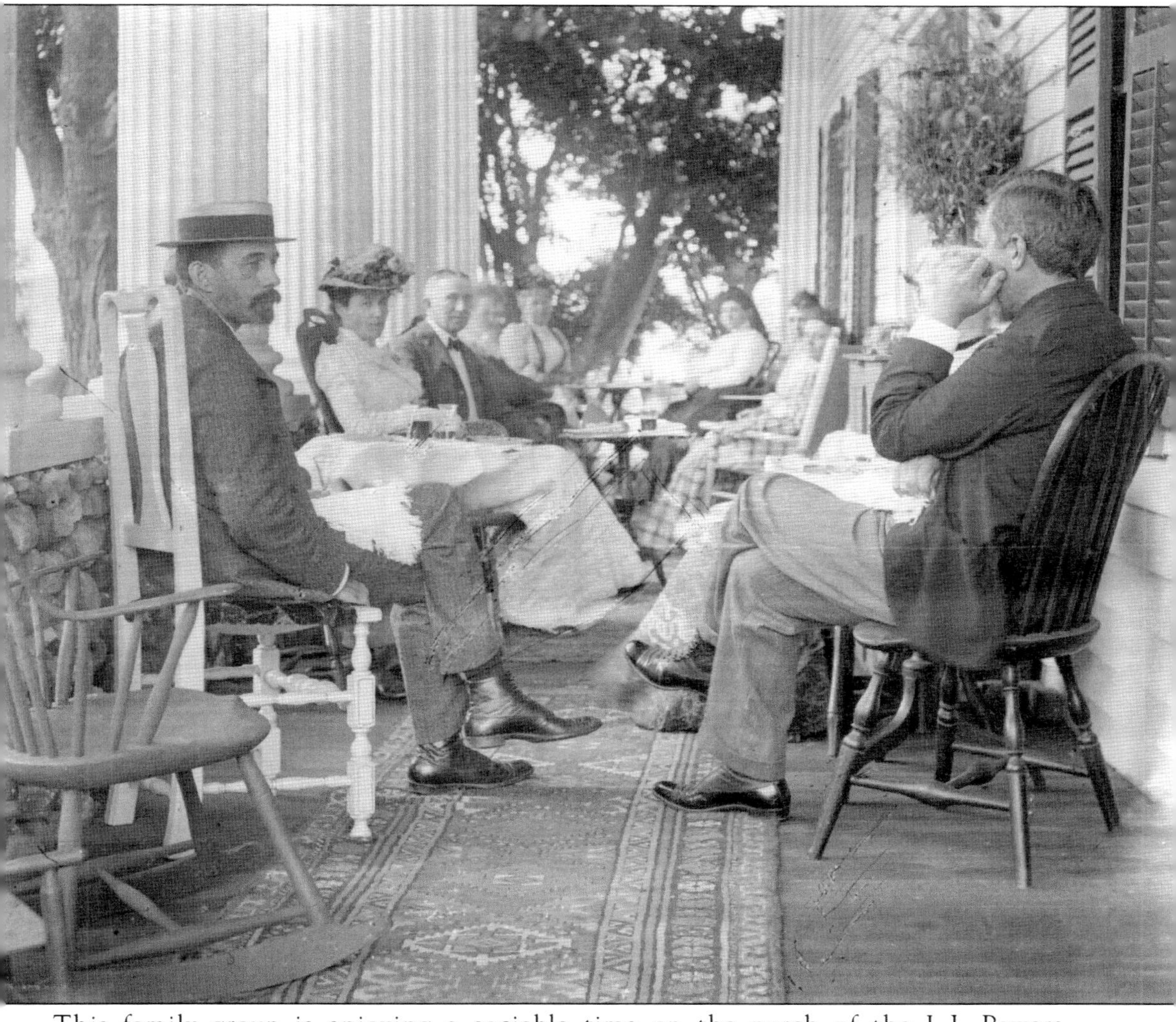

This family group is enjoying a sociable time on the porch of the L.J. Powers residence in Enfield.

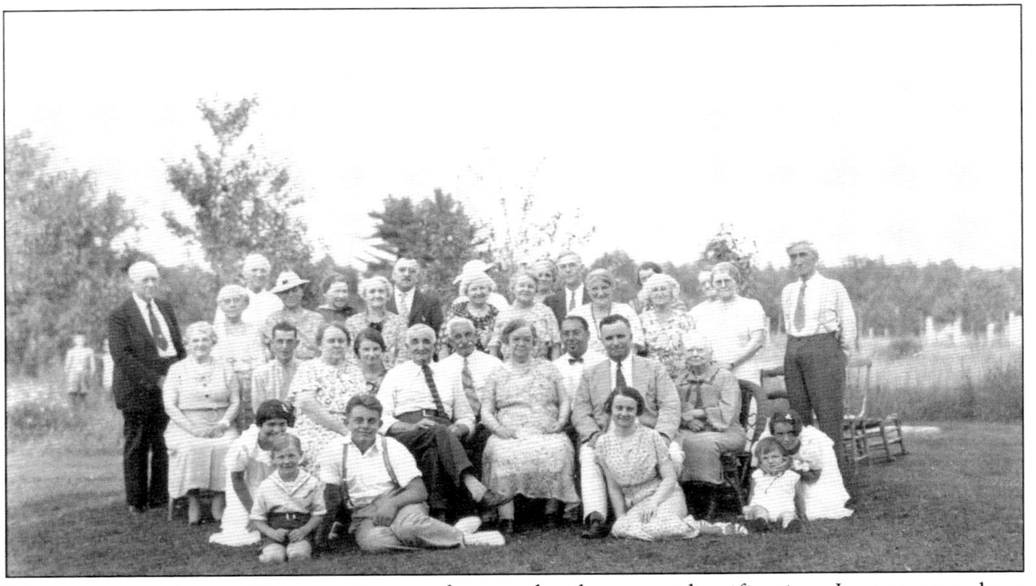

This picture, taken in Prescott, is one of many that have no identification. It appears to be a reunion, and a cemetery is visible in the background. The picture was probably taken in the 1930s era.

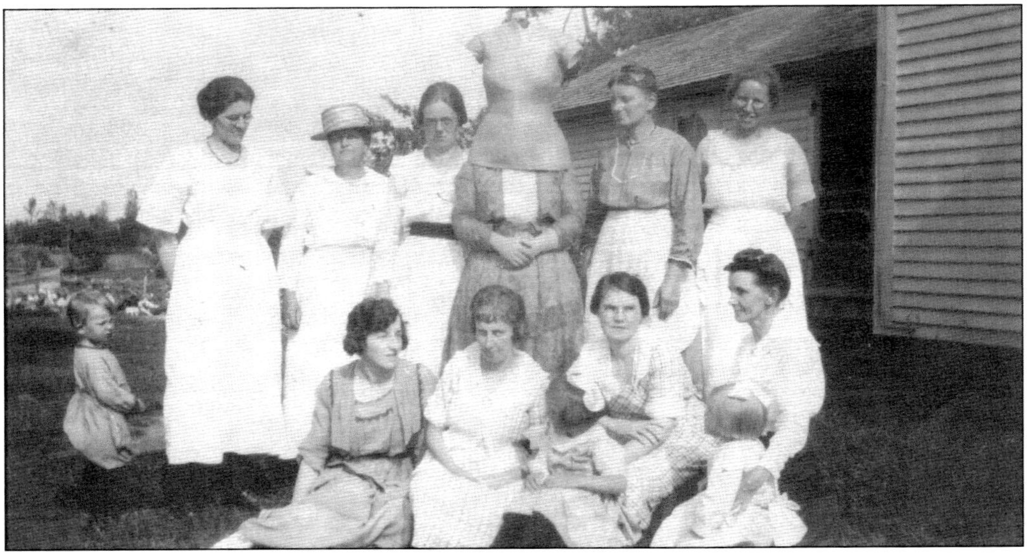

These Prescott ladies and children are gathered for an afternoon of sociability, sewing, and probably gossip. The women, from left to right, are (first row) Mrs. Allen, Mrs. Reed, Mrs. Parker, and Mrs. Peirce; (second row) Mrs. Fogg, Mrs. Gross, Mrs. Tinkey, Mrs. Barnes, Mrs. Mitchell, and Miss Thrasher. The children, from left to right, are Ginny Fogg, Elizabeth Reed, and Bernice Allen.

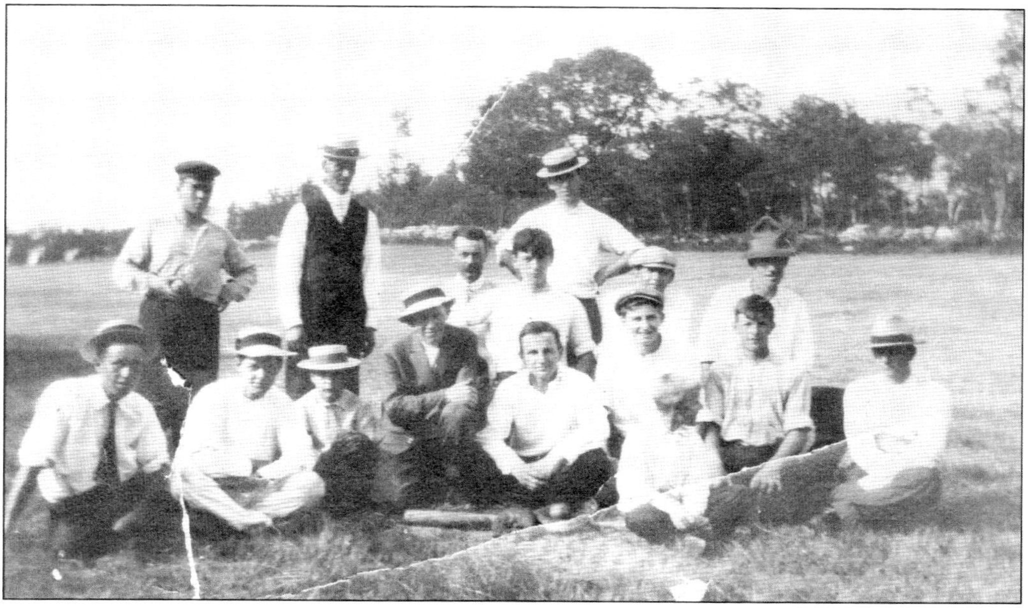

These men are preparing for a ball game at the Packardville Church Fair.

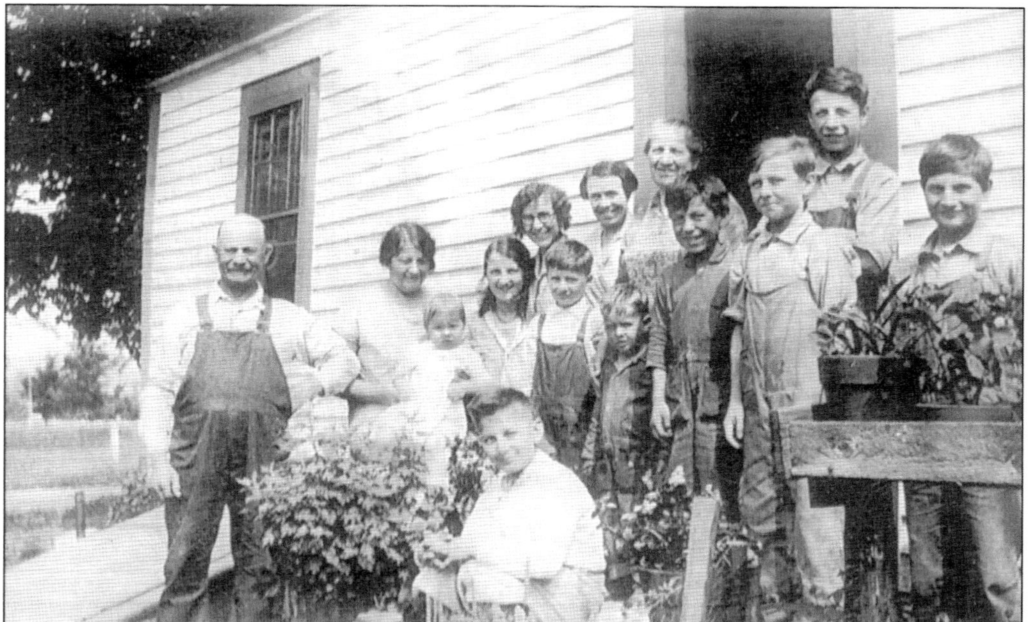

This family group is somewhere in one of the Quabbin Valley towns. It is uncertain whether they are related or are state wards. Many families cared for state wards or foster children. As no one thought to write on the back of the picture, the truth about this image may never be known.

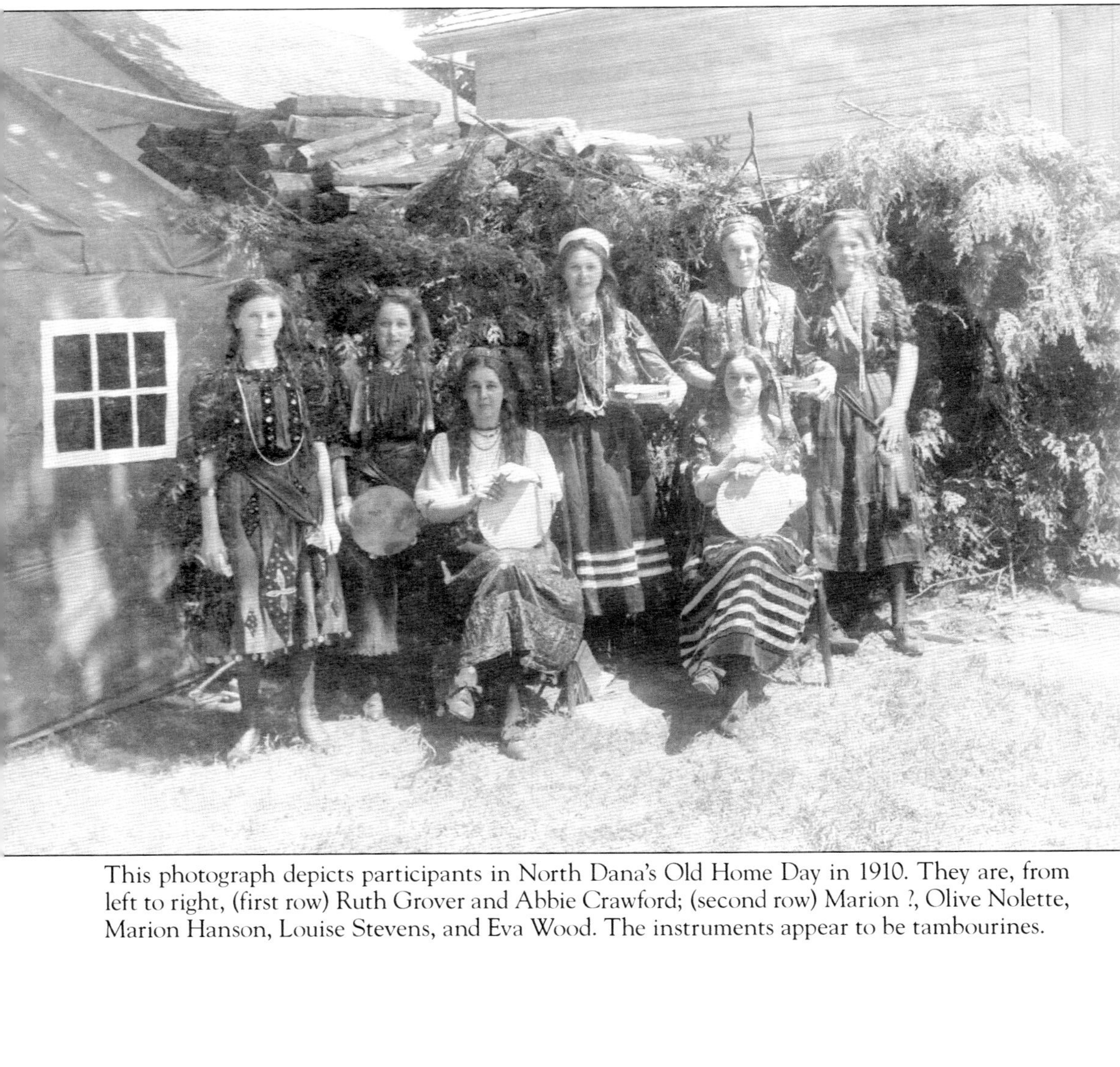

This photograph depicts participants in North Dana's Old Home Day in 1910. They are, from left to right, (first row) Ruth Grover and Abbie Crawford; (second row) Marion ?, Olive Nolette, Marion Hanson, Louise Stevens, and Eva Wood. The instruments appear to be tambourines.

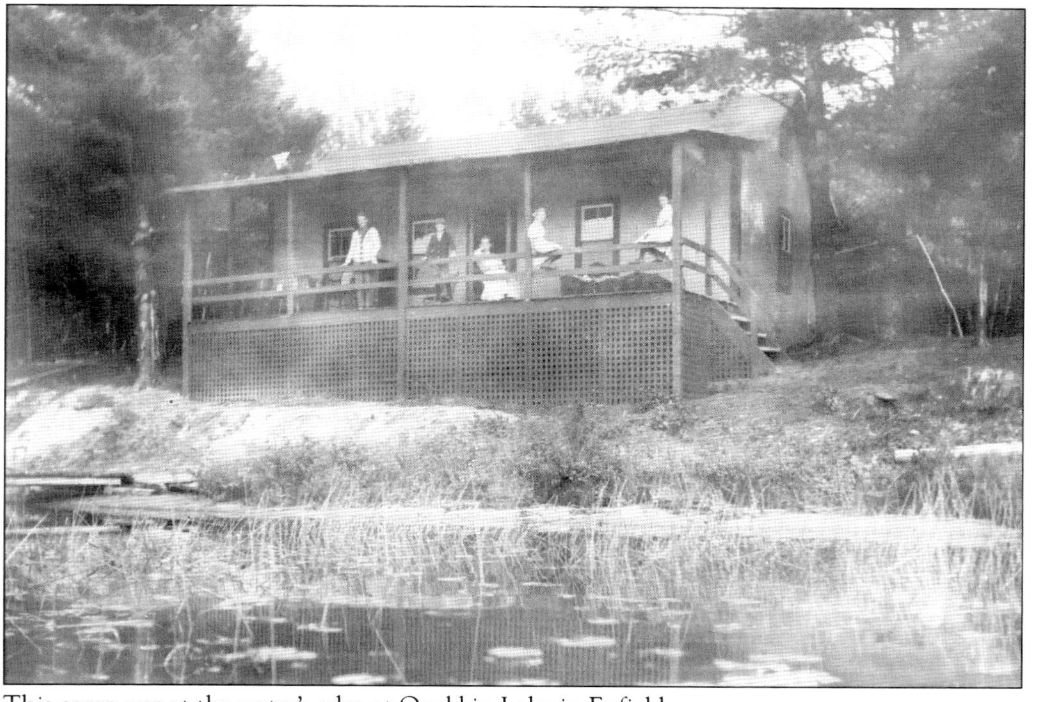

This camp was at the water's edge at Quabbin Lake in Enfield.

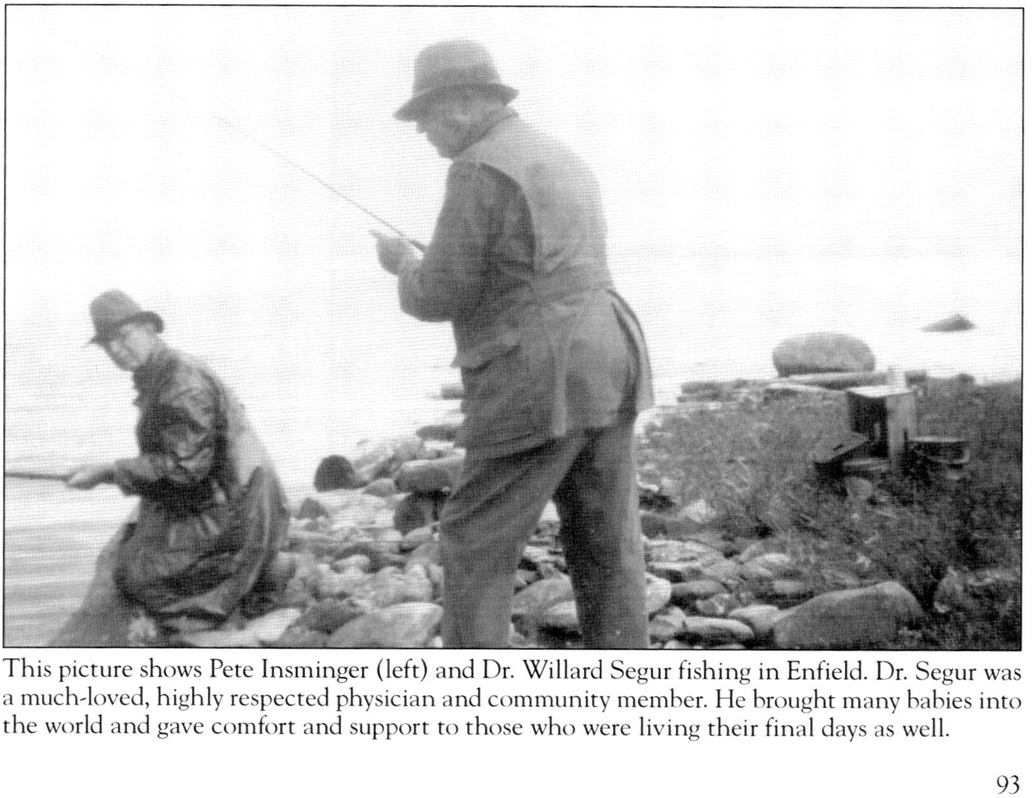

This picture shows Pete Insminger (left) and Dr. Willard Segur fishing in Enfield. Dr. Segur was a much-loved, highly respected physician and community member. He brought many babies into the world and gave comfort and support to those who were living their final days as well.

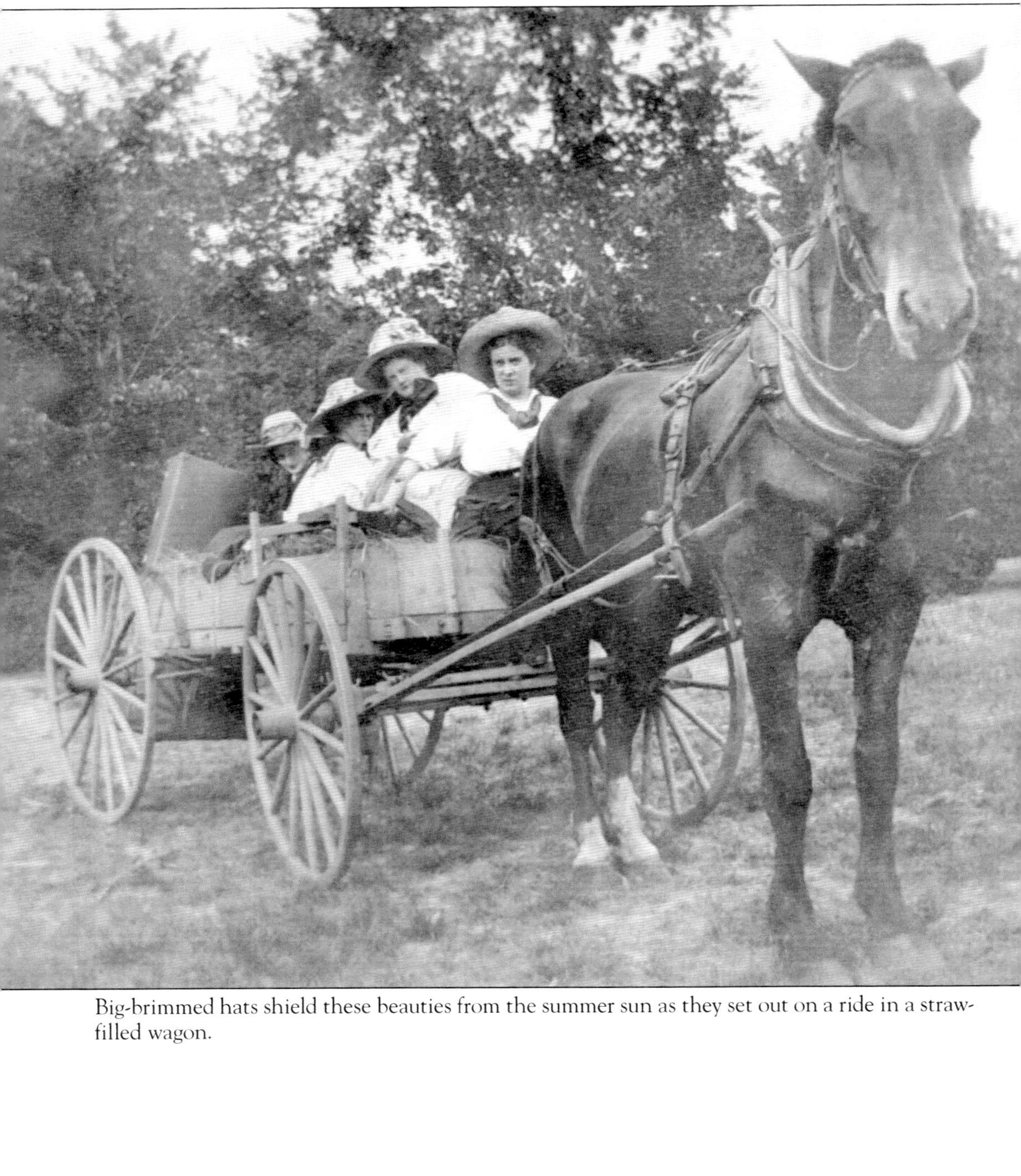

Big-brimmed hats shield these beauties from the summer sun as they set out on a ride in a straw-filled wagon.

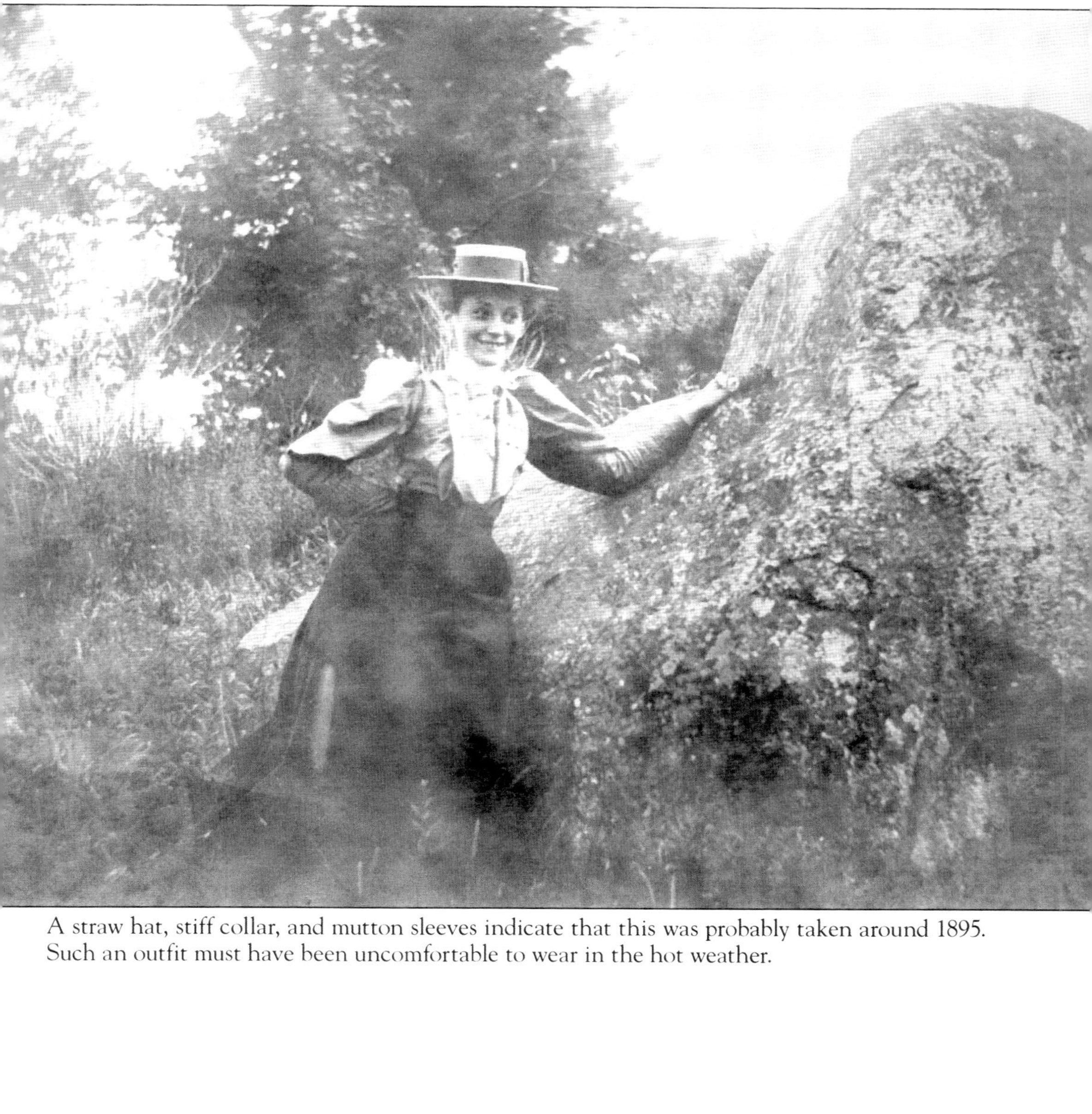

A straw hat, stiff collar, and mutton sleeves indicate that this was probably taken around 1895. Such an outfit must have been uncomfortable to wear in the hot weather.

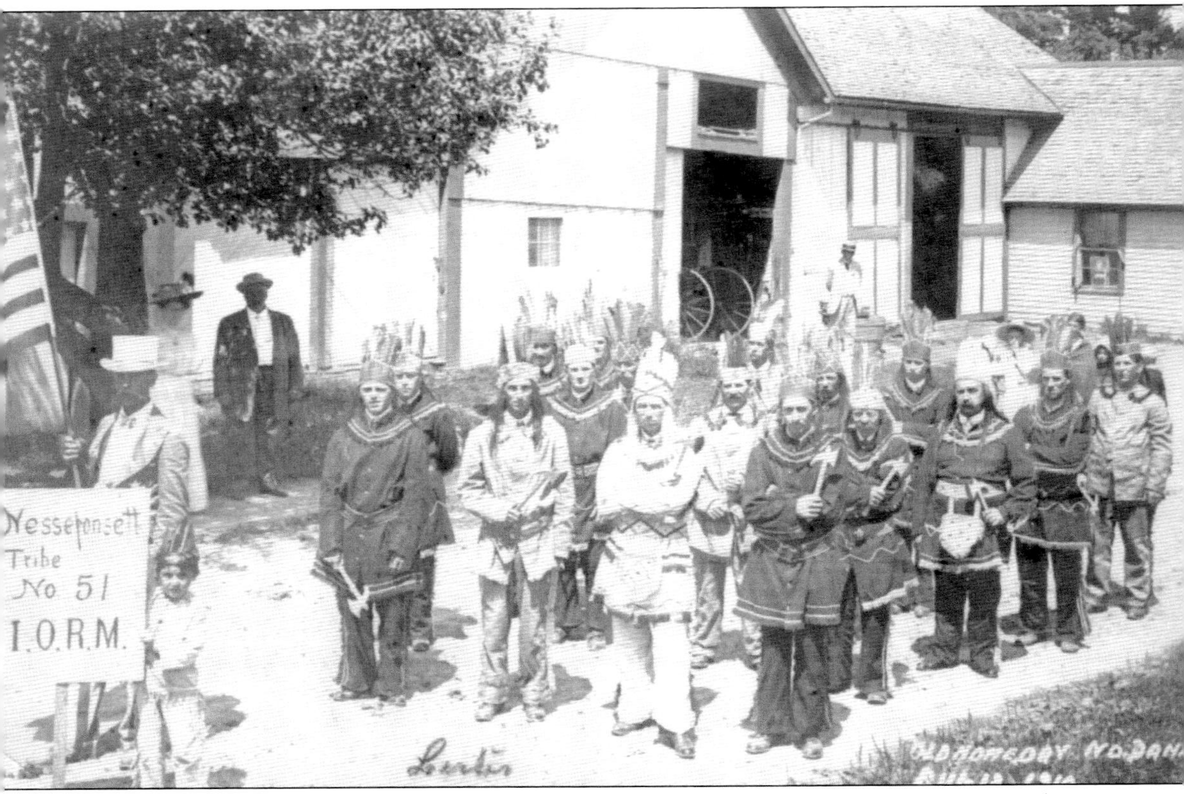

This picture shows the Improved Order of Red Men Nesseponsett Tribe No. 51 of North Dana. In full regalia, the men are participating in the North Dana Old Home Day parade on August 10, 1910. One of the purposes of the fraternal organization was providing help in times of need.

Three

To Be Remembered

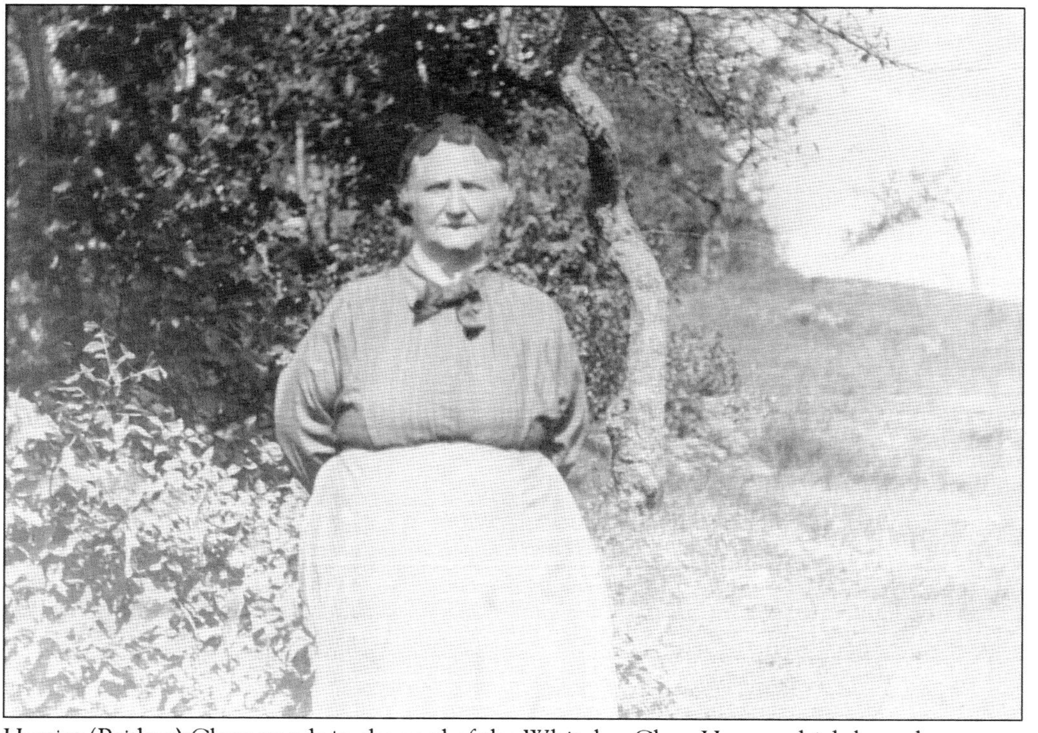

Harriet (Bridges) Clary stands in the yard of the Whitaker-Clary House, which bears her name. The Whitakers had the house built in 1816, and the Clarys purchased it in 1877 for a retirement home. Mr. Clary passed away in 1912, and Harriet continued to live here alone until she was nearly 98 years old. She was a no-nonsense lady with a very determined and active mind. She was born in South Deerfield into a family of 13 children. She loved birthday parties, and a celebration is held in her honor at the museum each year.

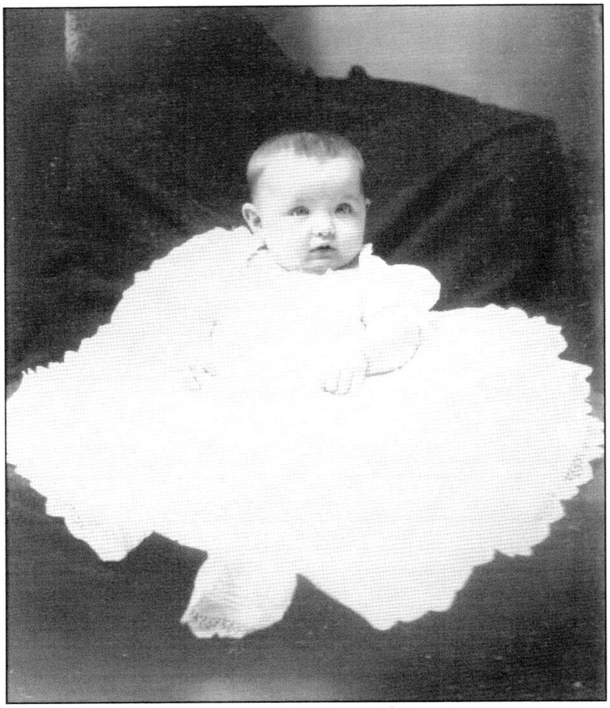

This beautiful baby in a gorgeous dress is unidentified.

Here is an exceptional photograph of some of the students at the Hillside School in Greenwich. They are waiting to attend a church service. The boys are not identified, but the lady is Charlotte Drinkwater, one of the founders of the school. The picture is dated 1915.

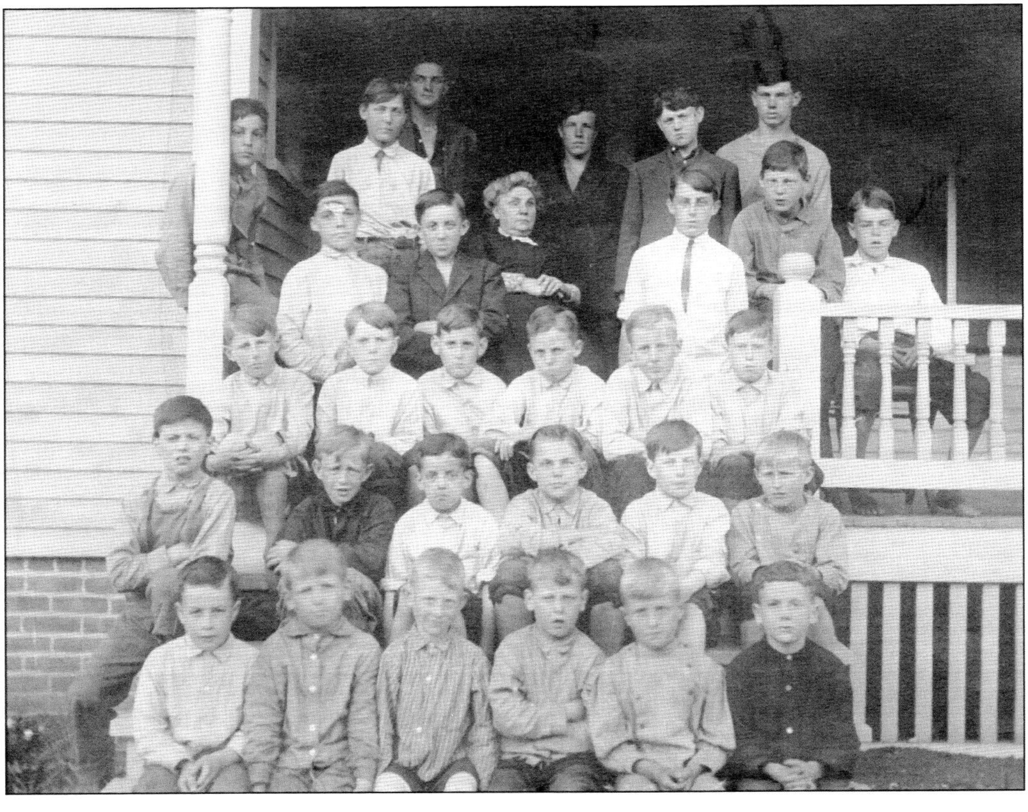

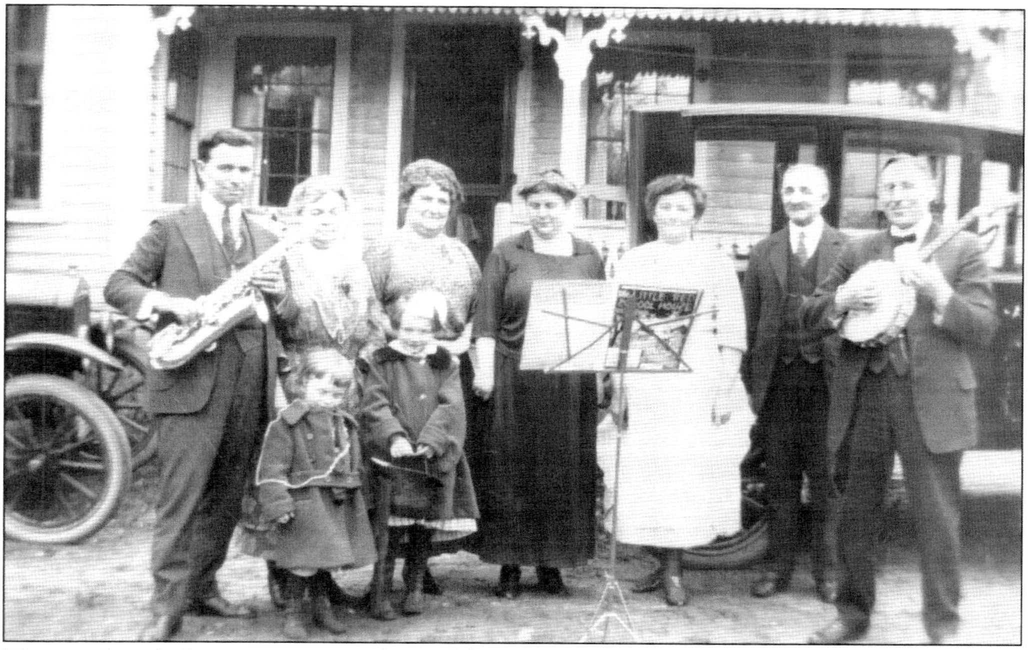

This unidentified group is prepared to celebrate some special occasion. The lady in the white dress is the soloist.

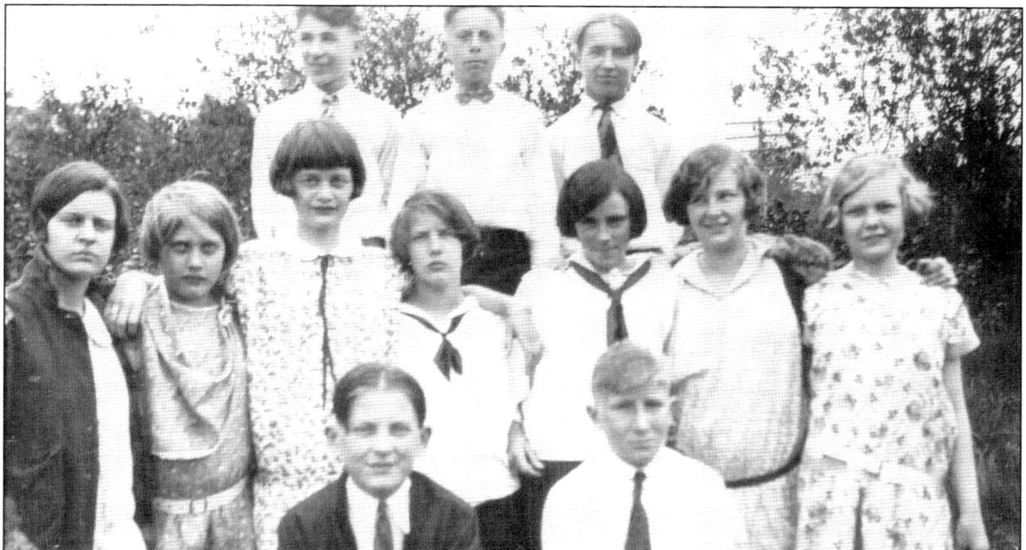

This is the sixth-grade class at the North Dana School in 1929. Pictured, from left to right, are (first row) Donald Roy and Andrew Loux; (second row) June Hanson, Bertha Olson, Florence Hunt, Virginia Jackobson, Margaret O'Brien, Gertrude Johnson, and Carol Anderson; (third row) Paul Pedrazzi, Bartie ?, and Maurice Ploof.

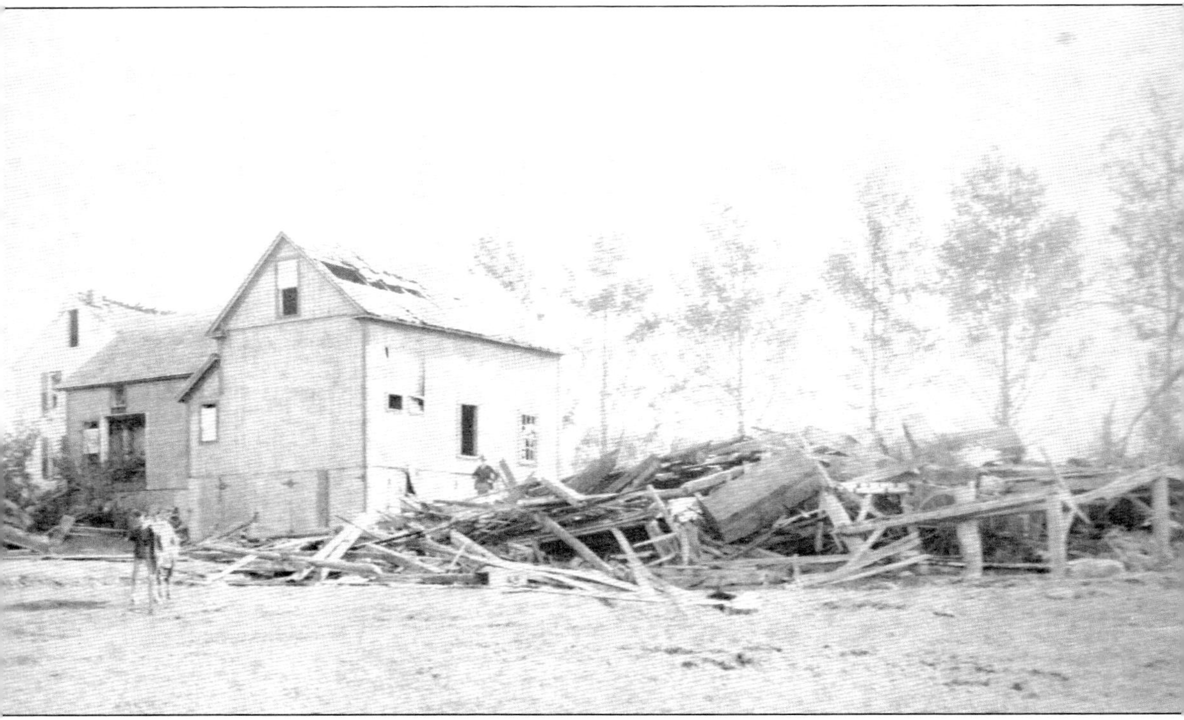

In 1894, a frightening tornado tore through the little town of New Salem, leaving a path of destruction in its wake. There was no way to warn people of what was coming. The one-room school was torn from its foundation and nearly turned around. With true Yankee ingenuity, it was righted and repaired. This picture shows the remains of a large barn reduced to a pile of kindling in a few seconds.

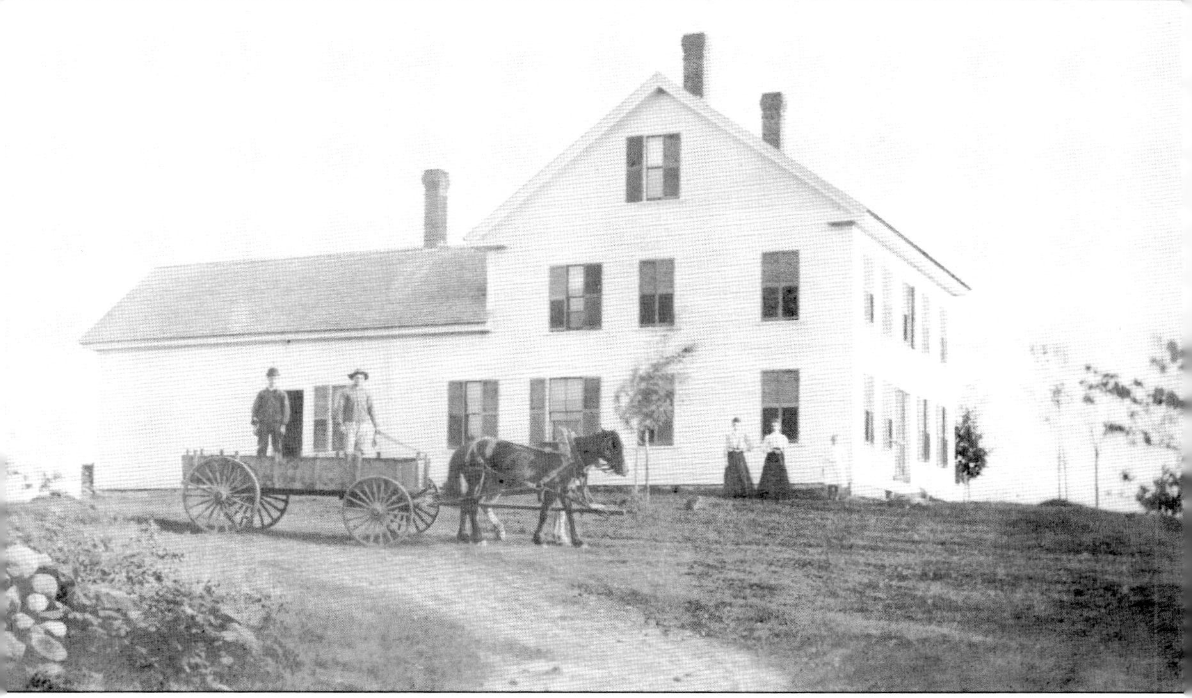

There were many enormous houses built to hold large families in Dana, Enfield, Greenwich, and Prescott. Since there was no insulation, storm windows, or central heat, most had several fireplaces and more than one chimney. It is no wonder that a home would use 40 cords of wood in a cold winter.

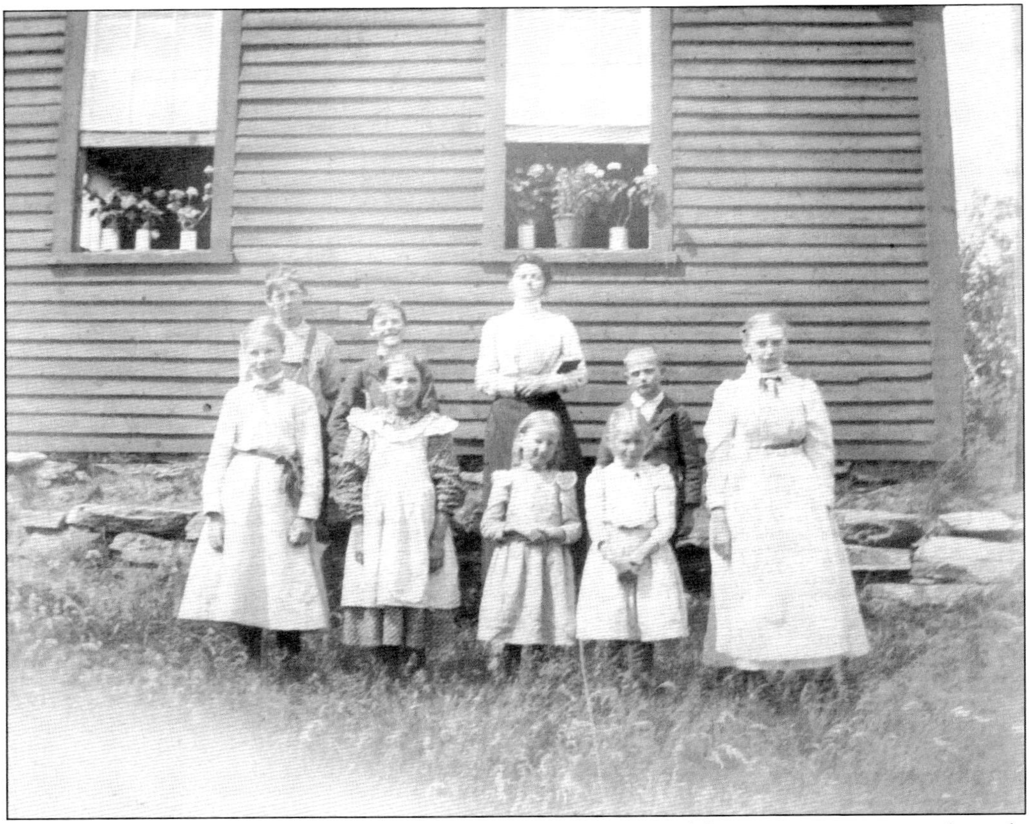

These children and their teacher pause for a picture outside one of the many one-room, multigrade schools in the valley.

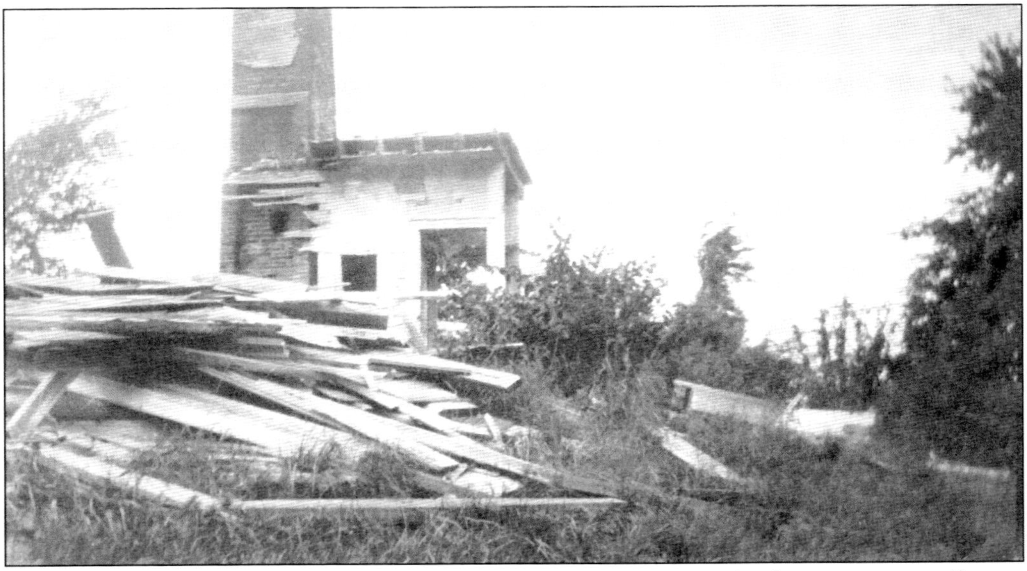

This picture of destruction was a common sight during preparation for the reservoir, as all signs of habitation were cleared. Salvageable boards were sold; what was left was burned.

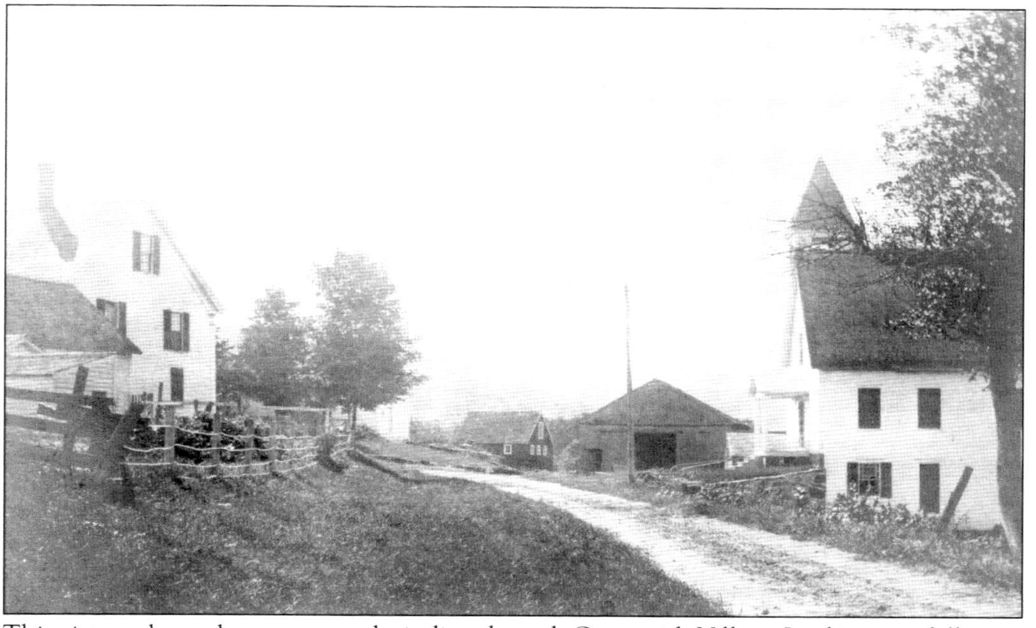

This picture shows the narrow road winding through Greenwich Village. Looking carefully, one can see the peak of the Independent Liberal Church on the right. This is the church that was built and later destroyed by Henry Smith.

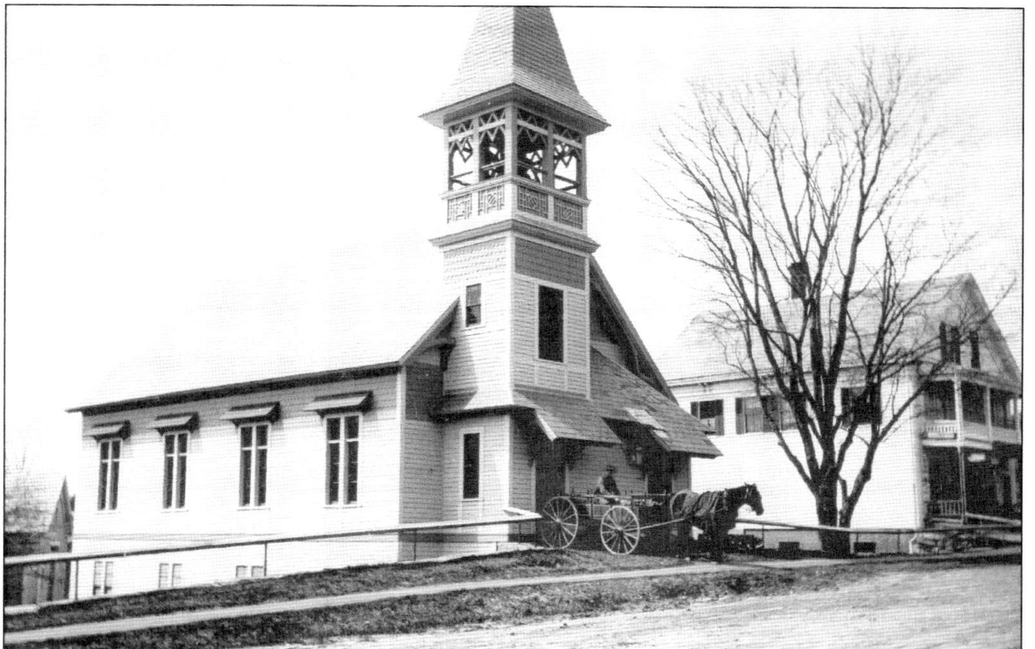

Here is another picture of the Independent Liberal Church built in 1885. Henry Smith was the leader of the church. After a few years, dissension broke out in the congregation, and Smith not only withdrew his support but also razed the church. In this picture, the horse and wagon are backed up to the front door, and the contents are being removed.

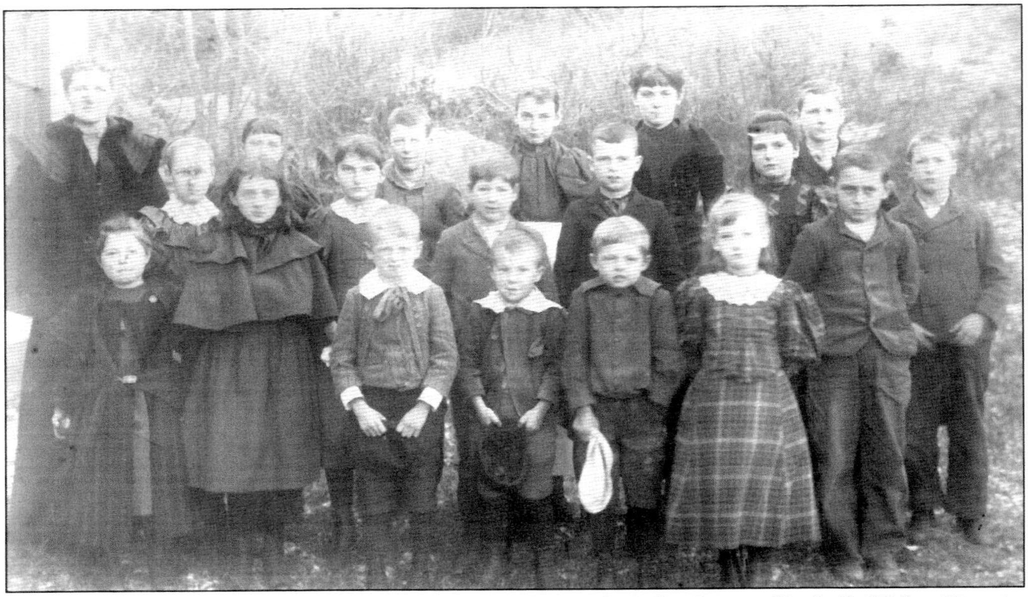

These children are Greenwich students. The teacher at far left is Jennie Haskell. Walter King in the second row at the far right. Unfortunately, not all are identified.

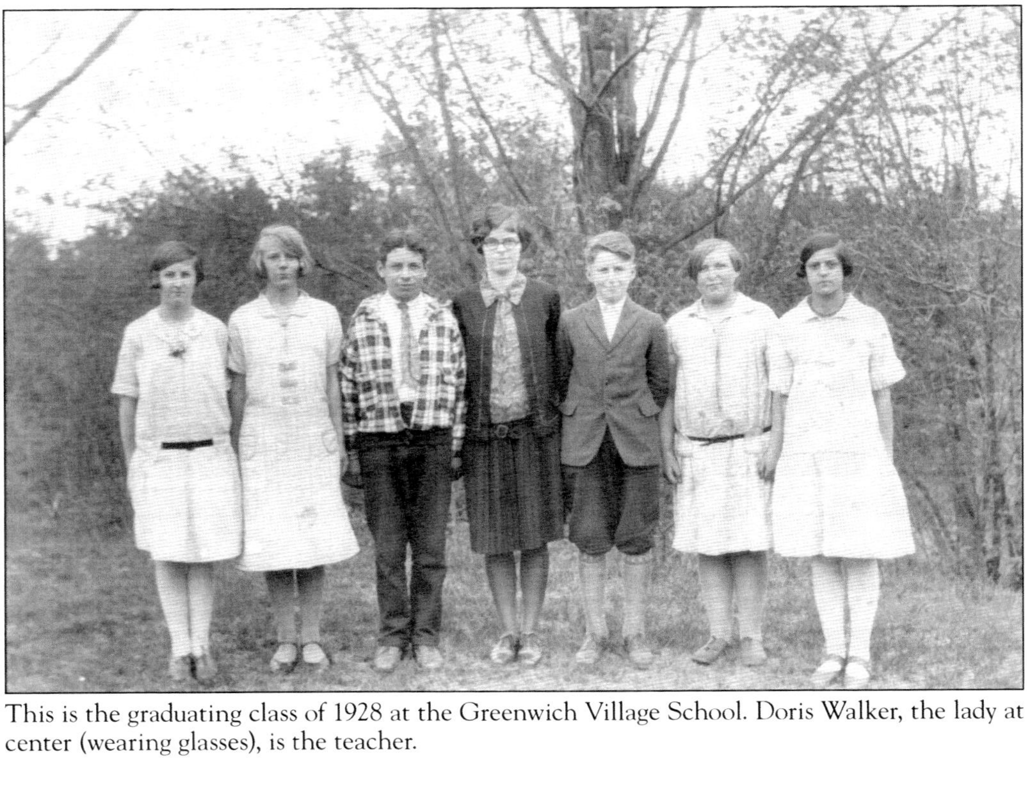

This is the graduating class of 1928 at the Greenwich Village School. Doris Walker, the lady at center (wearing glasses), is the teacher.

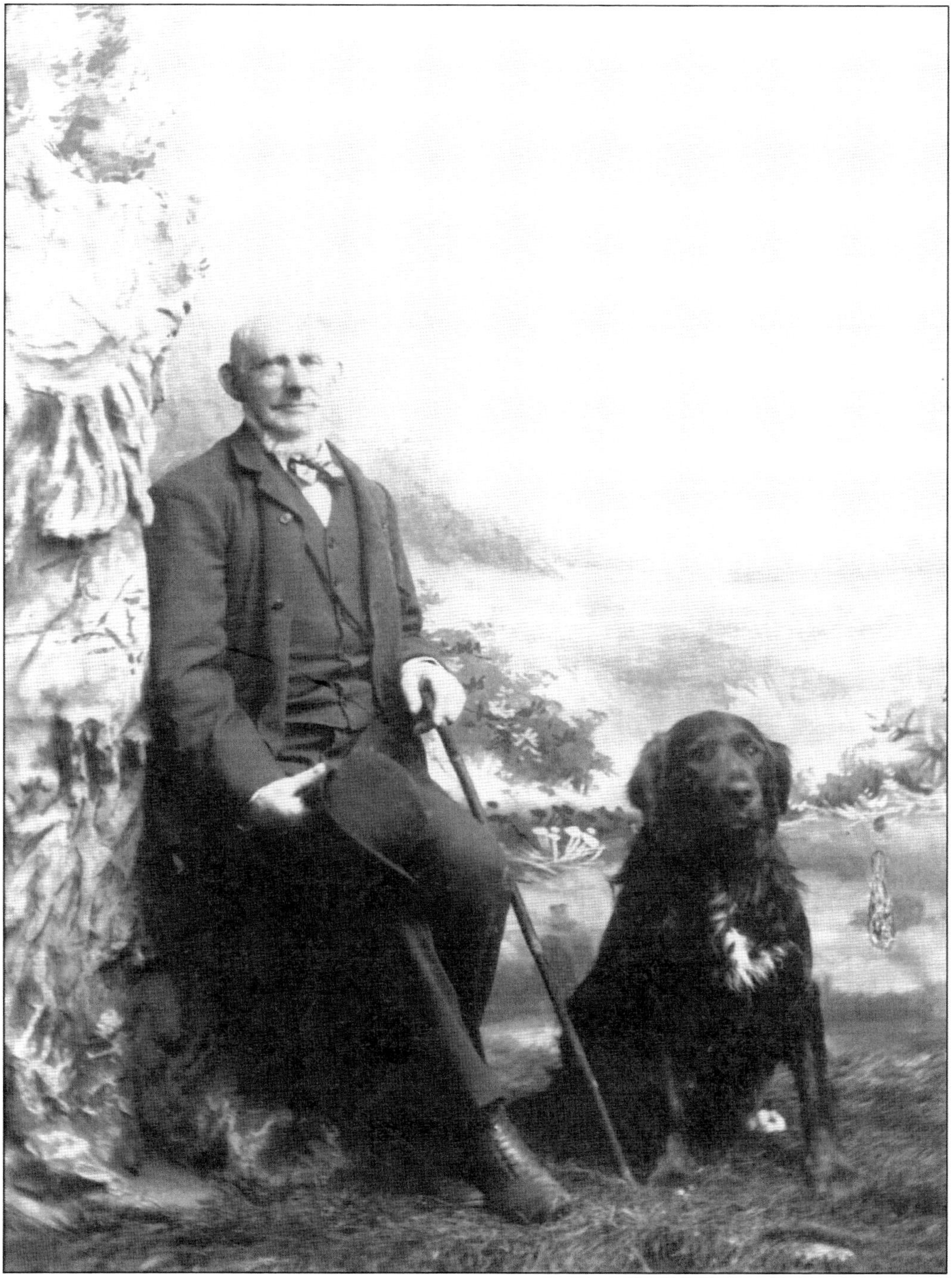

Adolphus Porter, a stonemason by trade, lived in North New Salem. He served and was injured in the Civil War. Following his discharge and recovery, he was hired by the town to build the Keystone Bridge connecting Millington to points north. He was paid $37.50. After building this bridge, Porter reenlisted.

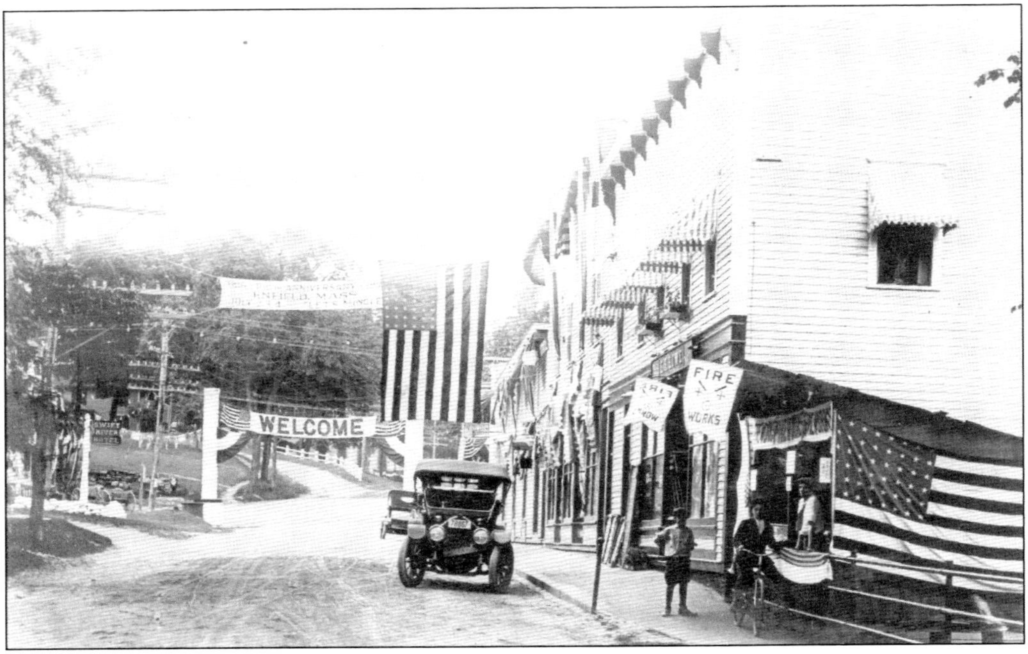

Above is a picture of the main street of Enfield before the destruction began. Shops and thriving businesses line the streets. Below is the same scene after the dismantling of the thriving town began.

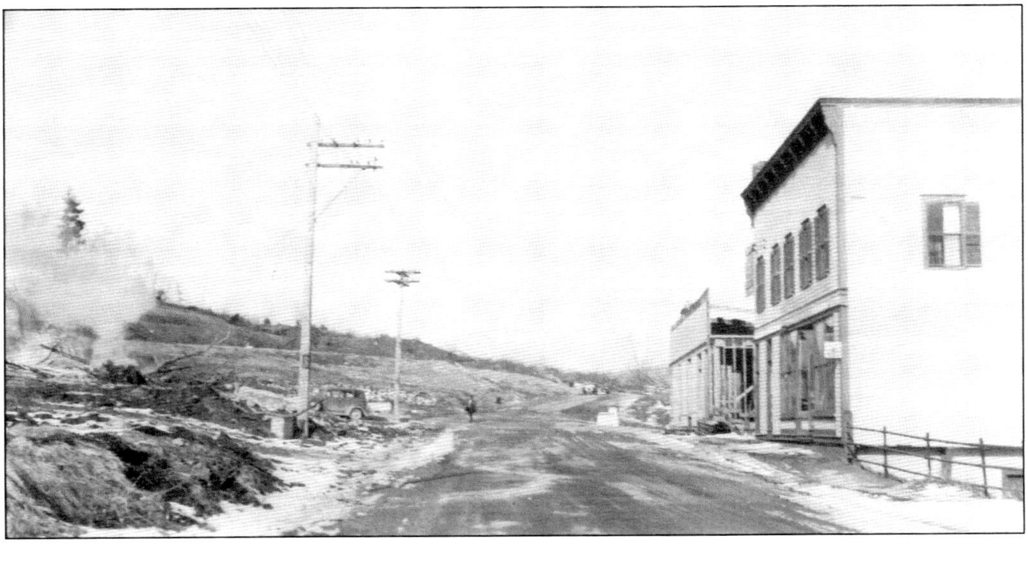

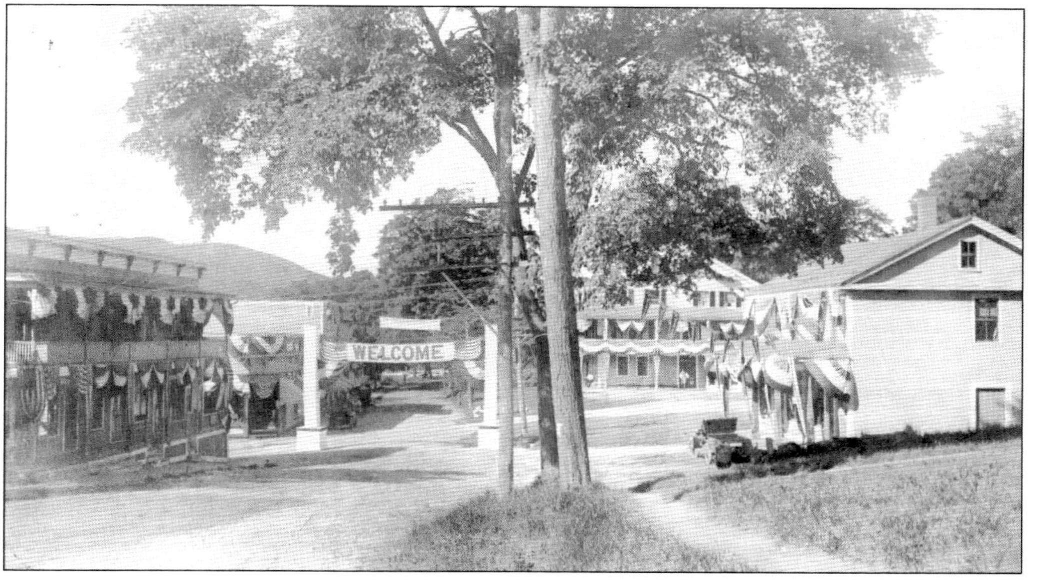

This is another view of Enfield's main street, taken in 1916. After the destruction, all that remained was desolation. In a few short years, only the peaks of the hills were visible above the rising waters.

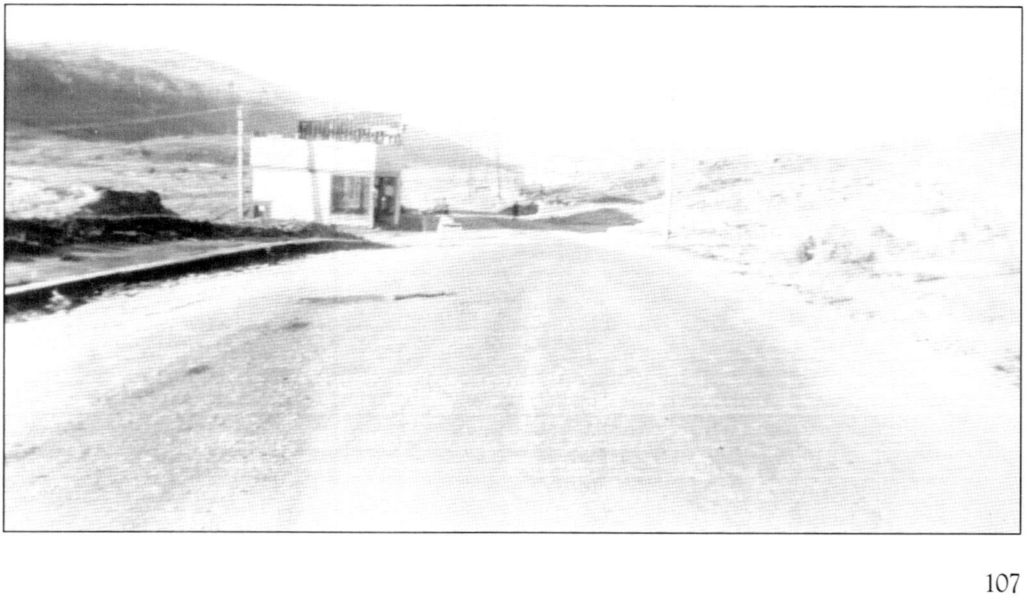

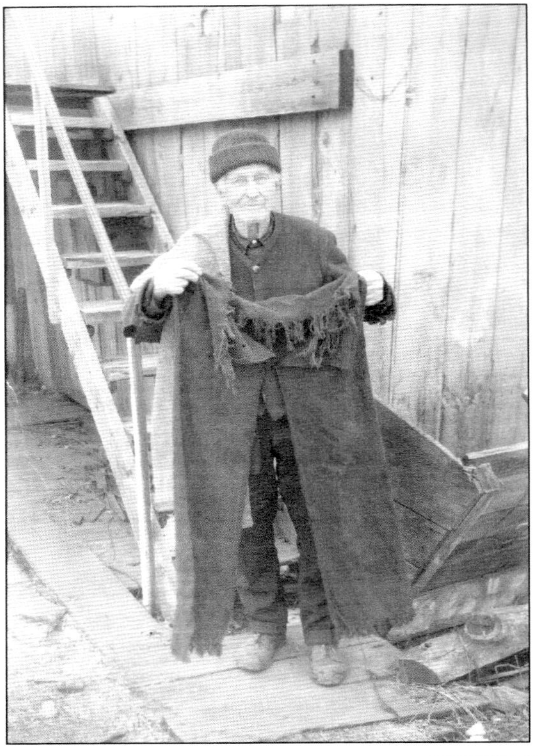

These pictures pose one of the mysteries of the Quabbin Valley. The man is identified as Albert Smith of Smith's Village in Enfield. Why is he showing this very large pair of trousers? Has he been on a diet? Are the ones at the far right his present size? Whatever the reason, someone recorded it with a photograph.

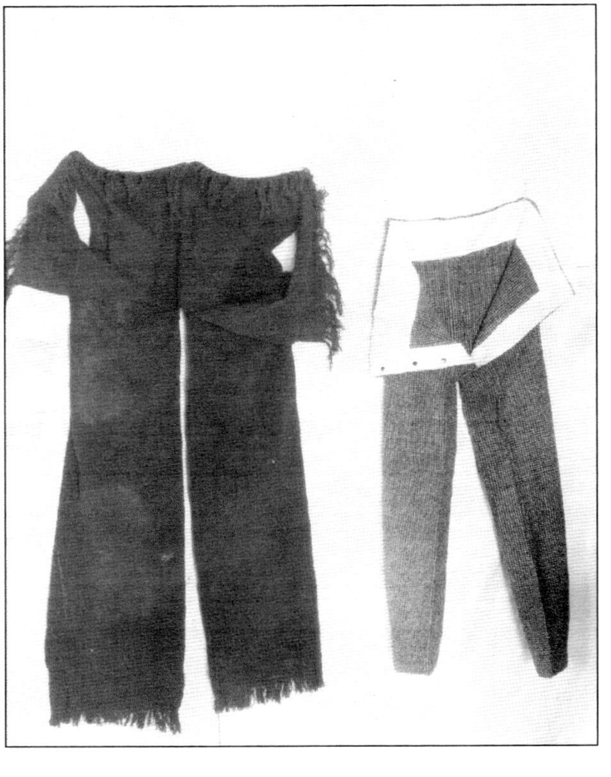

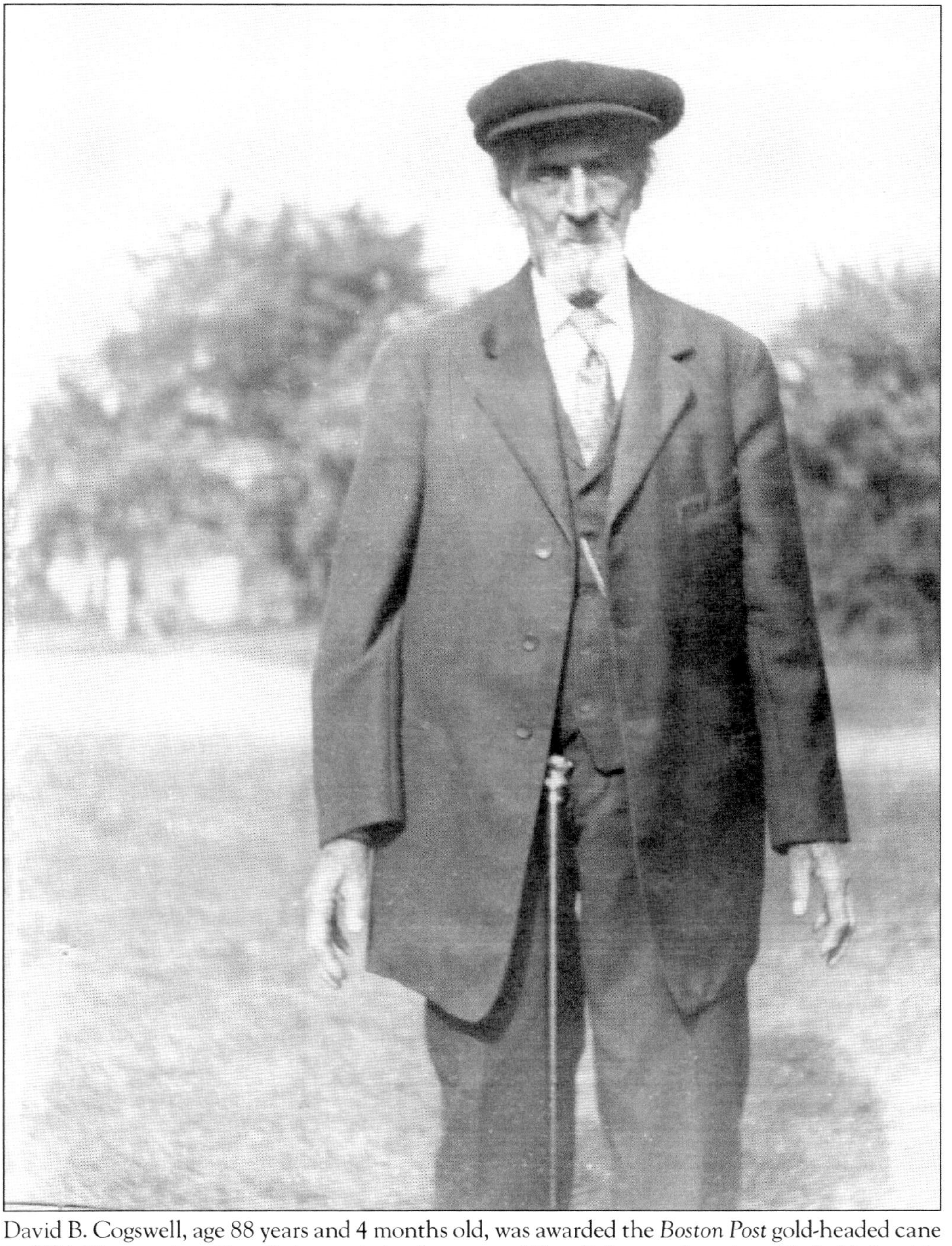

David B. Cogswell, age 88 years and 4 months old, was awarded the *Boston Post* gold-headed cane in 1914. He was the oldest living male in the town of New Salem at that time. He held the title for six years until his death on April 12, 1920.

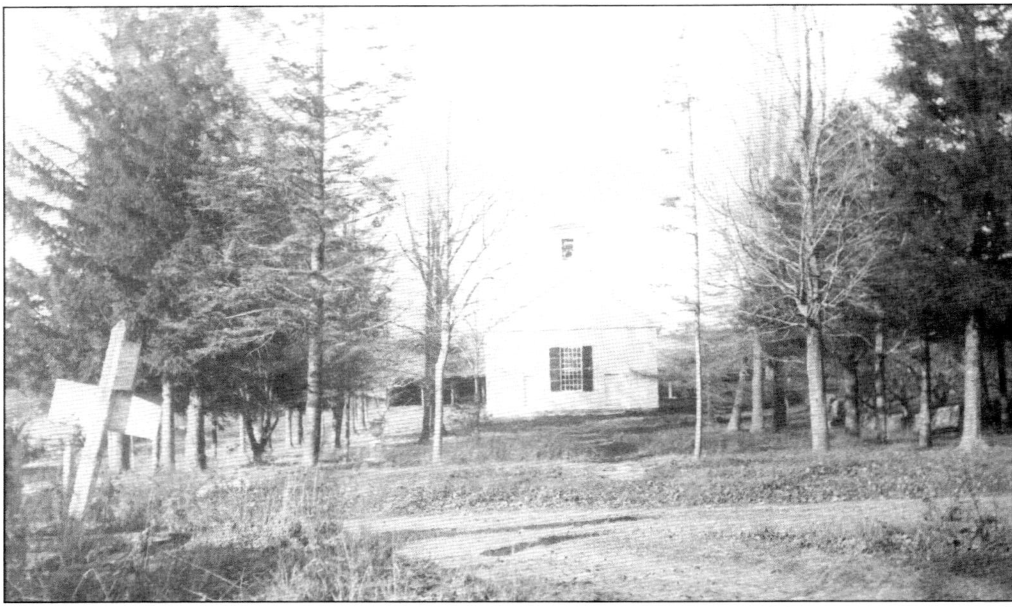

This picture shows the Congregational Church as it looked in its original home on Prescott Hill. It later became the Skinner Museum in South Hadley.

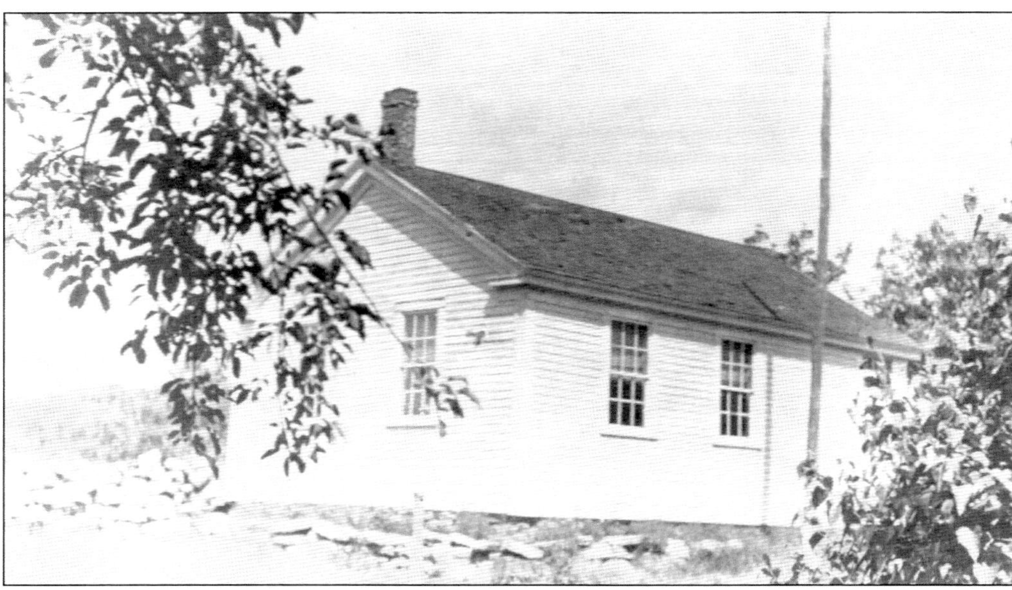

This is the No. 2 Schoolhouse in Prescott. In 1938, it was dismantled and moved to Conway, where it may have become part of a summer home on the estate of Ada MacLeish.

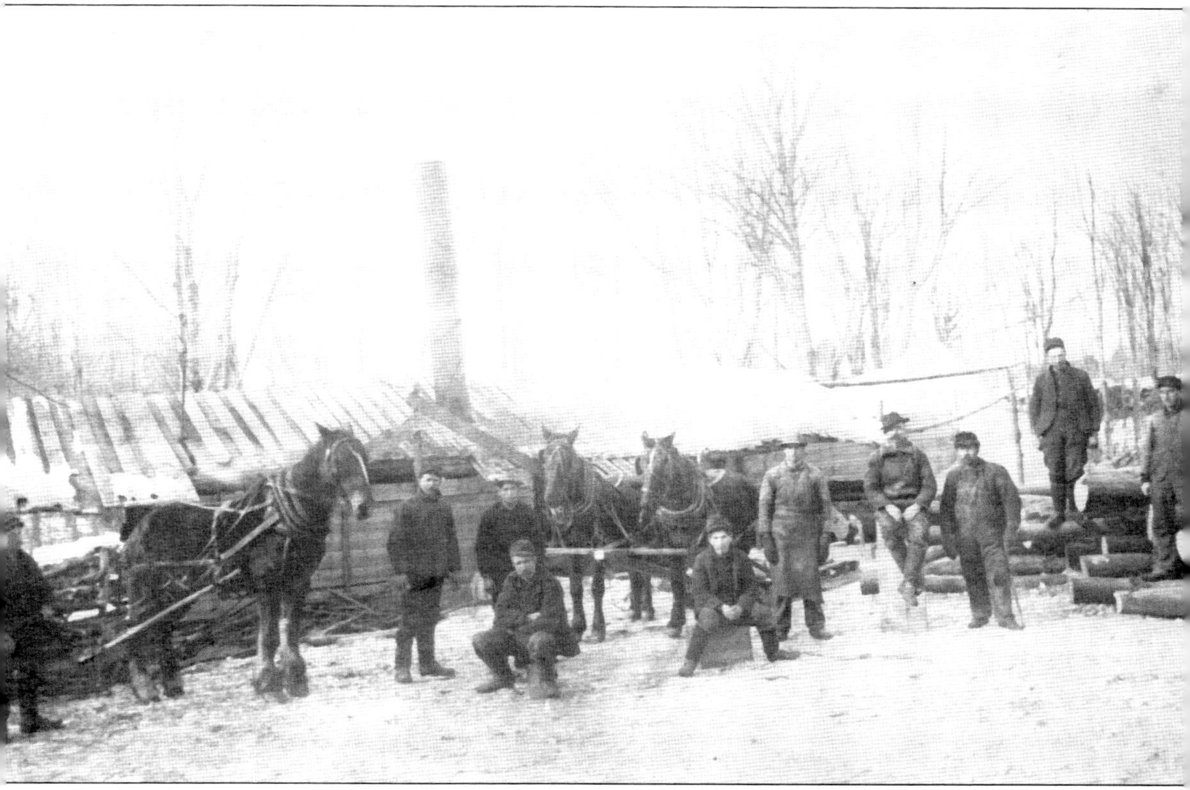

The abundance of trees in the Quabbin Valley provided plenty of work for sawmill laborers. Mills ran year-round; even snow did not stop the production of wood products for building.

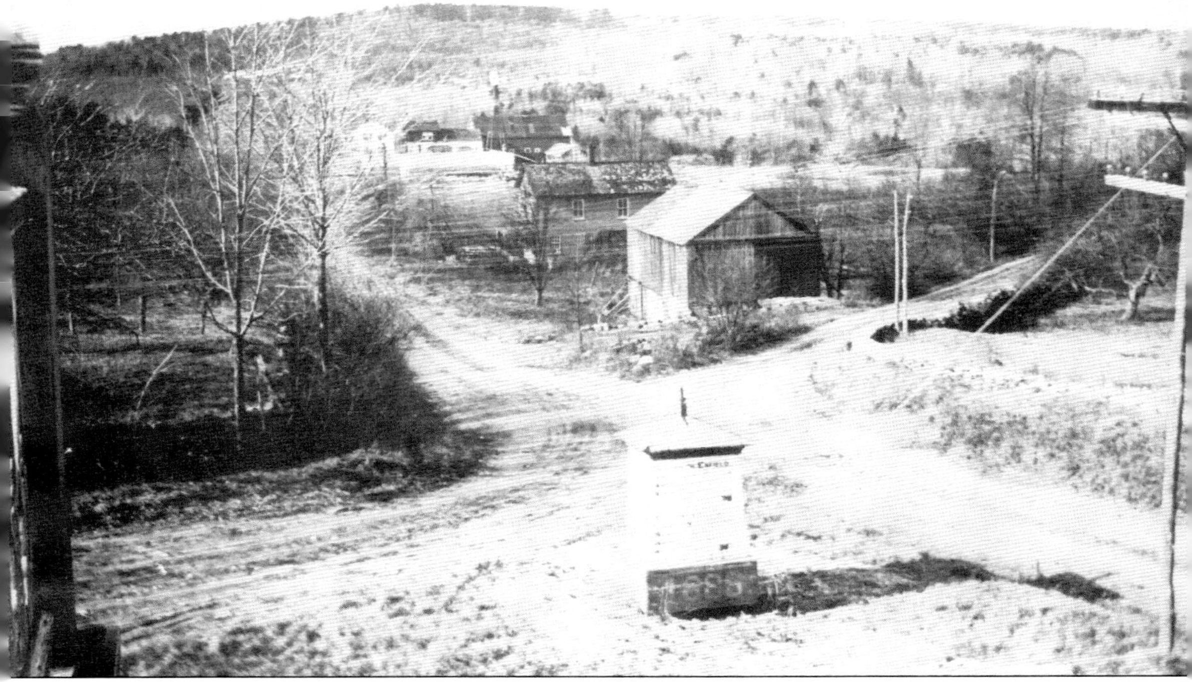

Before street signs, four-sided signposts were used at crossroads. Names of nearby towns were painted on each side, with arrows pointing in the correct direction for each. A lantern on the top would be lighted at dusk. This artifact can be seen at the Swift River Valley Historical Society.

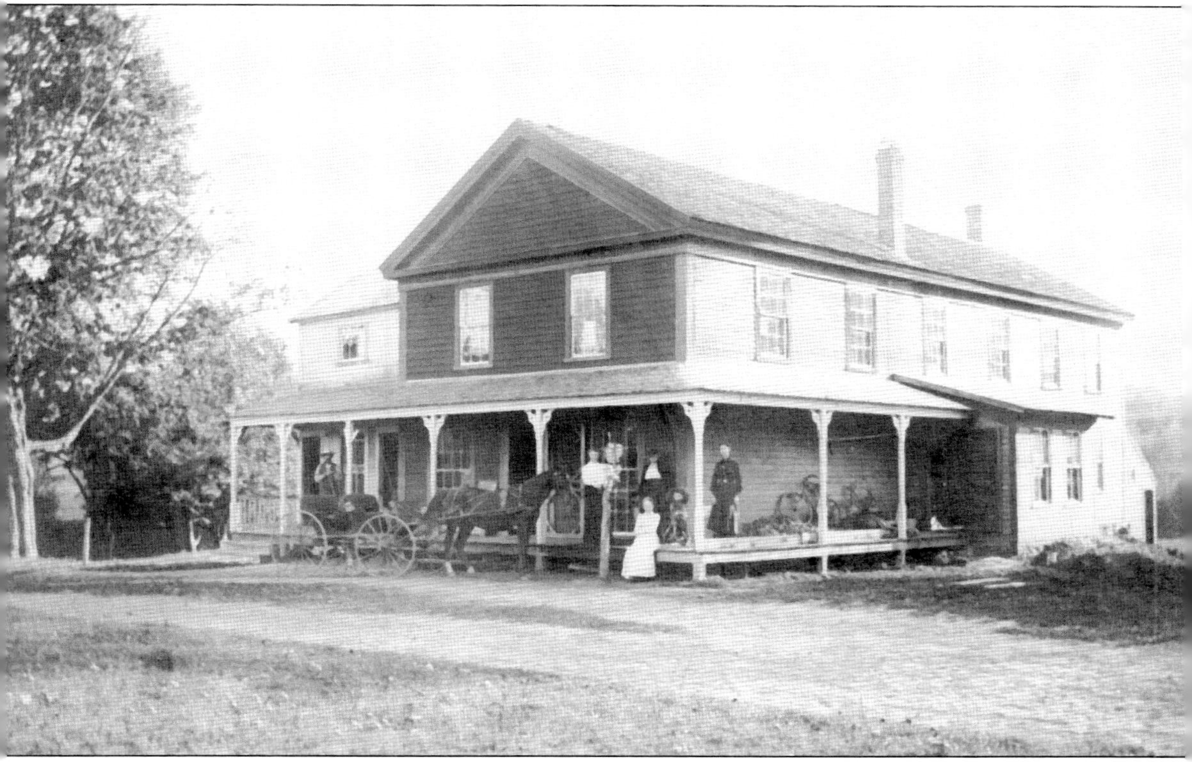

This building was the hub of the community in the Atkinson Hollow section of Prescott. It was the post office and general store where people could purchase everything from rubber boots and kerosene to patent medicines and lace. Upstairs was the Grange Hall, where town meetings and elections took place. It was also the site of many suppers, fairs, parties, and Saturday-night dances that lasted well into the night. The store was where people gathered to get the local gossip and maybe tarry a while for a game of chess or checkers. A pool table was also a big attraction.

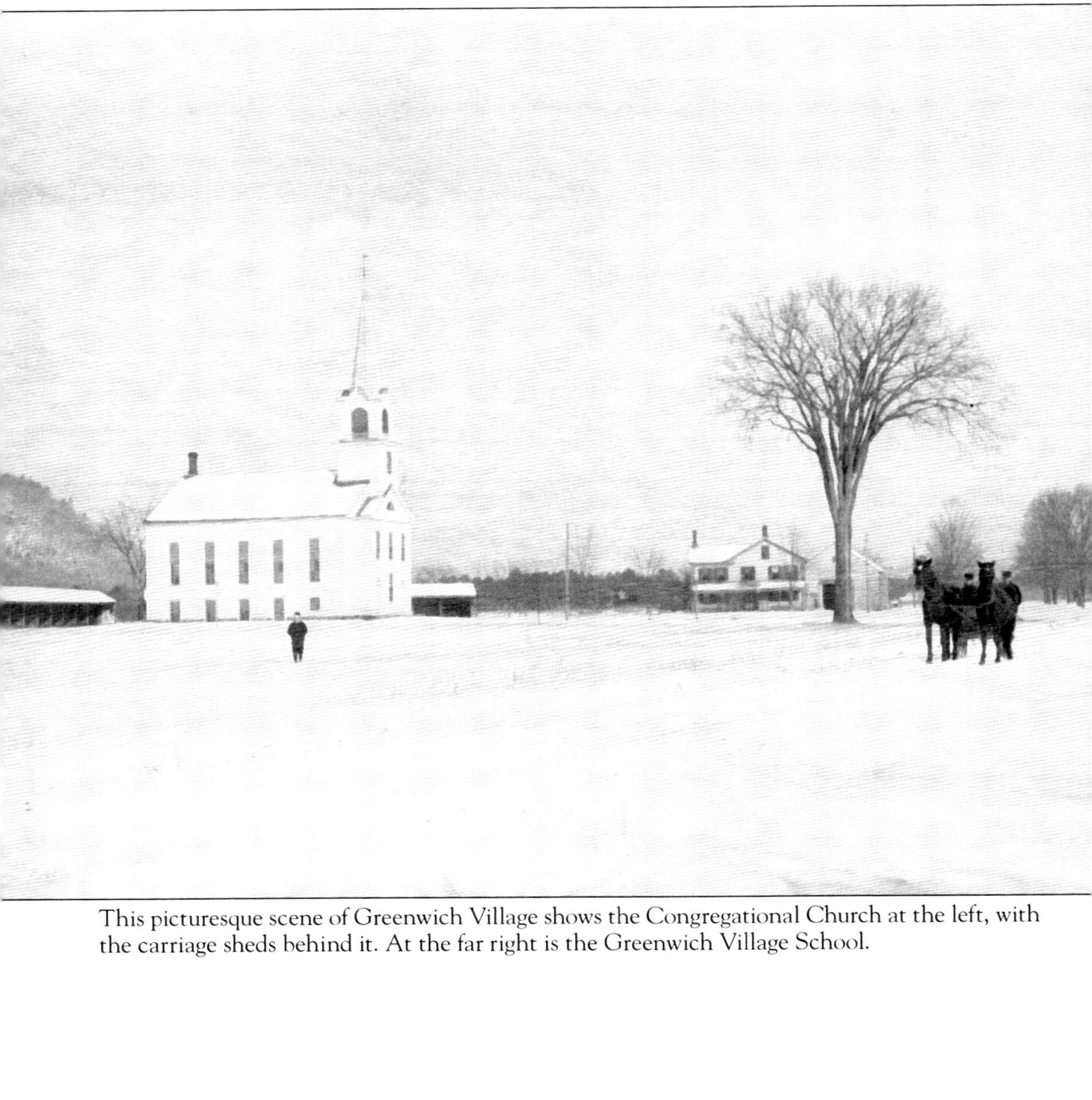

This picturesque scene of Greenwich Village shows the Congregational Church at the left, with the carriage sheds behind it. At the far right is the Greenwich Village School.

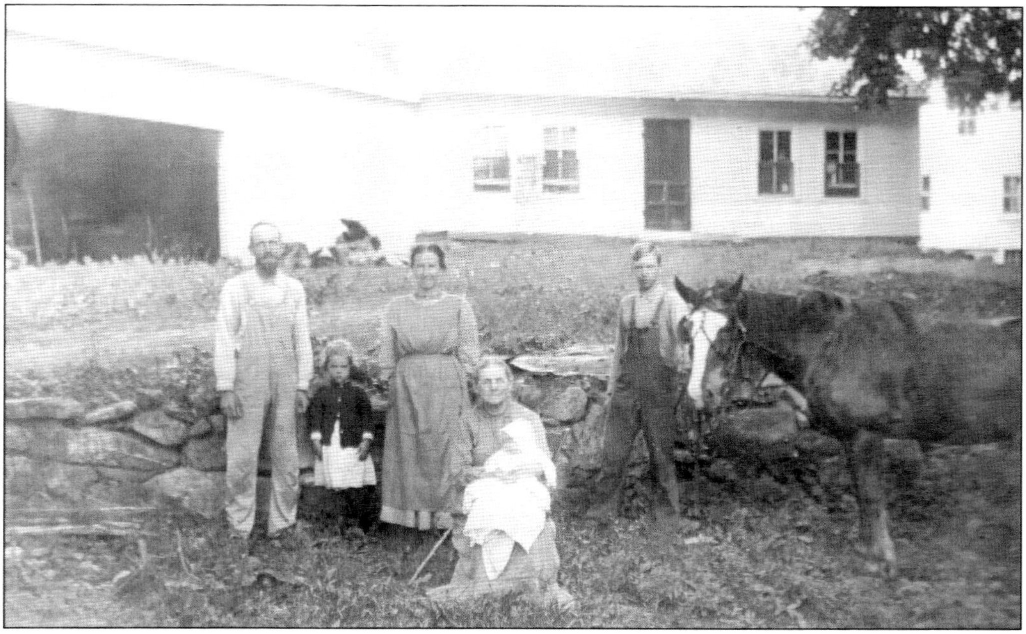

Here, a family poses for a casual picture to remember and enjoy in the years to come. The baby in this picture (being held by her grandmother) is Stella Eaton. As an adult, she was Stella Haney, the much-loved longtime librarian of the New Salem Library.

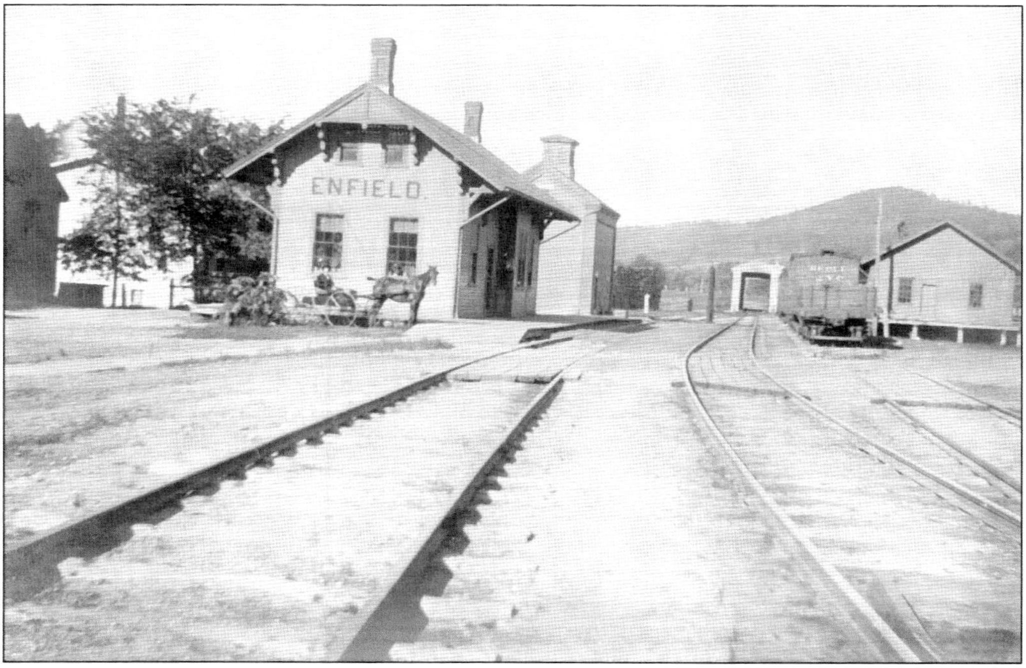

Here is the Enfield Railroad Station (all stations were built nearly identically). Trains were an important part of the daily life in the valley. Produce was sent to market, ice was shipped to the cities, and children who went on to high school rode the train to neighboring towns as there were no high schools in the valley.

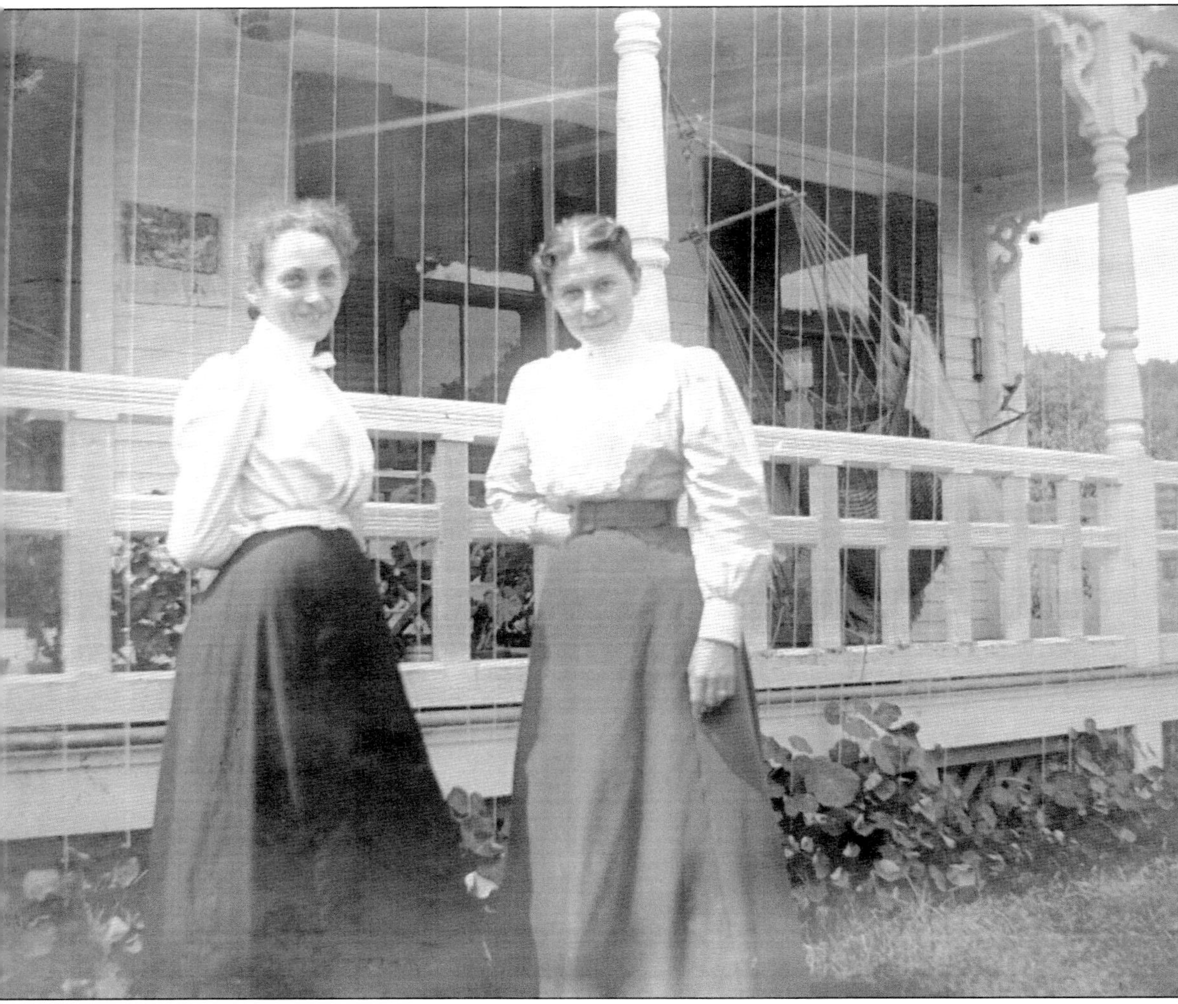

These two ladies are standing in front of the porch. Note the hammock in the background and the strings attached to the house and anchored in the ground. This was commonly done to train morning glories or other vining plants to help shade the porch on the hot, sunny days.

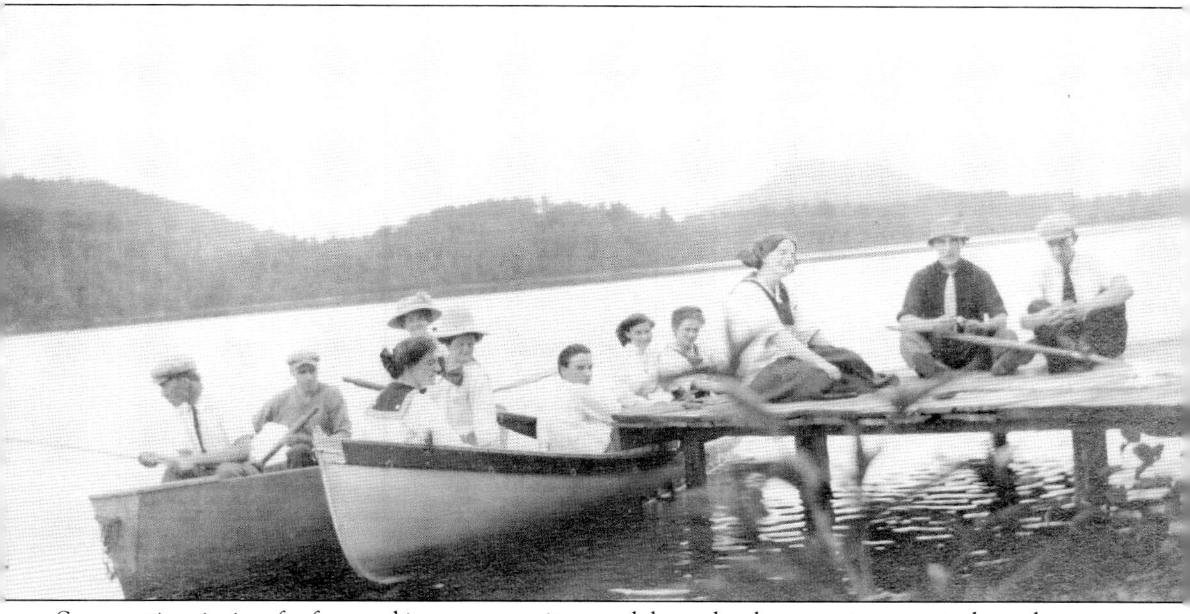

Summertime is time for fun, and in a community near lakes, what better enjoyment is there than boating with a group of friends?

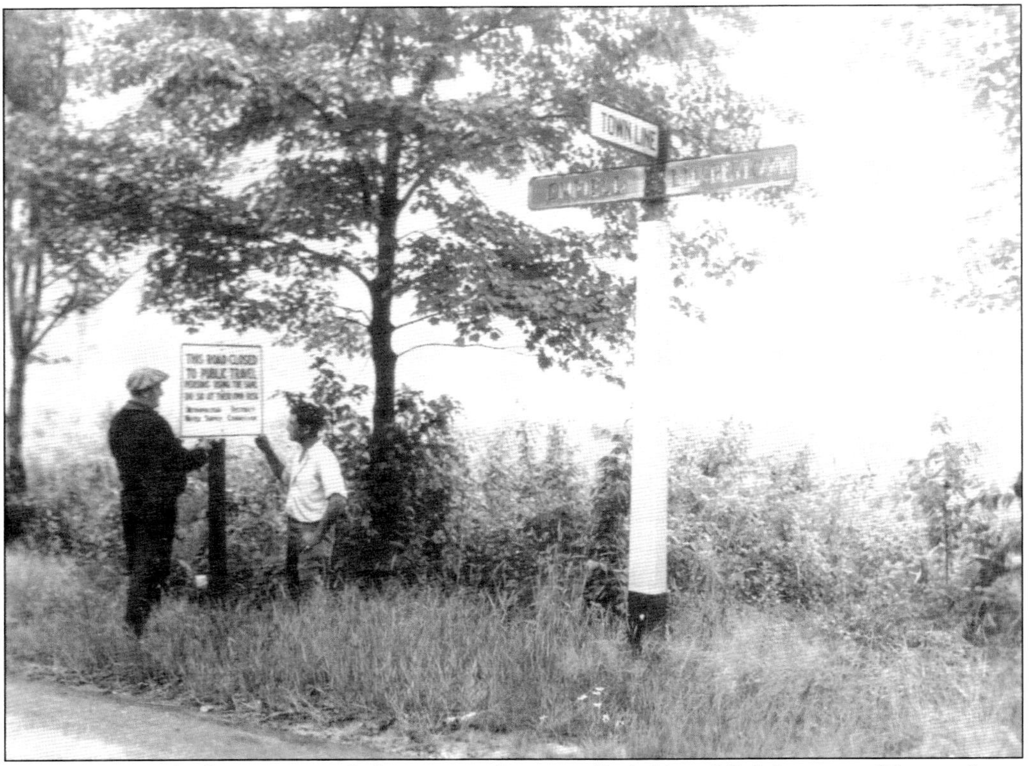

These men are looking at a road-closing sign between Enfield and Belchertown. The road was no longer needed: Enfield is not there any more.

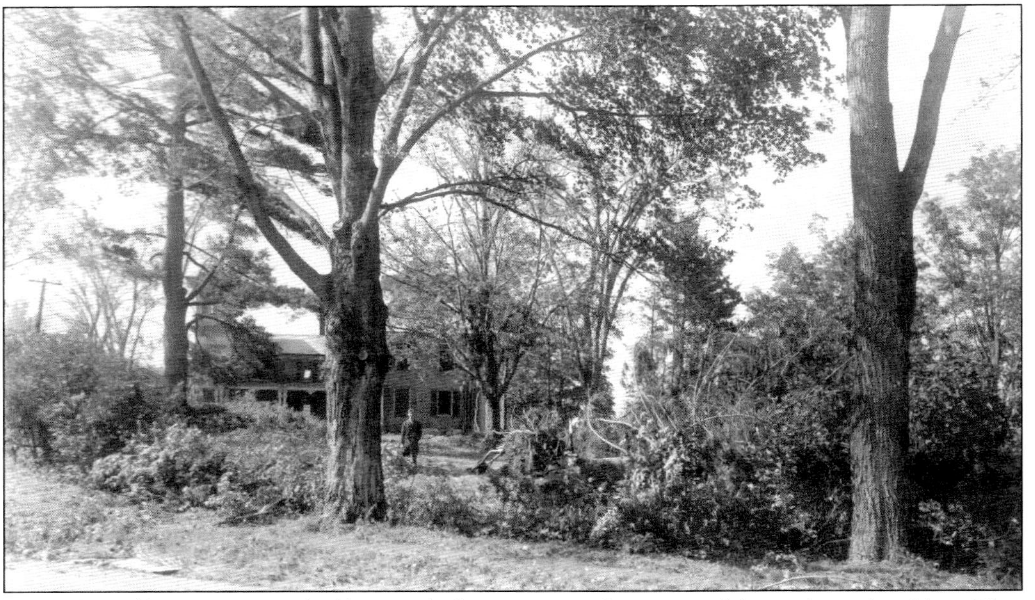

After the valley was emptied of human habitation in 1938, nature delivered another blow. This picture shows the damage caused by a hurricane in September 1938.

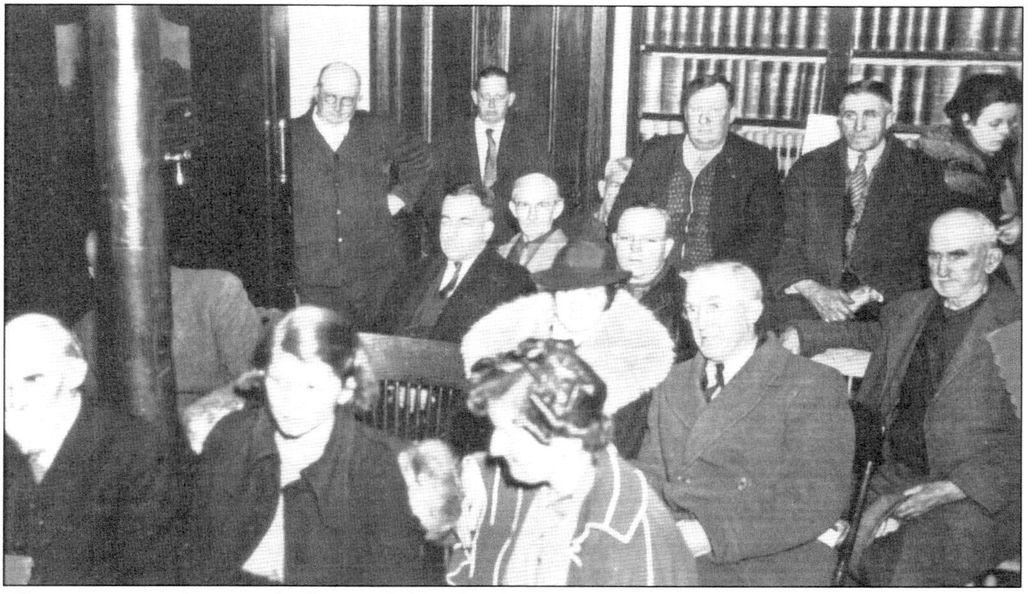

This scene is in the town hall in Enfield. The discussion is very serious. Note the expressions on the faces of the audience.

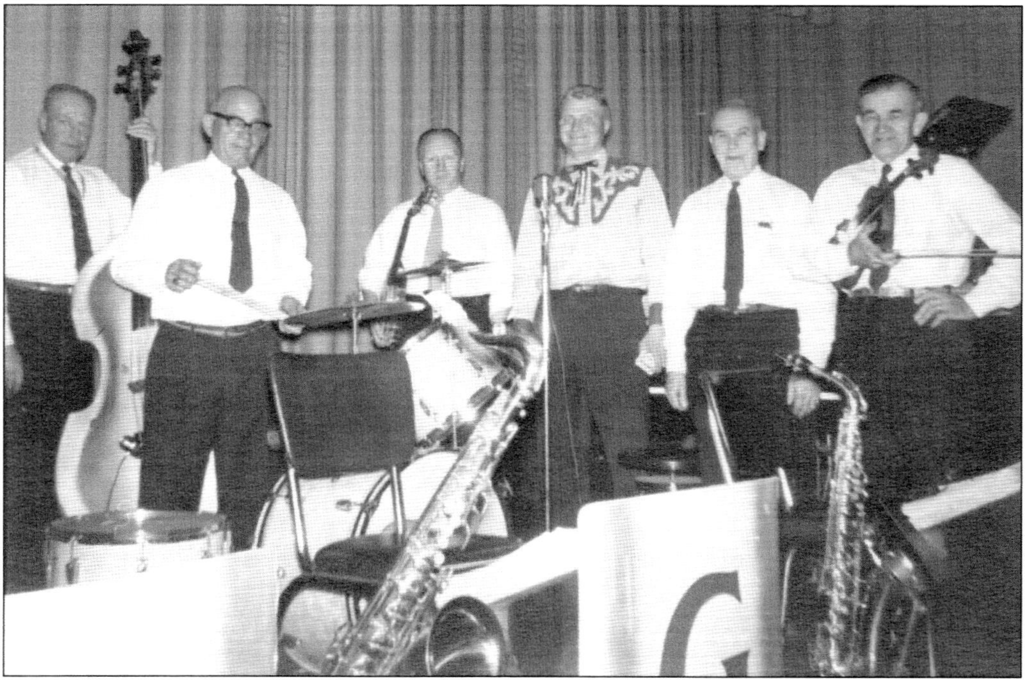

Goodnow's Orchestra was well known in the valley in the 1930s and played for many dances and other occasions. Pictured, from left to right, are Spencer Tandy, Charlie Fuller, Andy Anderson, George Hodgson, Errol Crowl, and leader Clarence Goodnow. This picture will stir the memories of many local readers.

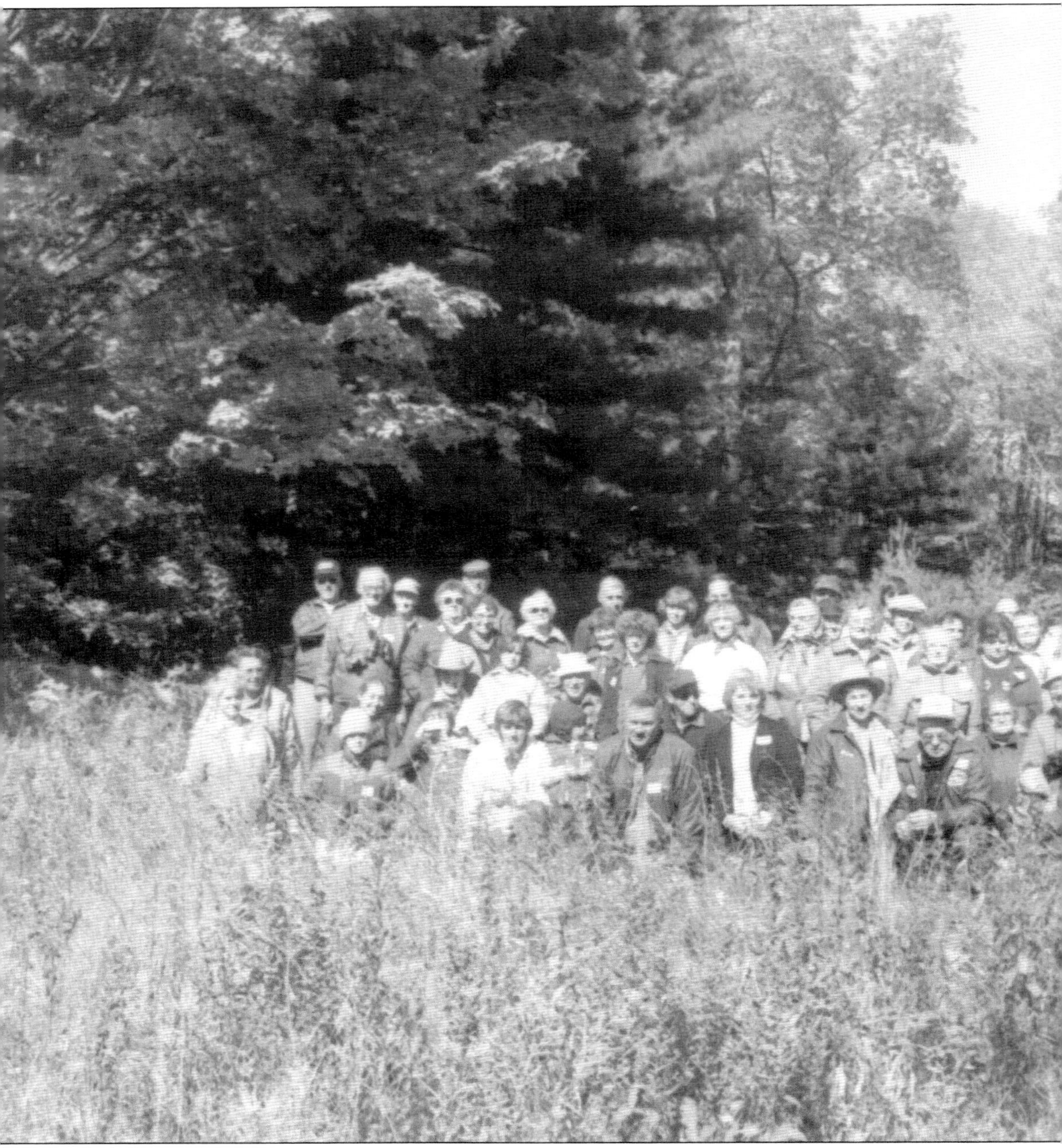

This picture shows friends, relatives, and descendents on a bus pilgrimage into the restricted area of Prescott in 1989. Pilgrimages are arranged each year by the Swift River Valley Historical

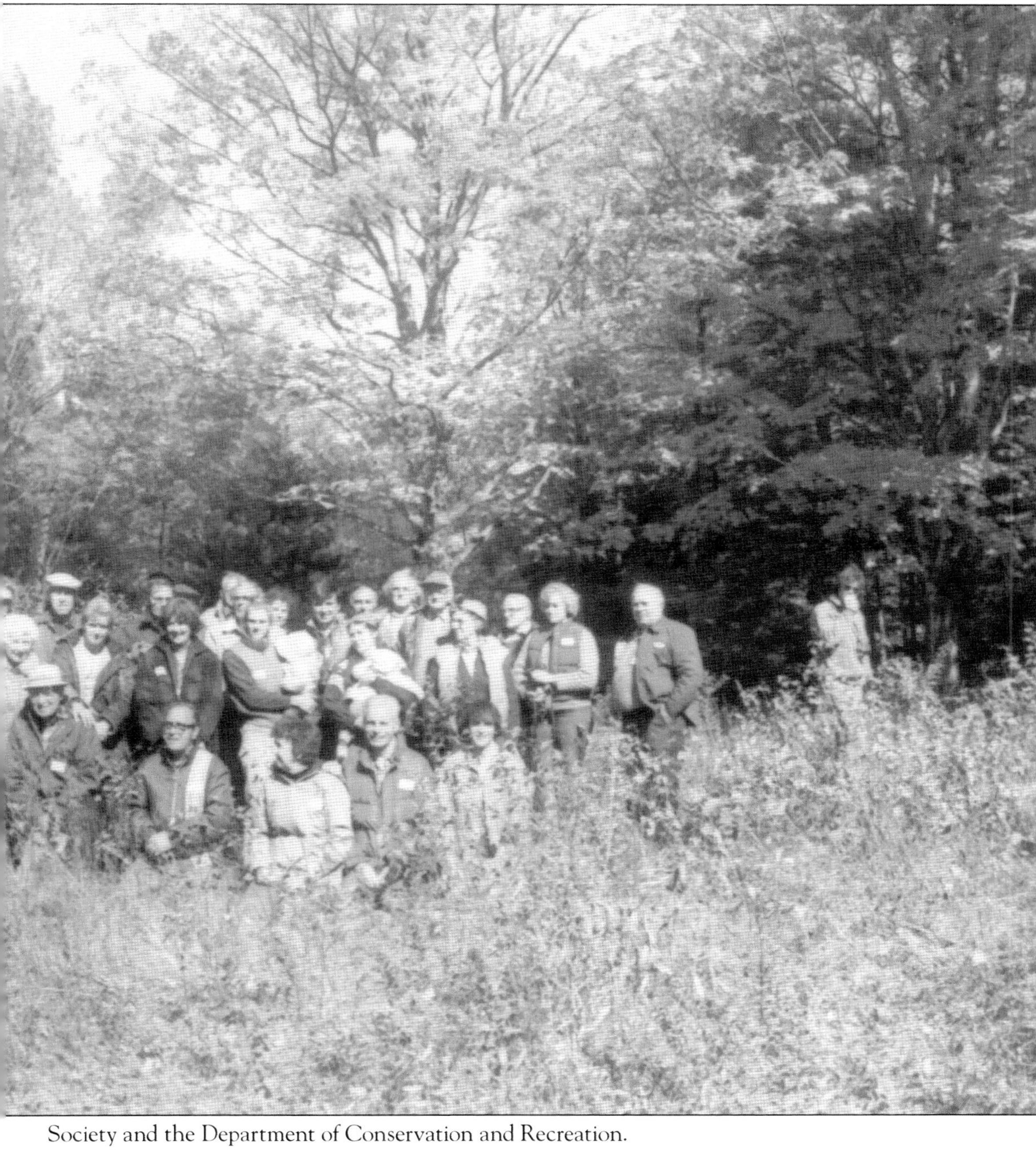

Society and the Department of Conservation and Recreation.

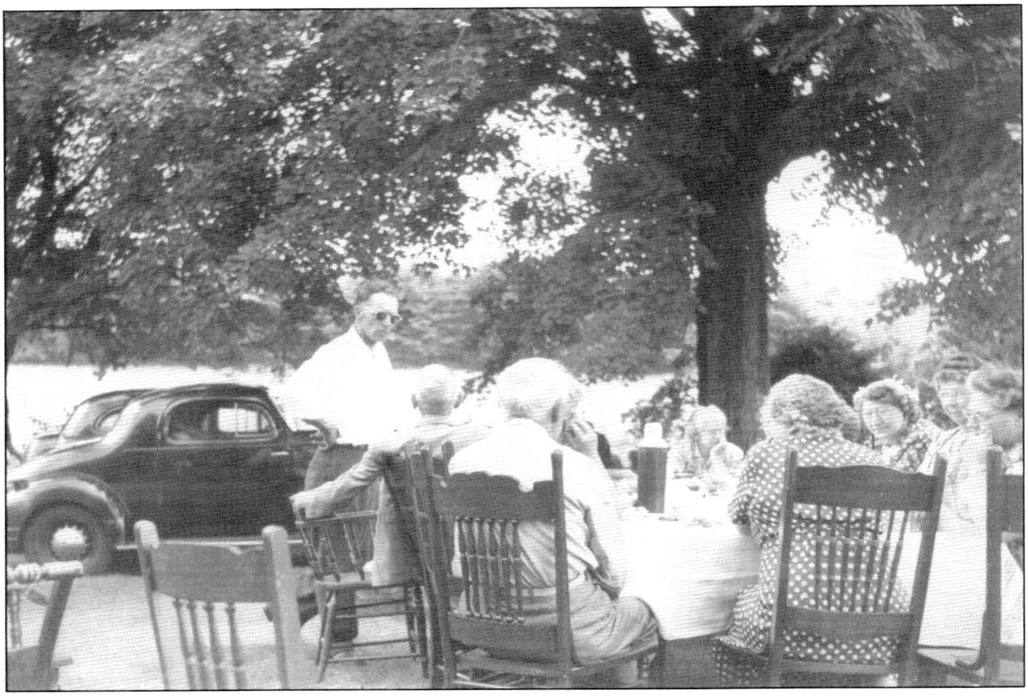

Before the Prescott Historical Society had its own building, members gathered in a variety of places. In 1946, they enjoyed a reunion at the Sago Sago Farm in New Salem.

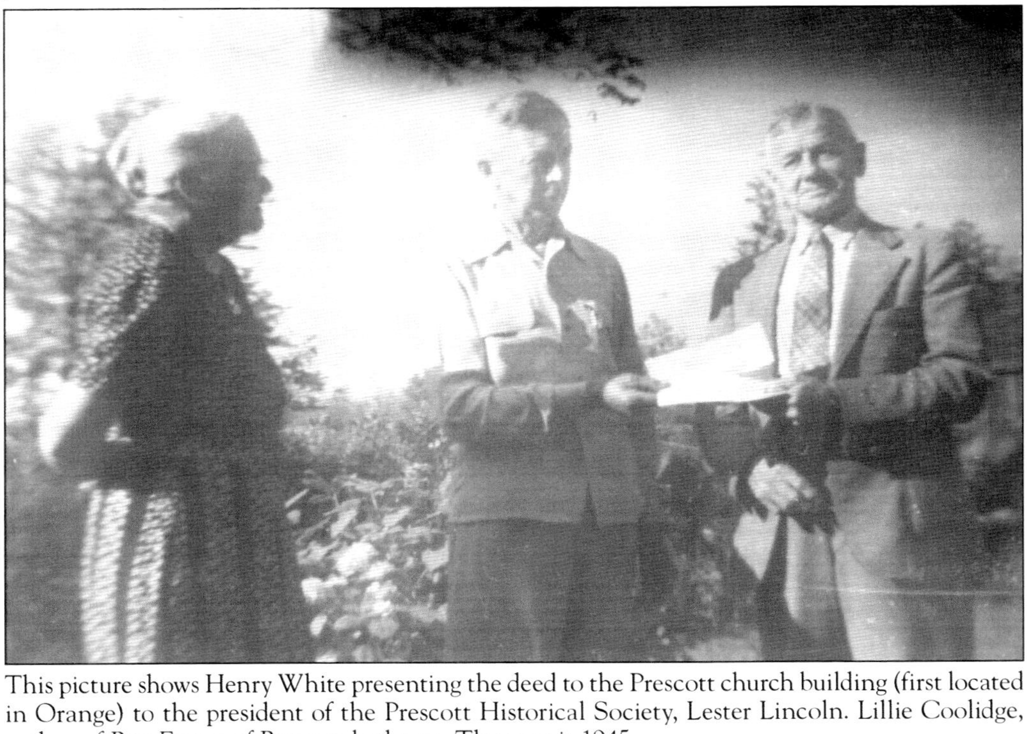

This picture shows Henry White presenting the deed to the Prescott church building (first located in Orange) to the president of the Prescott Historical Society, Lester Lincoln. Lillie Coolidge, author of *Past Events of Prescott*, looks on. The year is 1945.

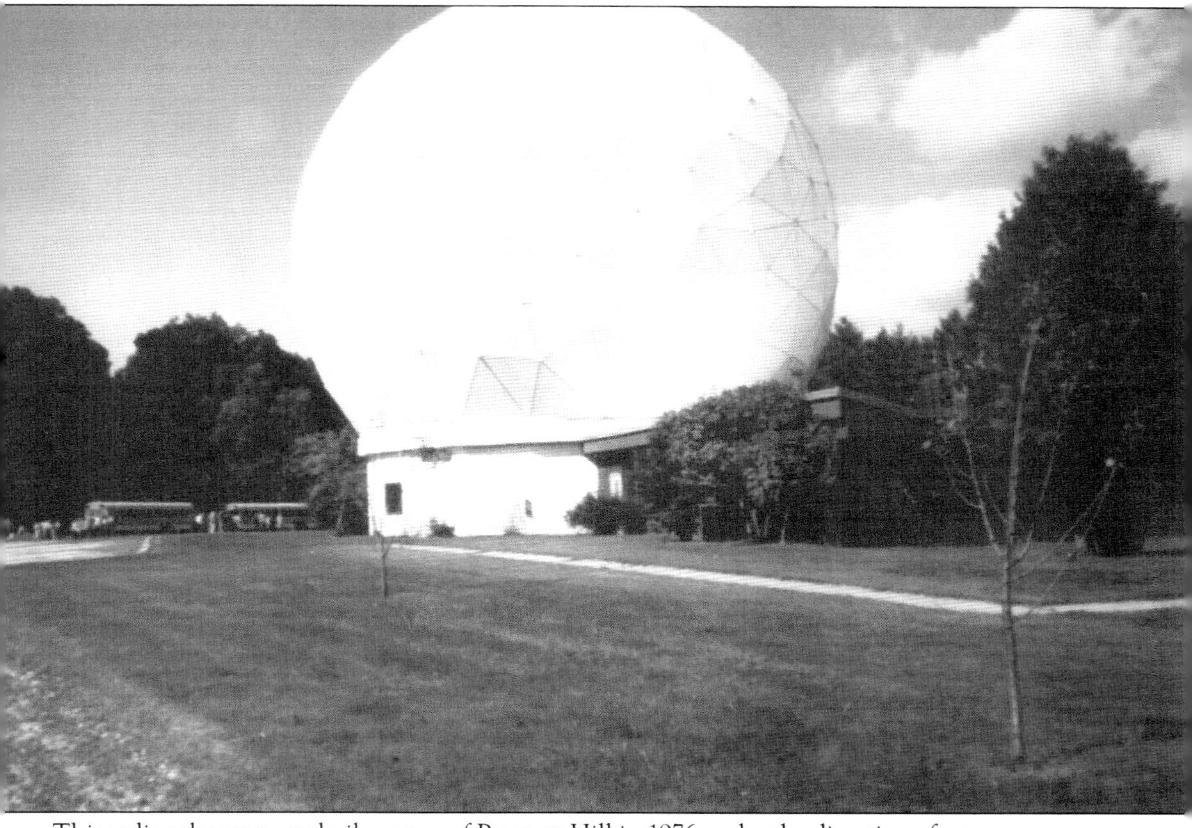

This radio telescope was built on top of Prescott Hill in 1976 under the direction of astronomers from the University of Massachusetts. It cost about $8 million and was capable of probing interstellar space, searching for clues to the origin of life. In 2011, it was dismantled, its capabilities being surpassed by a much larger facility under construction in Mexico.

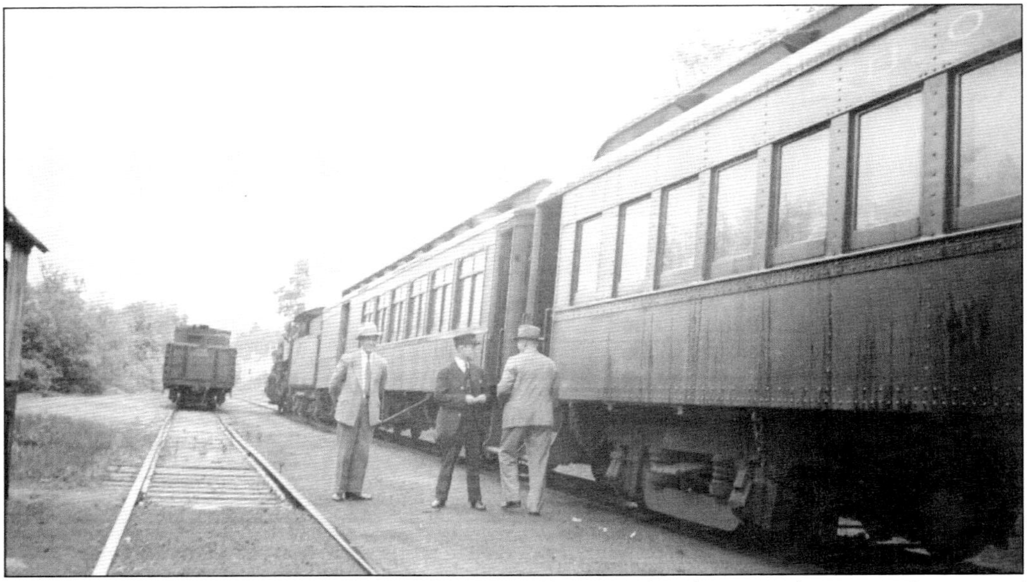

The "Rabbit Train," a branch of the Boston & Albany Railroad, received its name because of the many stops it made each day. Through the years, the train made two runs daily, carrying passengers to work, shop, or visit. The conductor in this picture is Joseph Sherman.

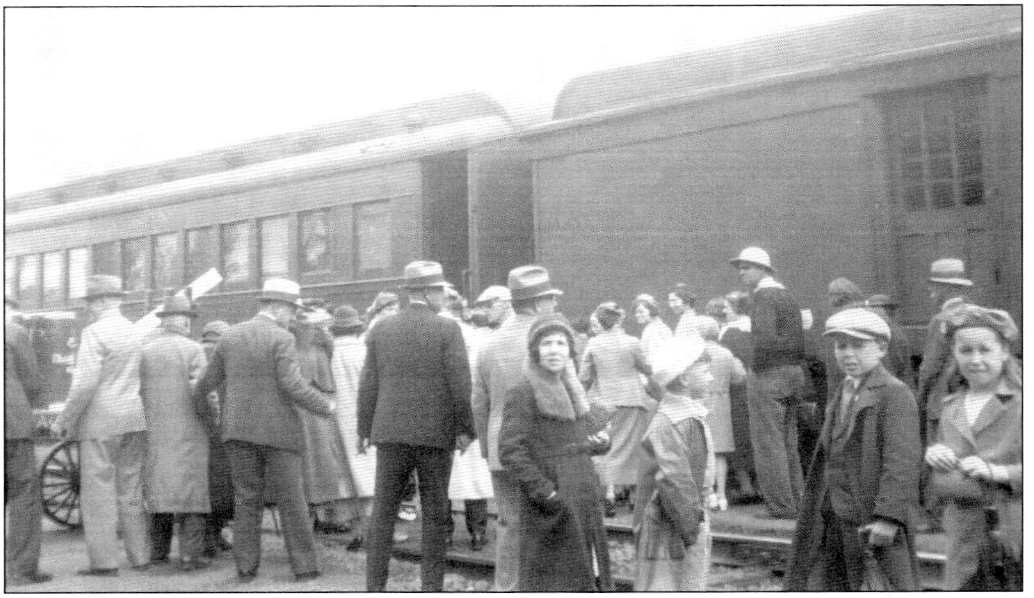

The "Rabbit Train" made the last run on June 1, 1935. A large crowd of enthusiastic people, many of whom were passengers on the first run 64 years earlier, made this trip.

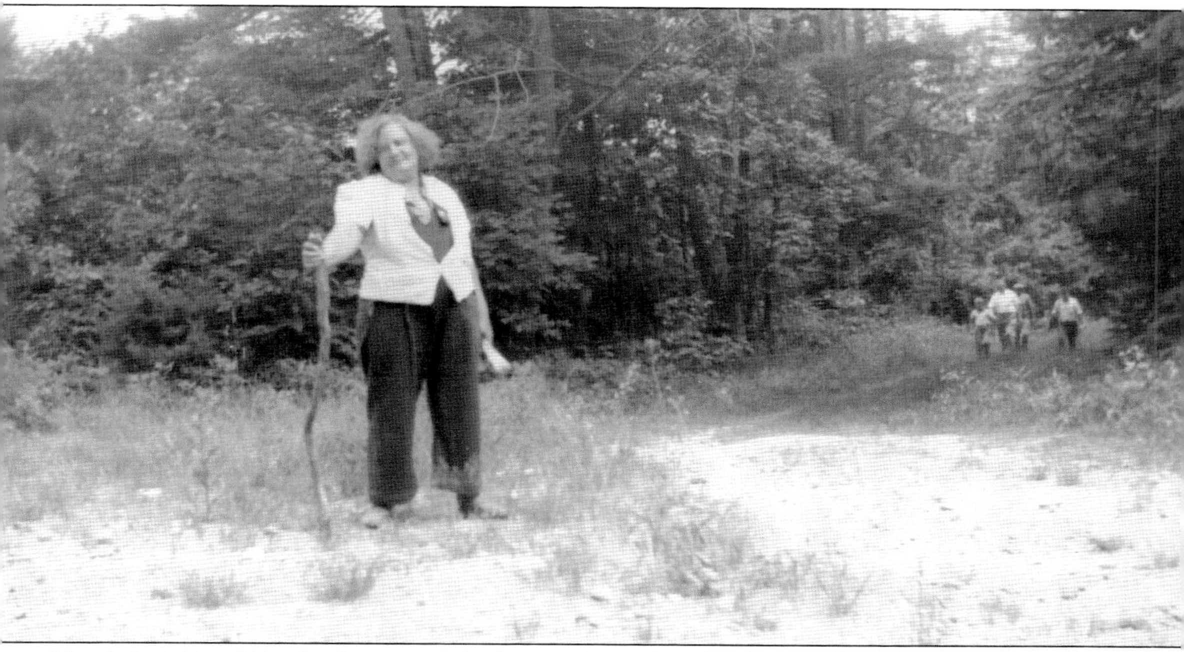

This lady is Etta Wheeler Berry, and she has just been for a Quabbin walk. A high wire fence, erected by the Metropolitan District Commission overseeing the Quabbin project (now known as the Department of Conservation and Recreation), now stands just behind where she stands. No entrance is allowed. Berry, whose home was next to the fence, was very bitter and very vocal about this.

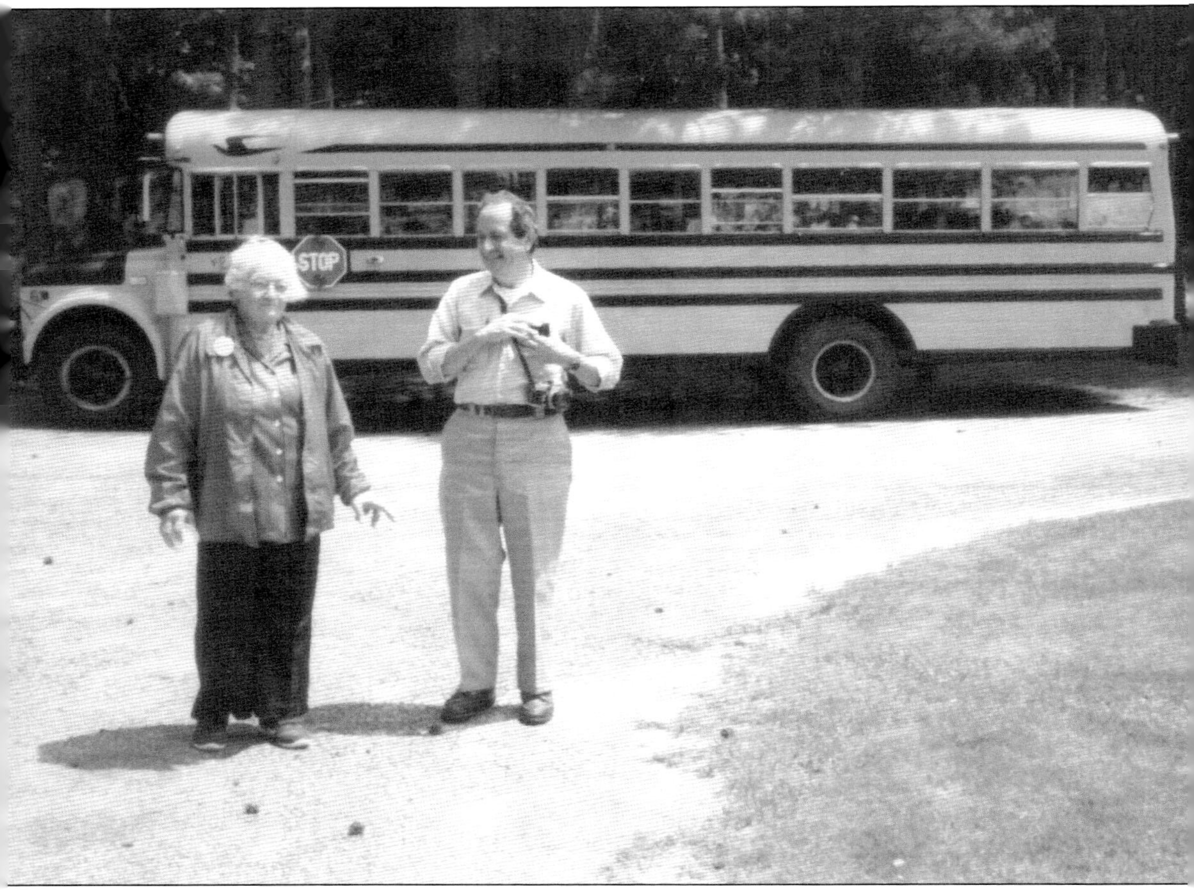

Eleanor Schmidt and Joe Cernauskas pose on Prescott Hill during a bus pilgrimage for members and friends of the Swift River Valley Historical Society. The pilgrimages were started by Eleanor. Joe was a storehouse of Quabbin history. Sadly, he was tragically murdered in 2010.

About the Organization

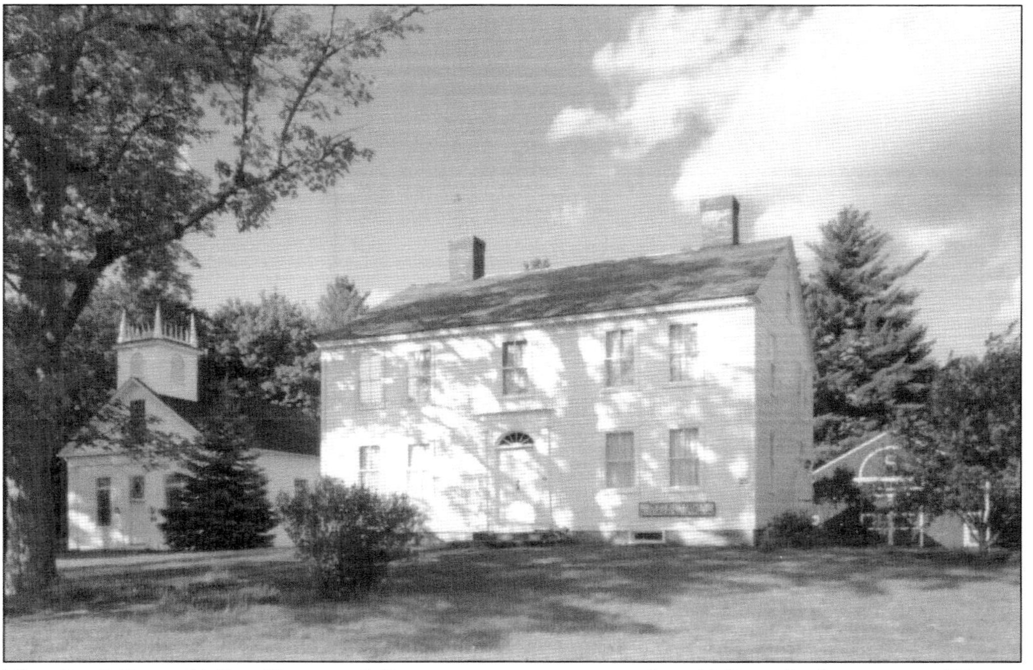

The Swift River Valley Historical Society was incorporated in 1962 with the towns of Dana, Enfield, Greenwich, and New Salem represented on this site in North New Salem. In 1985, the Prescott Museum (the former Methodist Episcopal church) was moved from Orange to the North New Salem grounds. The site now includes the Whitaker-Clary House (the original building), a red barn (not used), the Prescott Museum, and the Carriage Shed built in 1990. The three buildings are filled with artifacts and remnants to remember the towns that are no more.